"These vivid, well-wrought ess
and triumph of others and deli

Carol Henderson, www.carolhenderson.com, Author of
Farther Along: The Writing Journey of Thirteen Bereaved Mothers

"In *Speaking Your Truth*, you will be taken on an exhilarating soulful ride by the words, wisdom and stories of others; heart words, some of which, will no doubt seem to be spoken as if your own."

Vanessa Talbot, Success Creation Guide,
Author of *Extraordinary YOU ~*
The art of living a lusciously spirited vibrant life.

"Thomas Merton, the renowned author and Trappist monk, once said: "We make ourselves real by telling the truth." By this standard, this is a book chock full of real women and two-hundred proof truth. Sip slowly and be amazed."

Joe Zarantonello, M.A.,
Director of Loose Leaf Hollow Retreat Centre

"Much of history has silenced the wisdom of women, but these inspirational authors remind us that by sharing our joys and sorrows we become stronger, more tolerant and more compassionate with ourselves and with each other."

Delinda Korrey, Publisher of the South Platte
Sentinel in Sterling and author of *The Neverending Journey*

"Every once in a blue moon, someone comes along who shares a story that makes you delve deeper into your own spiritual journey, triggering self-reflection and ultimately taking you down a path of peace. Praise to the authors of this book for creating this gift and for having the courage to share this poignant journey with its readers."

Lisa Krug Avery, Writer; Fiction

"This title stretches the boundaries of giving and sharing, with personal stories that will touch your heart and raise your awareness. A wonderful gift that fits everyone."

Nancy Naigle

"Bearing their souls through story, the women of *Speaking Your Truth* reveal wisdom that comes from sadness, growth that emerges from grief and motivation found in inherent strength, in hearing one's authentic voice, in God. Their messages are intimate, uplifting, inspiring."

Robert M. Weir, writer, author, speaker, coach and editor for emerging and established authors. www.robertmweir.com

"Just like the first and second volumes of *Speaking Your Truth*, this third remarkable compilation of authentically and wonderfully written stories from courageous women deeply inspired me and warmed my heart. Read these stories slowly, drinking in the beautiful wisdom and insights. You will be truly enriched!"

Kate Heartsong, author of *Deeply We Are One* and contributor to *Speaking Your Truth, Volume 1*

"What a wonderfully moving and inspirational book. The stories will resonate with anyone who has lost someone they loved. The stories will pull at your heart and inspire you to pick up the phone and tell someone you miss them, love them and appreciate them being in your life."

Jan Tucker, Ph.D., Higher Learning Institute

"*Speaking Your Truth* is a spiritually galvanizing, heartfelt and authentically expressed gift to the world. These courageous women offer their personal life experiences in a way that will deeply touch you and empower you to speak and live your own truth."

Diana Drake Long, Speaker, Coach & Author, www.DianaLong.com

"The stories in this publication speak from the heart. The writing alone took courage, and for many, the ability to set their ego aside. I found inspiration and hope within these pages and the validation that strength can be gained from some of the most unsuspecting sources. This is a book that will touch men and women alike."

Melissa Foster, Bestselling author and founder of the World Literary Cafe, Melissa Foster

"What greater service can women provide for women than to share their stories? *Speaking Your Truth* shares poignant, first-person accounts that other women can use as a source of strength, direction or encouragement. It helps to know that other women have experienced similar things as we have. Their words can help us see greater possibilities. This is a must-read for women of hope or searching."

Sharon Simpson-Dogon, RMT, CR,
and Certified Rossiter Coach

"Many women believe secrecy is the price they must pay for the past. The authors of *Speaking Your Truth* decide that secrecy is a prison. By airing out the skeletons in their closets, they discover how different the truth is from what they were told. And they learn to love and value themselves—no matter what. Women who read this book will feel admiration for these authors' courage, as well as inspiration on their own journey."

Carol Marleigh Kline, author of *Streetwise Spirituality:
28 Days to Inner Fitness and Everyday Enlightenment.*

"In reading the many stories, I was struck by how many of the experiences were similar to ones I have gone through in my life—the loss of a child, the loss of a dear parent, abuse by a loved one, loss of a true love. More than any other book, I was overwhelmed by how courageous and vulnerable these truly remarkable women have made themselves—for a chance to change someone else's life. It helps me to know that women of faith and courage are strong enough to speak their truths. I will never forget them. I cannot recommend this book enough. It is a voice for those of us who have none."

Dr. Jeanine Zinner

"This is a book filled with love, tears ,laughter and hope. It takes you on a journey that will inspire you to find your inner truth through the deeply moving real stories of its amazing authors."

Sue Crosbie, Contributing Author of *Extraordinary You - The Art
of Living a Lusciously Spirited, Vibrant Life*

"These stories remind us of the elegance of simplicity; that we experience moments, not days; that we remember instances rather than seasons in our lives; that we understand by making an experience a story. For some of life, words are not important enough— yet these stories show us in a very real sense, they are."

David Krueger MD, Executive Mentor Coach, www.MentorPath.com

"*Speaking Your Truth* is a compilation of motivational and inspiring stories about incredible women facing life's challenges head on. Each story is filled with a heartfelt experience that we can all benefit from. A must read."

Susan Dintino, author of the Hay House book *Songs of My Life...Slightly Out of Tune*

"Wow! Inspiring, touching, heart breaking. As I read each story I felt as though a bit of my own story was being told. Women seem to have this incredible ability to articulate, relate and understand one another's lives, if we will let it in; letting our hearts be broken open. Welcome to the wonderful world of being a woman. My heart was broken open."

Marsha Sage

"Facing these challenges would be daunting and overwhelming for some people, but these women manage with courage and dignity and without glossing over the difficulties to take us with them on their journeys to personal triumph. A very moving book!"

Betty Cannon, President of the Boulder Psychotherapy Institute and author of *Sartre and Psychoanalysis*

"I was riveted. Direct, clear storytelling. Amazing narratives with the flavor of their particular lives. You want these amazing women to be your friends, colleagues and neighbors."

Helene Sorkin

"*Speaking Your Truth* is just that...truth. Real women, amazing stories and a realization that we are not alone on this journey called life."

Stacy Graham

Speaking Your Truth

Courageous Stories
from Inspiring Women

Volume III

Compiled by
Lisa Shultz & Andrea Costantine
Illustrated by Janice Earhart

www.speakingyourtruthbook.com

Copyright © 2012 by Self-Publishing Experts, LLC

Illustrator: Janice Earhart, iZoar
Book Cover: Nick Zelinger, NZ Graphics
Editing: Donna Mazzitelli, Writing With Donna
Layout/Design: Andrea Costantine
Author Photograph: David Weihnacht,
David Marc Photography

Printed in the United States of America

First Edition
ISBN 978-1-478-16167-7

*To my daughters and to the women readers looking
for hope and inspiration.*
- Lisa Shultz

*To my mother, Taryn, for believing
I really can change the world.*
- Andrea Costantine

Contents

PART FOUR
DEFINING MOMENTS

PART FIVE
RELATIONSHIPS

FOREWORD

I find myself writing in a sacred grotto. It is a curious synchronicity that I have been asked to compose the foreword for the third and final edition of *Speaking Your Truth*. Truth comes in many forms, as subjective as the individual expressions of it. Finding truth may be an unexpected and delightful discovery. Truth can also be joyful or wise. Yet, there are times when a difficult truth wells up from deep within the core of one's belly and simply refuses to be stifled any longer. It is this kind of insuppressible truth that has brought me deep soul searching on the impact of keeping secrets—the *opposite*, really, of speaking your truth.

It often takes a strong act of courage to speak out, perhaps breaking generations of silence. To speak publicly, as the women in this anthology have done, takes even more boldness. For some of these women, this is the first time they have ever been published. Others are speaking about personal and family circumstances never before shared with such a broad audience. Each of them is expressing their unique perspective. Each of them is speaking their truth.

We are the better for these intimate words offered between friends we may never meet. Their stories provide a key into a healing and transformative portal. Their stories trigger memories and contemplation into our own stories; their challenges and successes highlight our own life experiences. We can learn so much from one another.

I offer gratitude to Lisa Shultz and Andrea Costantine who had an inspired vision to publish this gathering of women's words. Historically, it has often been the men telling the stories. Women spoke in hushed whispers to share confidential matters between caring for children and hanging the laundry. Certainly, there have been women writers; yet, not too long ago, some of those women took male pseudo-names in order to give their birthed works a chance for public embrace.

We now live in an age where women have been speaking for decades with clearer voices and an expanded platform—brave women who cut a difficult trail through dense and resistant thicket to make way for what we have to say today. Now, more than ever, in 2012, it is important to tell our secrets, to share our insights, and to express our unique wisdom. We need to ask questions and share our deepest pondering in order to explore possibilities for a healthy and enlightened future. Speaking our truth tips the balance of some of the wrongdoings in our world. Truth spoken shines light on even the darkest of places. Truth also encourages our thoughtful meandering to further develop, and celebrates our golden triumphs.

In the little grotto where I write there is a mixture of sturdy rocks and potted ferns. To me, the rocks represent the ancestors with tales of times past, times we will never see, even though their strong history continues to support us. Natural patterns of black and white with shades of grey, kissed with the occasional hint of a muted mauve—exquisite patterns of life's unfolding. Yet these old stones, as well as old stories, may wall off our ability to see the vast horizon beyond. Tall structures built by others can block our personal view.

We must look beyond the constraints of our past, and those of the ancestors, to bring forward new and healthier ways. We are the ferns. Our task is to awaken to the new growth. Our seeking tendrils bring healthy green shoots among the contrast of the dark and weathered stones. The delicate fern in front of me has berries; like us, it holds the promise of yet-ripening fruit.

Our words, like those of the ancestors who have come before us, will one day turn to stone, so they may stand the test of time by living beyond the constraints of our human existence. Unlike us in this human form, the impact of our writing may last forever. Our words become the foundation for others, as again and again, the new "ferns" brighten the grotto with evolved ideas and inspired growth.

In this sacred sanctuary I notice an impressive archway. Its open mouth reaches for the sky, beckoning infinite potential. And the beauty of the inner garden is exposed to the outer world, inviting us to soak in its sweet presence. In that archway, there is a keystone. It is the central stone at the summit of the arch, which locks together the whole. Without the keystone, the arch would crumble; with the supporting element the arch stands focused and firm. May the precious words of these courageous and wise women touch your mind and your heart this day, as together, we celebrate the human birthright of true expression. Perhaps one or more of these precious stories will become a treasured keystone in *your* sacred grotto.

Wishing you success and joy beyond your wildest dreams!

Donna DeNomme
Award-winning, internationally-published author
President of Wild Success 4U, Inc.

INTRODUCTION

REFLECTIONS from the Editor

"There is no greater agony than
bearing an untold story inside you."
"A bird doesn't sing because it has an answer,
it sings because it has a song."
- Maya Angelou

I intended to write my own story for the third volume of *Speaking Your Truth*. But then something happened. I was asked to edit this anthology. And, as a result, I found I could not write a piece about me. In the process of midwifing and tending to the stories of the brave women in this volume, I knew that my role was to support these amazing women—to hold space and help bring their stories of truth, courage, and transformation to life.

I don't know what the experience is like for other editors when they edit a book, but for this editor, I can't help but take the stories into my heart and work with them from that space where love and compassion begin. When I rounded the corner to be with the last couple of stories, I found that I had a lump in my throat and a heaviness in my heart. It wasn't necessarily that the last two stories were any more emotional than the other 40-plus, although they were profoundly moving. I believe my swelling emotions represented all that I'd carried for the past few months—and the time I'd spent with a piece of each woman. As I neared the end of my time with this book, I felt the cresting wave of everything that had been revealed within these pages.

It was a truly sacred moment when I realized how much I would now take with me as a result of nurturing these pieces. So much took place in the lives of each of the women contributors. Some experienced powerful life events. Others persevered and faced intense emotions and opportunities to "become." In the

15

context of their life experiences, many stood up to speak their truth for themselves and on behalf of others. Most had deep spiritual stirrings, leaving them forever changed. I too will never again be the same.

For a brief time, I lived with each of these stories. Some made me cry. Some made me smile and laugh. Some made me gasp and took my breath away. All have touched me deeply. Each one has entered my heart and spoken to me in intense and profound ways. As a result, every woman who contributed their story of experience, strength, and inspiration is now connected to me, whether they know it or not.

The women you'll meet in the following pages have been willing to share their "in betweens," often in their raw and exposed states. It's what happens *in between* the beginning and getting to the other side where we experience the most potential for possibility, growth, and change. It's also the hardest place to be and the most difficult to share with others, but it's the space from which all of us are able to connect the most deeply with each other's humanity, vulnerability, and incredible power.

This anthology of stories represents a circle, a gathering of women, strong enough to allow each person to take her turn in the middle, to stand tall, and to proclaim her truths. As each has come forth, they've revealed their authenticity and declared that there will be no more secrets, no more shame, no more fear, and no more victimization. Instead, there will be love, connection, peace, hope, courage, strength, and healing. Each woman understands she is ultimately responsible for her own life. Each, maybe unknowingly, claims the power of her story to heal and transform herself as well as the generations that came before her and those that will follow.

The women in this book, who span in age across five decades, leave me humbled and in awe of their bravery and courage. Every woman has willingly revealed her intense desire to be healed, to inspire, and to be instruments of healing and hope for others. And no matter her age—no matter how young or old—each woman has shared her amazing wisdom and shown us that when we're willing to walk through the fires in our lives we can rise out of the ashes to be glorious.

The stories you'll encounter in *Speaking Your Truth* have been offered and intended as a source of insight and inspiration for others. We can all be inspired by the power of each other. We are all capable of seeing that when one of us has overcome a seemingly impossible situation, we too can make it to the other side. My hope for you the reader is that you embrace these stories with the intention that the healing of ourselves and our world will continue to expand in an ever-widening circle. May we each be a ripple of love, authenticity, and hope.

In loving service,
Donna Mazzitelli
The Word Heartiste
June 2012

Healing

WINGS OF HEALING

Kathy Sommer-Buss

It's in the early hours of the day, when the sun has just raised her brow, that I find myself with coffee cup in hand exploring my garden. I delight in the fullness of life, in its myriad of form, texture, and color. The birds greet each other as they converge on the feeders, and the trees are full of song. Nature's classroom has and continues to be an integral part of my wholeness…within her I find such clarity…

I converted a butterfly house into a tri-level birdhouse late last fall and attentively watched with delight as many families of sparrows were born and cared for in their beautiful little home. I enjoyed countless summer hours quietly in wait to capture the perfect photos of the love and care that went into raising fledglings. The cozy nest that was lovingly woven with every detail, including soft grasses, plastic ribbons, and feathers, has now been home to three different families of sparrows. Both parents were very dedicated to caring for them all and boldly took them into the world with precision.

The last clutch, however, may have been the one that required more work, as tirelessly the parents attended to their needs until that day when two of them popped out to follow their father and one remained. The others were nearby tweeting away, as if to say, "Come on. You can do it. Come on little one!"

After two days of bouncing and bounding around in the shrubs, and countless attempts to encourage him to follow, the three of them disappeared altogether, leaving one baby behind. I could feel the longing in this little one…the sense of belonging, the sense of mattering, all shattering in the quiet.

Cowering in the recesses of the birdhouse with seeming confusion in its eyes, I could feel the dialogue, *"Where is everyone?" "Why have they left me?" "What am I going to do?" "How will I manage?" "I'm scared…and hungry."* The loud cries for assistance were not met with food for a full day, and it became too difficult for me to observe without offering aid. Too small to venture out and retarded in growth, he had become "my little one." And indeed, how profound "my little one" has proven to be.

His wobbly little head, big wide beak, and tiny fear-filled eyes were met with compassion from this goliath at his front door. Not knowing what to do, however, trusting that I was to do something, I began hunting for ants...and this is where my healing journey began.

I have always had interconnectedness with animals that I liken to being "hardwired." I "know" their need, and if I can assist, I do so without hesitation. This would be no exception!

A small narrow straw was fashioned into the perfect tool with which to feed my little one. Out came the sunflower seeds, bread, water, and cache of ants found after scouring the yard front and back. Feeding was a beautiful success. Each time he realized I meant no harm—I was a bit clumsy but consistent! Every few hours I chirped to him as I approached, and he eagerly replied, knowing it was time to eat. He slept soundly after eating and seemed very content to be cared for.

After three days, it became obvious to me that the sustenance he was receiving was keeping him alive and energetic and allowed him to gain a bit more size. His appetite was hearty, and he turned away once he received his fill. Knowing that the desire to fly was a short ten to fourteen days off, I purchased a special preparation for baby birds and added that to his mealtime. He loved it and ate more voraciously than ever, making quite a mess of his cozy place. As the last hint of sunlight lay across the front lawn, I sat and pondered the quality of my experience.

In those nine days of relentless care for the little one left behind, I realized the magnitude of the love shared between us. Filled with deep gratitude for the opportunity to be a part of this amazing connection, I sat awhile reflecting on the many stories of my own life that were being mirrored in this unfolding. I became deeply saddened by the entire experience...the conflicting pieces were all hitting me.

I love animals deeply, and I show compassion without hesitation. And yet, was I getting in the way of life? I felt so deeply compelled to comfort, care, and nurture. But I also felt a deep sadness about the outcome...will my little one survive? What will he do when he gets out of the nest and no one is there to care for him? Having observed the birds throughout our yard for years, I felt some kindred spirit might assist.

He struggled to chirp that morning, so I held him cupped in my hands, praying he would feel a sense of comfort and warmth. He seemed to relax, and after five minutes he didn't want to go back into the house alone. Gently I scooped him back in. I wanted to continue to cuddle his little frail body, and I could sense his heart's longing and saying, "Stay here with me."

A rush of sadness enveloped me, my eyes filled with tears as I felt the immensity of what I had projected onto him...and mirrored for myself. This is all about *my* "little"...what deeply pains *me* as I feel this experience. As a young child, my daddy died, my mother was distraught and withdrawn, and my brother left. *"Where is everyone?" "Why have they left me?" "What am I going to do?" "How will I manage?"* The familiarity was stunning and heartfelt. I knew this sense of abandonment. I knew the pain of it. I had lived it myself. As the recognition flooded in, I cried. The confusion of a wobbly little head, big wide beak, and tiny fear-filled eyes seemed to make perfect sense to me. It's no wondering this "little one" stranded in the birdhouse out front was to be here for healing. I deeply understood the experience and opportunity. I had a readiness to heal what was still painful for me.

Weeping with grief, I longed for the mother who had abandoned me, the father who was now gone, and the brother who had left. There I sat, my sad self in a puddle of tears, crying and cuddling the pain to my chest. All the years of masquerading about with a mask of togetherness, balance, and perfection were crumbling before me...and it was ALL beautiful. I saw myself in my "little one," trying to be strong and not knowing what lie ahead.

Neither of us did. He might not make it, and I was willing to accept that. It would be painful indeed for me if that were the case. I was grateful beyond words, however, for the healing beauty in this otherwise conflicting experience—of what it had felt like to carry my own wounded "little" with the love, compassion, kindness, and acceptance that I realized had always been within me. To uncover the depth of my being, to embrace what had always been here, and to release what I had carried for so many years. To open my heart and fully experience the amazing synchronicities in life…they are constantly flowing and offering opportunities to find the magnificence of what we really are….in this humanity….this flow of life.

The truth, with great clarity, was that what I had been searching for outside of myself from my youngest years, I had always held deep within me. The strength to go forward, the love to sustain me, the knowing that all would be provided for as life unfolded—the gift of wholeness!

Dusk of the tenth day, I knew by his independent actions and increasingly anxious state that the time was near for him to take flight. Excited and anxious myself, and knowing he had everything already within him, my husband and I sat outside marveling at the result of love's touch. I felt tears run down my face as I took in all that I'd been a part of, knowing the following day would likely be the day.

And indeed it was. I went out first thing to feed him, and as I chirped, he rustled through the nearby shrub, out with his wings vibrating energetically, his mouth wide open as if to say, "I did it! I'm out and soon to be on my way!" The expression of love deepened, as the connection to this little one was much grander than I had first imagined. It's as if the assurances were there before me that Spirit's way is to speak to our hearts in subtle, yet beautifully inspiring ways…in each and every moment of whatever gift is present.

I would be remiss to not share with you the joy I currently have months after, as I observe my "little one's" escapades in our yard. He is exuberantly flying about with his downy feathers full, displaying a blend of seemingly reckless yet very skillful flight patterns of a young and vibrant bird! He is easy to recognize with a faint "S" shaped dark patch on his chest. I feel freedom and peace deep within, as I recognize and embrace the healing that has occurred in me. Grace has shared clarity once again in the most amazing of ways! The ever-present, deep experience of Oneness in everything before me fills me with an unfailing sense of gratitude.

It is with great joy, now a year later, that I share an update to this precious experience. Early this spring, there was my "little one," perched atop the converted butterfly house in jubilant song!

I was heart-struck to witness the wisdom shown in nature; the flow, as he has built and now raised two families in the very home where he was born! The joy from these experiences comes simply from the ability to have them, the ability to be alive and experience them.

I'm realizing that life is an experience...that's all it is! Embrace it, in its complexities, ups and downs, and its constant change. The more you flow with it, the more it moves you into understanding the true majesty of being YOU! I have a treasured video of my "little one" before flight, and a few still photos of our kinship to add to my collection of the many ways that I have found wholeness and clarity in nature's classroom. With deep gratitude and much love, I offer that perhaps you will too!

Kathy Sommer-Buss believes our lives are our message. Her life is all about love, compassion, kindness and acceptance...as we are all ONE. She is a seeker and a free spirit—ever curious and enamored with life. Since the beginning, Kathy has been an artist and creator. She loves people, animals, nature, and all aspects of the divine. She lives her life each day in gratitude for all things...and all experiences... She enjoys sharing her life with a loving husband, her sweet animals indoors and out, friends and family! Kathy reminds us that each moment brings wonder, so drink up! She calls herself "The Compassionate Creative." You can reach Kathy at KathySommerBuss@gmail.com. Please visit her website, www.thecompassionatecreative.com.

HOLDING HANDS IN
THE CEMENT

Tresa Martindale

Her life came to a sudden end in the ICU when a pulmonary embolism broke free from her lung and seized her heart. She was three months pregnant and only twenty-nine years old. My mother was found lying on the floor of the ICU. No one knows for sure how long she had been there. My father was like a deer in headlights with five children, ages eighteen months to eight years. I was the eight-year-old. His eighteen-month-old child was in diapers. Almost instantly, his four other children became bed wetters, a symptom of bereavement. He was not emotionally equipped to take on this task that was so much bigger than him.

There was help, but it was a band aide. His own fears of being alone, as a single parent, led him to find a "replacement." She came into our lives with the velocity of a tsunami, washing in with fury and destruction. In an attempt to stop the bedwetting, she withheld water after four in the afternoon. Liquid deprivation seemed like a quick fix to the messy sheets of five additional children. She was a young single mother around 23 years of age. She had two children of her own, with no support from her ex-husband. She was poor and struggling. I imagine she was also desperate. My father was attractive, owned his home, had money in the bank, worked for the electrical union, and could provide material stability to a woman willing to sign up for his situation.

We put my mother in the ground September 2, 1977. Swaddled in a cotton candy pink casket, I think she would have loved it. She didn't look at all like my mother. The mind plays tricks, and my limbic brain was telling me that my mother was breathing. I even said it out loud, "Look! She is alive!" Like an oasis, I was sure that I could see her chest rising and falling. The adults tried to quiet me but I had to let them know she was alive. My oasis disappeared as swiftly as a finger touching a hot stove. I reached my tiny hand out to touch her hand. It was stiff and cold, her skin felt like rubber. My arm recoiled, and it was in that moment that

I felt death in my hand. It made my small body dizzy. I knew she was gone, and it would haunt me for years.

Not much time had passed; my mother's sisters and her mother came to our house. They went through her clothes and belongings, taking them from the closet. My mom had a great sense of fashion, and I'm sure her clothes spread joy to all who inherited them. By the end of the year in December, a cyclone had passed through the house. All evidence of my mother was removed. Photos, decorations, personal things, and non-personal items. Everything she'd ever touched was gone. The house had a haunting echo. It caused great confusion.

In the middle of the storm, with that echo in the background, my father introduced us to our new "stepmother." My mother had been buried only three months, her loss still raw, and the grief unexplored. They were getting married in a week and needed a clean slate for her to bring "her" things into the home. We were instructed to call her Mother. She brought her two children along, and they became our instant brother and sister. My entire life felt fake. I lie in bed at night wondering where my real parents were. I knew for sure that the ones living in my house were impostors.

A lot changed in the year 1978—a stepmother, two "new" siblings, new decorations, furniture, and food. I became the Cinderella archetype overnight. I cooked, cleaned, did laundry, and cared for the younger children. We were told not to talk about our real mother. My grandparents and aunts and uncles, all from my mother's side of the family, were asked not to visit anymore. It created contention with the stepmother. I even remember being told to "hide" when my grandfather came knocking. We were stuffed into a closet where we had to be silent. I had never hidden from them before, so I didn't understand. After many rejections and being turned away, they stopped coming by. I did not see them again until I was 18.

There was one particular event that burned an image in my memory. I was with the stepmother and we were driving in the car. A deep sadness welled up inside of me. It was my first sign of grief. I longed for my real mom. I said that I was sad and asked to go see where she was buried. By the time we got home, I was grounded and told never to speak of her again. It was that day, as an eight-year-old child, that l suffered a soul loss. It was not safe to remember my mother out loud, and I even wondered if I would be caught thinking about her in the quiet moments to myself. Fear quickly replaced mourning and remembering.

The years progressed. I often thought of my mother and missed her tremendously. I became so fearful that I forced myself to not think about her. I forgot what she looked like, and I could no longer hear the sound of her voice. With no photos anywhere, she slipped further away, like sand between my fingers.

There was, however, one place my siblings and I could go. It was dangerous if we were caught, but I snuck there from time to time and shared a moment with my mom. Before her death, my father had poured a cement slab next to the driveway. We had all embedded our handprints in the cement and inscribed our names underneath. When the coast was clear, I snuck out to this patch of cement and put my hand into the imprint of my mother's hand and held it for as long as I could without being seen. Holding hands with my mom in the cement was the only link I had to her. My other siblings often visited her handprint as well.

As the years passed, my hand outgrew its original print and started to catch up with the size of my mom's. I always felt the lump in my throat when I put my hand in hers. I tried to remember what she looked like, imagined the similarity in the knuckle size and shape of her fingers. I had silent conversations with her in my mind and told her how much I missed her. We had been forced to suppress our memories at such a young age, and I hoped that holding her cement hand would help me remember. It offered a connection and comfort, and although the memories had faded, I knew that the handprint in the cement belonged to the woman that was my real mother, and I knew that she loved me.

I will never forget one particular day, burned into my soul like a fire-hot branding iron on flesh—the smell of smoke in the air, the sound of the power tool roaring, the dust cloud. When I realized what was happening, it felt like my soul's scream was being ripped out of my body, and I could not run fast enough to stop the insanity. The power tool was a sander. The smell of smoke was the friction of the sander on the cement as it removed my mother's hand. By the time I got there, both my father's and my mother's hands were gone. The dust cloud swirling around in a thick plume were the ashes of her hands as they were taken away by the breeze, leaving behind a deep and twisted wound, so deep I let out a primal scream. My father looked up. Tears streaked his dusty face, leaving muddy trails as the stepmother watched like a thief in the night. My brother was there, too. We both screamed, "NO, what are you doing?"

It was too late—she was gone. I would never hold her hand again. I lost her twice, and for the second time, didn't get to say goodbye. Apparently, the stepmother had a problem with my mother's hand being there—it was a reminder that she was not the only wife and mother who had been a part of this family. She believed removing her hand would remove the fact that my mother had ever existed.

My father, it seems, lived in fear of his religious beliefs. They held him prisoner in this marriage. In his mind, divorcing her would have been worse than watching his children being abused, worse than removing our final connection to our mother. His emotions and ability to connect with others were locked in a vault that contained his lifetime of hurts. He was unplugged, numb.

As I stood on this holy ground now defiled and sanded, hot from the friction, I was orphaned. Covered in the dust of my mother's hand, I felt so alone. I hated him in that moment, but I hated the stepmother even more. Monsters were real and they didn't hide under beds. They went about their business to hurt children in the bright light of day.

It was then that the culmination of abuses and my mother's death all melted together. It was on that day, when fear, abandonment, and loss of control settled deep into the canyons of my bones. My soul now contained an imprint deeper than my mother's hand in the cement. I would spend a lifetime recovering from the collateral damage of death, abuse, divorce, abandonment, and neglect. This moment changed who I was. A part of my soul died, and simultaneously, the birth of the survivor and self-made woman took root in the core of my being.

The stepmother finally divorced my father and left. She took everything. She had been collecting tin cans full of money over the years and buying everything from new furniture and cars to a new nose and wardrobe. The past came knocking, delivering the reminder of a now familiar and haunting echo in the walls of our empty home. And for the first time in eight years, at sixteen years old, I could breathe.

My father pushed me to continue my duties as his Cinderella. I was expected to maintain the balance of a broken home. My own heart had been broken, and deep inside the caves of my soul, I heard whisperings from the skeletons buried there. "You are a chain breaker. You are not meant to be in this box."

Conflict with my father reached a breaking point. I felt like my fuse had been ignited and I was going to blow. I left home at sixteen and did not speak to my father for three years. In that time he got married again, divorced, and then remarried for a fourth time. Grace saved me, when a dear friend's parents took me into their home and provided food, shelter, and love. They had ten of their own children and found space in their heart and home for one more. This act of love provided me with a course correction, a chance to rewrite my story.

I worked after school to pay for a car, clothes, and extra things. Wherever I fell short, they made up the difference. I had two choices. I could be defeated and orphaned with no hope, or I could use my struggles as the octane fuel to help me find the gifts, learn the lessons, and rise triumphant. I instinctively knew that each struggle visited upon me was my teacher. Somehow I knew that I needed to look for the gift in every disappointment. There was darkness and danger inside, and I knew that if I was to heal, I would need the courage to invite my devils to the table one by one and make peace.

I found escape in the crevices of my imagination. I believed that there was a sacred contract made between my mother and her children. I imagined that she knew her life would be short. She came to give us life, to create a legacy that would change the future. She promised us that after she died, she would never be gone. I imagined her as a constant companion that I could call my angel. She would protect us from danger and help us navigate our way through life. She knew it would feel like an impossible journey, but she promised that we would be surrounded by her love, and that we would rise up as we each earned our wings and learned to fly.

I knew the message that told me I would be a "chain breaker" was a significant part of this contract and a very important piece of my purpose. With this belief, I knew that my life was important.

I had my own holy grail that needed to be discovered and the journey to find this treasure would define not only my life but forge a new path for future generations.

This may have started as an imagined story in my mind, but over time it became real. It was my elixir of courage, tincture of strength, and potion of forgiveness. I had to give up hope that my past could ever look any different. I had to forgive myself for hating the adults that had been in charge. I learned that I'd had magic powers all along. The power was realizing that I could be in charge of my own life and script it any way I wanted. For years I searched, trying to understand the mystery of the message that was on a loop inside my brain. "You are a chain breaker."

Clarity and understanding began bubbling to the surface when I became a mother. I started to see how my children were living a life with entirely different lenses and that the ancestral cycle of abuses handed down for generations could start the process of healing. I didn't want to be known as the victim of a sad story. I want to be remembered as a survivor who rose up and would not be defeated. When I fall down and think I can't get up, I feel my mother picking me up, dusting me off, and whispering to me, "You are breaking that chain."

I can see broken links lying on the ground every time I share a story of my youth with my children. It is so unfamiliar to them, and when I see their confusion, I can feel light shining in the once dark canyons of my bones. The horrendous deeds of my past have been my greatest gifts and teachers. I honor my lessons and hope to inspire others to honor theirs.

> *"You may encounter many defeats, but you must not be defeated. In fact, it may be necessary to encounter the defeats, so you can know who you are, what you can rise from, and how you can still come out of it."* - Maya Angelou

Tresa Martindale has been married for 14 years to her husband John. They have four children. She is a jewelry artist who combines vintage and found objects, gemstones and crystals, to create talismans, "wearable art." She also enjoys photography and storytelling. Tresa is a certified Dying Consciously teacher and mentor, where she assists the dying and their families make their journey beyond death a peaceful and conscious process. She also studied at the Four Winds Society and is a certified energy medicine practitioner, helping to heal the light body using cutting edge neuroscience to create transformation and healing at the level of the soul. You may contact Tresa at: theearthrocks@gmail.com or www.arealjawbreaker.blogspot.com.

THIS I BELIEVE

Melissa Grosboll

When my daughter, Danielle, was little, I remember how blessed I felt that she was a happy, healthy child. I also remember some of my friends having special needs children and children with chronic illnesses. I was in awe of these parents and had so much respect for what they had to endure on a daily basis. I remember thinking that I didn't know how I would handle it if I had a child who had a special need. Over the years I've discovered that God has a sense of humor and we must be careful what we wish for, even if we don't realize we're wishing for it...

In early 2010, Danielle, 11 at the time, started complaining of chronic diarrhea. She went to the bathroom a few times a day, which didn't seem to be cause for too much concern, but she didn't have any solid stools. As a chiropractor, I believe that health comes from within and the body can heal itself, as long as there's no interference to that healing. My first thought, of course, was that she needed to be adjusted more often. She was otherwise completely healthy. In my mind, there was just this one little issue that needed to be addressed.

Adjustments by themselves, however, didn't get rid of the symptoms. A friend of mine suggested that it might be a stress-related or emotional issue (not the last time I would hear this diagnosis) and did some energy work on her. Danielle's spirits lifted, but again, no change. During these first few months, I didn't really think it was that big of a deal. I thought it was mainly due to stress and if she just learned to manage her stress better, she would get better. If only...

Later that year, as her symptoms continued to worsen, I took Danielle to her pediatrician. The doctor examined her, took some blood, and collected some stool samples. All tests came back normal. Not knowing what else to do, the doctor referred us to a gastroenterologist. Meanwhile, the symptoms started to become a real hindrance. She needed to stay close to the bathroom because

35

she never knew when she was going to have to use it. I began to realize that she truly had a problem and we needed to find out what was wrong. The gastroenterologist suggested Danielle had irritable bowel syndrome after only one visit. I said, "Thank you, but I don't accept that generic diagnosis," and moved on.

The next place we turned was a doctor's office highly recommended by several of our friends that focused on nutrition. We thought this was where we would find the answers. They used a bio-meridian scanner to check all the internal systems of the body. Their guess at the time was that Danielle was allergic to gluten, and a company in Texas tested her stool for gluten, along with cow's milk and genetic testing for celiac disease. The test came back positive for gluten sensitivity, although she did not have celiac. This was the answer! Cut out gluten and everything would be healed!

While Danielle was less than thrilled about a gluten-free diet, at this point she was willing to do just about anything to feel better. She wasn't gaining weight, she was chronically dehydrated from the diarrhea, and she was just plain embarrassed about this problem. Danielle was also given several supplements to take daily to help support her healing. Apparently, it can take six to nine months of gluten-free eating to resolve symptoms. I decided to make it a game. I started a blog with recipes that I found. I scoured the library and the Internet for gluten-free ways to cook our favorite foods. I met several amazing people during this time that I am so blessed to call dear friends today.

Let me tell you, living gluten free is a lot of work!!! We bought gluten-free flours to make our own food; we bought gluten-free foods. We discovered that some gluten-free foods are delicious; some are not. Gluten-free foods can be pretty expensive as well. I was extremely grateful for our local natural food stores that did periodic gluten-free fairs where we were able to taste some of the products before we bought them. I did extensive research on all the different names gluten hides under, and I read every label of every product we bought.

Simple things that you never expect to contain gluten were Pringles, Doritos, Rice Krispies, and most processed foods. Even shampoos and hand sanitizers can contain gluten. I learned about that in the doctor's office when there was a note on their hand sanitizer indicating that it contained gluten. Sometimes I felt that I couldn't win. Gluten was everywhere! If it didn't specifically say gluten free on the label, I didn't buy it.

Six weeks later, Danielle was retested. Her internal systems were coming more into balance, which was good. Her symptoms had not changed a bit, which was not so good. The next step, they said, was to get rid of the candida, or systemic yeast, in her body. She was given more supplements and medication to take for the following 30 days, also with no change. I called the doctor's office to let them know. Their response was to add even more supplements to her daily routine. Although I am a big supporter of supplements, after three months they weren't making a bit of difference. Danielle's diarrhea was just as bad as when we started. I was beginning to get very angry. I said, "I don't want more pills! I want someone to tell me what's wrong with my daughter!" They had no response.

Meanwhile, we were still eating gluten-free. We were finally getting the hang of it, and eating at home was easy and even fun. We found lots of gluten-free foods and snacks that tasted really good and enjoyed transforming recipes into gluten-free meals. Outside the house, however, was a different story. It was difficult to find gluten-free entrees in restaurants, and Danielle stopped going to birthday parties and other outside events because she couldn't eat what was served. She also felt weird bringing her own food.

As a mom, this was difficult. I watched her withdrawing from some of her friends and lacking in that social time. It was also difficult for my marriage. My husband and I rarely did anything as a couple because we were constantly focused on Danielle. But we were committed to the process and knew we would soon see results.

One day, after about four months of being gluten-free and still not seeing any positive changes, Danielle had a particularly difficult day at school. My husband was out of town and we were looking forward to a girls' weekend. She came home from school that Friday crying and in pain. She cried every time she went to the bathroom. I looked at her, in agony myself, and asked, "What can I do?" Danielle said to me, matter-of-factly, "Mom, there's nothing you can do."

Now, I knew that she meant there was nothing I could do about the pain she was in at that moment, but in my heart, she voiced exactly what I had been thinking for the past year. I felt completely helpless and unable to do anything to help my daughter. After being strong and not letting my pain and sadness show in front of her for so long, I completely broke down. I fell to the ground sobbing. All those months of acting strong, of not showing her how upset I was so she would stay positive, just crumbled. I couldn't stop crying.

All of a sudden, my 12-year-old daughter began to comfort me. She sat down next to me and held me as I cried. Her words of comfort and encouragement made me cry even harder. She told me that she was going to be fine. She was not going to let this stop her from living her life and she wouldn't give up until she was well. She told me she knew this was her cross to bear right now and she was strong enough to get through whatever was thrown her way. I don't think I've ever been more proud of or amazed by her than I was in that moment. When had my daughter grown up? Who was this strong young woman in front of me? She knew we would find the answers and she would be healed. My daughter's strength in that moment renewed my strength and perseverance and we ended up having a great girls' weekend!

After more than seven months of gluten-free eating, with no changes and other alternative therapies that didn't work, my husband finally put his foot down and said it was time to take Danielle to Children's Hospital. I had a hard time coming to terms with going back to medical doctors. First of all, they hadn't helped her in the past. Second, I was afraid they would just stick some label on her and make her take medication for the rest of her life instead of looking for the real cause. Third, my chiropractic training taught me to be skeptical of medicine and always look for the natural way. My husband, in his infinite wisdom, kindly told me to get over myself, put my ego aside, and do what's best for our daughter. I had to admit the alternatives we'd tried so far hadn't worked either.

The earliest appointment we could get at Children's was a month later, and that gave me the time I needed to "get over myself" and be open to listening to the doctors. It wasn't easy, but I was finally able to put my pride and ego aside, along with my ingrained training, and ask for help. I was still my daughter's biggest advocate and would question anything I didn't agree with, but I was also open to their testing and expertise.

Our appointment went well. We both really liked her doctor. She took a very thorough history, examined Danielle, and took some blood. The doctor suspected she had Inflammatory Bowel Disease, most likely ulcerative colitis. I wasn't ready to accept that diagnosis without proof. She just didn't have the classic symptoms. Her doctor ordered a stool test to rule out a bacterial infection before doing a colonoscopy/endoscopy. She also wanted Danielle back on gluten so they could biopsy for that as well. Needless to say, Danielle was thrilled about that. I don't think she ate a single thing that weekend that wasn't full of gluten! It also helped to take her mind off the upcoming procedure.

Thankfully, the stool test came back positive for C. Diff bacteria. Apparently, C. Diff is an infection that can cause the same symptoms as ulcerative colitis, and hopefully, getting rid of the bacteria would get rid of the symptoms. This result was the first definitive positive result we had received.

When Danielle went back to eating gluten, believe it or not, there was absolutely no change in her symptoms. Nine months of living gluten-free and it hadn't been the cause of her issue! Oh, I'm sure she has some sensitivity to gluten. Up to 80% of the population does. Gluten was just not giving her chronic diarrhea.

Danielle went on antibiotics to get rid of the infection and probiotics to replenish the good bacteria. Within a week of being on the antibiotics, her stools were solid. Two days after stopping the medicine, her diarrhea came back. They tried a stronger antibiotic. Within two days, the diarrhea was gone. This time, it took a week for the symptoms to return after the medicine was gone. Obviously, the medicine was working on the symptoms, but it wasn't fixing the problem.

After three months on antibiotics, Danielle finally tested negative for the bacteria. The infection was gone, but not the diarrhea. Her doctor was becoming more and more convinced that she had ulcerative colitis, even though every blood, stool, and physical examination came back normal. I was beyond frustrated! I asked the doctor, "How many negative test results do you need to see before you start looking at other options?"

She responded, "Well, there aren't really many other options." I refused to accept that. I told her that she needed to start looking for other options because in my gut I knew she didn't have this disease.

Finally, on December 30th, almost two years after her symptoms started, Danielle had a colonoscopy/endoscopy. The pictures showed widespread inflammation over her entire colon! Had I been wrong all this time? Had my intuition failed me? Looking at those pictures, I couldn't think of any answer other than ulcerative colitis. I wanted to know the biopsy results but started doing research on this disease and natural ways to treat it. I knew there had to be something better than putting my daughter on medication for the rest of her life.

I learned a ton in those few days, and Danielle started taking anti-inflammatory medication to treat the inflammation. The doctor called me mid-week with the biopsy results showing that she definitely did NOT have ulcerative colitis!!! My intuition had been right! The inflammation was damage done by a long-standing C. Diff bacterial infection, and with a few months of treatment, she should be healed completely. We had finally found the answer. She is now taking a combination of medicine and natural supplements to heal her colon.

The last two years have taught me many things. I learned that God never gives us more than we can handle. I'm pretty sure He has a lot more faith in what I can handle than I do most of the time, but we took things one day at a time and made it through. I learned that intuition is a powerful thing, and I should always listen to that little voice or feeling. My intuition kept us from accepting the easy answer and we didn't quit until we found the real cause. I learned that searching for and finding the truth, no matter what it takes, are more important than ego and pride. And, finally, I learned that traditional and alternative medicine can work together. It doesn't have to be one or the other.

Danielle wrote a paper for school called "This I Believe." It was her story. Her "This I Believe" was: <u>Never give up hope.</u> No matter how bad it got, she always knew she would get better. Her parents never gave up hope, and neither did she. The last paragraph of her paper read: *"Having hope can really help anyone. It was particularly hard for me, but this whole experience taught me that you should never give up hope no matter how dark the situation may be. There is always an answer if you continue looking for it and never ever give up. This I believe."*

Dr. Melissa Grosboll has been practicing chiropractic since 1997 and her office is located in Lone Tree, Colorado. She is certified in prenatal and pediatric care through the International Chiropractic Pediatric Association. Her mission at Grosboll Family Health Center is to assist people in achieving their health, wellness and performance goals. She also offers nutritional cleansing coaching, as well as exercise and stress management techniques. She and her husband, Jon, have been married since 1993 and their daughter, Danielle was born in 1998. She loves all things outdoors, as well as reading and discovering new ways to get and stay healthy. She can be reached at drgrosboll@grosbollhealth.com or www.grosbollhealth.com.

GOOD ENOUGH

Shari Mitteco

I remember, from as early as 12 years old, what happened each day when I returned home from school. I arrived completely ravenous for food and then ate anything I could get my hands on to satisfy my hunger. The soft lemon cookies with the thin layer of icing were my favorites. I'm not sure when I switched from simply being a hungry kid, but at some point that hunger for food became an intense craving to sooth my anxiety and stuff my emotions.

Maybe it was the feeling I got when I ate that sweet sugar. I would "zone out" as I ate, and my feelings of anxiety would melt away, replaced with a sugar "high" that was as quick as turning on a switch. I would then feel on top of the world and turn into the happy girl I was supposed to be. Unknowingly, this behavior was my preliminary training for the terrible downward spiral of binge eating I did to feed my emotions and hide from the discomfort of my true feelings. I became stuck in this vicious cycle for many years.

My junior high and high school years were painful; many things that I found dramatic and intense plagued me at that age. I struggled to find and fit in with a group of friends to feel better about myself. I had floundered around in school due to reading and auditory comprehension issues. I hid these issues because I wanted to be normal and didn't want to bring any extra attention to myself—especially over something negative like being "stupid" in school. Those kids who need extra help are made fun of, and I wasn't willing to be one of them. Instead, I always did my best even with my learning disabilities.

Additionally, I was very hard on myself about my body because I didn't look like the girls on television. All of this added up to me not being or feeling good enough. My way of dealing with these feelings of inadequacy, including the belief that I

43

was "less than," was to *not* deal with them. My feelings made me uncomfortable so I avoided them. The quickest and fastest way to cover them up was through food, especially sugary stuff. When I went into the kitchen and ate sweet sugar, my anxiety melted away and I felt good again (at least for a while). A cycle of bingeing began, which caused an increase in both my anxiety and my weight. This fueled more dissatisfaction and discomfort with myself and increased my self-consciousness, and that led to more bingeing. As time passed, the cycle took a deeper hold on me.

I started exercising at the age of 14. Aerobics was an option for gym class. Since I was very uncomfortable with myself and my body, I signed up for it. I fell in love with that class! I especially loved that it took away some of my anxious energy, and over time, I could feel my growing confidence as my body changed shape and size. I also discovered that I was actually good at something in school. I enjoyed it so much that my teacher noticed and began to have me occasionally assist with instructing the class. Up to this point in time, I had never liked having attention focused on me; however, because I was able to do something right and help others at the same time, I found that I enjoyed being noticed.

With some of my anxiety diminished, the bingeing didn't happen as often, but I didn't get away from it completely. Every time I did binge, I made myself exercise really hard to burn off what I had eaten. Since my body had begun to change through exercise, I wasn't willing to let go of the noticeable improvement. So, when I binged more, I exercised *even* more. Sometimes, to compensate for my bingeing, I exercised twice a day for an hour each session. Thus began a new cycle—bingeing and purging through exercise. Although I never actually threw up my food, my mentality was the same. I needed to "make up" for something I had done wrong. In my mind, exercise was a good thing to be doing for myself (after all, I wasn't throwing up like the girls they talked about on television). I told myself that I was doing something healthy to rid my body of those extra calories. The exercise that began so positively became an unhealthy obsession.

After I graduated from high school, I joined the local gym and began to learn from various people how to incorporate strength training. I loved working with weights even more than the aerobics classes. The new shape my body took on as I gained muscles and got stronger was totally empowering. I soon found myself hooked on bodybuilding. And I began to research exercise and nutrition to learn everything I could. Of course, this new direction carried its own set of problems. The strict lifestyle I demanded of myself expanded my compulsiveness. Additionally, since I still hadn't managed to kick the bingeing, in my own mind I still wasn't good enough. *What was wrong with me?* I knew so much information about how to eat and how to care for my body, yet I continued to struggle and was extremely frustrated with myself—the cycle continued.

By this time, I had taken a job with a large biotechnology company. I really enjoyed what I was learning there but wasn't doing well assimilating into the corporate lifestyle. I became so stressed about my job that each day as I drove to work, my stomach became upset. I wasn't able to eat much and definitely wasn't eating very well (I was actually so stressed that I even stopped bingeing). Some days I felt so ill, I actually threw up my breakfast once I arrived at work. I was very unhappy and knew I had to find something else to do with my life. My health and happiness were just too important to continue living this way.

My passion for exercise and nutrition began calling me. I knew I wanted to become a personal trainer. I started to train at the local gym and put some of my co-workers through the paces in their homes. With my new decision and a way out of the corporate environment to do something I loved, those stresses of work went away. I began to feel happy again. I would be able to help others feel more confident and become healthier through exercise. After a few months, I knew it was time for me to quit my job and begin my life as a full-time personal trainer.

Although I felt I was a good trainer, I still struggled with my bingeing, and my weight continuously went up and down. I felt like a fake. Here I was—a personal trainer who told people to eat healthy and exercise—with a secret life. For the most part, I ate and exercised in healthy ways, but I continued to binge.

An all-too-common scenario came in the form of a bag of Tootsie Rolls. One night, I had eaten almost an entire bag and to hide from my husband what I'd done, I got in the car and drove from our mountain home to the "local" grocery store—a 30-minute trek—in order to replace it. To cover my tracks further, once I got back to our house, I ate more of the Tootsie Rolls so that the new bag looked like the old one—with the same amount as had been in the previous bag before I ate them. After hiding all the evidence, I felt like a total loser—a failure to myself, my clients, and everyone who knew me.

Once again, as I'd done so many times before, I told myself this had been my last binge. Yet, it wasn't. I continued downward on my spiral of bingeing and getting angry at myself for a while longer. Even after scenarios like the Tootsie Roll "run," I just couldn't stop.

The stressors of a bad marriage didn't help either. As the pressure from the arguments and misunderstandings continued to build, so did my anxiety and uncontrolled eating. This was a time of major insecurity, pain, and frustration for me. I was exercising a lot and bingeing even more. My weight was at an all-time high, and I was very unhappy with myself and my situation.

It was finally time for me to take drastic action. I moved out and after filing for divorce, I moved in with a good friend who happened to be involved in a 12-step program. She suggested I take a look at Overeaters Anonymous. I went to a couple of meetings, sat in those groups, and listened to the other stories. I cried so hard I couldn't even speak. I couldn't believe there were people just like me out there. As I worked through some of the steps, however, I knew this wasn't quite the right place for me. Yes, I related deeply to the individual stories and struggles, but I couldn't get past one thing taught there—that I was powerless against this. Although I believed I was powerless against the cravings and the way I had taught myself that food would make me feel good, I didn't believe "I was powerless." Yes, I handed over my anxiety to my higher power, but ultimately, I was the only one putting that food in my mouth and I was the only one who could decide to do something different. This realization was what changed my life.

I finally recognized it wasn't about the food but about my fears, my anxiety, my anger, and even my happiness. I was uncomfortable with my feelings—all of them—even the good ones. The first step for me was to decide to accept who I was and how I felt about anything and everything. So began my process to feel those emotions and be comfortable in them (or at least be comfortable in the discomfort) and to change my relationship with food.

Each and every time I walked into the kitchen, I asked myself, "Are you really hungry or is something else going on?" If I didn't know the answer, I left the kitchen and didn't return for 20 minutes. This gave me time to think about what I was feeling instead of just diving into food. If the answer was, "Yes, I'm feeling uncomfortable with something," I either called my good friend and chatted about it or wrote my feelings in my journal in order to get them out of my head and gain some perspective. Sometimes, the answer came back as, "I AM really hungry and need to fuel my body, not my emotions." As a result of all these changes, my bingeing started to fade away, and I began to look better and feel good about myself.

Through this process, I became a better trainer—even GOOD ENOUGH. My weakness in life had become my strength. What I lived through has allowed me to help others. Through understanding my own process, I have been able to empower others and teach the tools I used to get myself out of that lonely downward spiral with food and emotions. I have been able to support them every step of the way and understand how they feel because I've been there.

I do not simply teach them from a book, but from my own experience. I walk with them as they ask themselves, "Am I really hungry?" I help them see that making a new choice with food is worth it because *they* are worth it—they *are* GOOD ENOUGH.

My clients, in turn, help me remember where I've been and where I choose to be today—healthy, happy, and free to be me and continue to help others. Each and every day, my clients offer me the opportunity to continue to see myself and them through eyes of compassion, understanding, and acceptance for where we've been and where we want to be. Knowing that I have been able to transform my past experiences to help myself—and in turn help others—has made it all worth it. For that I am forever grateful.

Shari Mitteco is the Owner of Your Fabulous Body, LLC. She helps her clients with exercise, nutrition, and getting past emotional eating. The Your Fabulous Body studio is a private, state-of-the-art facility where Shari teaches individuals and small groups. Visit www. YourFabulousBody.com or call Shari directly at 303-408-0321.

STILL

Jerri Lee George

One Saturday evening in early November 2009, my life was suddenly altered. Like a tree whose leaves change colors and drift slowly to the ground each fall, my existence as I knew it was stripped clean and lay bare.

A practicing caterer for over twenty years, I had just finished serving 200 guests at a wedding reception in the snow-dusted Rocky Mountain foothills. Catering was a job I loved with all my heart. Utilizing a talent I considered to be God-given, I had been operating for nearly five years in the Denver area after relocating from Florida. I was quite proud of my growing reputation in an entirely new market. My sons, Ethan 16 and Zachary 14, made new friends, settled into their school routines, and our family had just opened a storefront in a local strip mall, confidently forging ahead.

Being a Christian woman, I was familiar with biblical scripture and verse. A favorite of mine was and still is, "Be still, and know that I am God," although I had never applied it literally. That was about to change.

The weeks preceding the epic blow to my life were a bit out of control—similar to a runaway freight train, twisting and turning at breakneck speed. Our busy holiday season was approaching on the heels of a crazy event-packed summer, and my uncle, my mother's only sibling, died the last week of October. Although I love my family and would normally jump at the chance to visit New England, I simply did not have the time nor the extra money to run off to Massachusetts. My Uncle Jack, however, had been the most important man in my life ever since my own dad died; so after some consideration and discussion, off we went. The stress of the loss notwithstanding; the two four-hour flights in as many days, along with hotel rooms, fast food, relatives, friends, and memorial services did me in physically and emotionally.

In retrospect, I thought I had been still...at the funeral, on the planes, between flights, and I was certainly listening to God. I was praying...praying for my family, my cousins' grief, and my uncle's peaceful rest for eternity. I wasn't working, and I was definitely grieving, though questioning God's fairness and timing as most of us are inclined to do.

My uncle knew how to be still and he definitely *knew* God! His life and death were a testament to what God promises His people. He served in the Navy at 18, became a husband, father, and bank officer for more than 40 years. He was active in his church, the president of his model railroad association, a first-prize winning photographer in his camera club, a travel photographer, and public speaker about trips he made "round the world." He survived a wife dying of cancer and even married again but never really retired. In later years, he still worked part-time and sat on a council overseeing the operation of the town cemetery—the one where he was ultimately interred at the age of 86. He died a month after returning from a two-week cruise to Nova Scotia and only two months before another—planned for Jamaica. He was survived by three adult children (my cousins), six grandchildren, two great grandchildren, several nieces and nephews, my mother, and me.

Obviously, my uncle was not "still" in the literal sense, but he attended church with great regularity, sat in his peaceful home, often read the bible, and KNEW God! He was found curled up in bed, having gone comfortably to sleep following a conversation with his only daughter about plans for his next trip, a photo show he was hosting at the library the next day, and the proud completion of a newly-made engine for his model railroad village completely hand-crafted and on display in his cellar, filling it to the rafters. I am convinced the only way God could take my Uncle was to catch him while sleeping.

The funeral was held on a Tuesday. My return flight was Thursday, just in time to prep for a wedding that coming weekend. The next few days were daunting with menus to create for holiday parties, staff to schedule, regular orders to deliver, tastings to hold, and a grieving family of my own with at-home demands. Stopping to be still was not an option!

I squeezed every last ounce of energy I had into my business but somehow managed to show up for the long-anticipated premiere of the tribute movie "THIS IS IT," created to honor the legendary Michael Jackson. At that time, I was blissfully unaware that Jackson's once-in-a-lifetime vocals would be the last pieces of music my ears would ever hear. Two days after the hillside catering job, I was rushed to the hospital, fever rising and delirious.

I woke from a coma in an intensive care unit one month later. I had somehow contracted Bacterial Meningitis. Doctors subsequently shared that I had presented with three different forms of the killer infectious disease...bacterial, viral, and something named Meningococcal Sepsis. Meningococcal Sepsis is a strain of the infection that causes the formation of sores on the body. The sores were of varying severity and size, which grew just centimeters from one another, ravaging my body from head to toe. I think one can best describe my body as covered (except for my face, praise the Lord) with open, oozing adhesions, the likes of which I imagine lepers bore during the time Jesus walked among us.

One of the few memories I have of my hospital stay was when an ER doctor initially roused me enough to get permission to run a main intravenous needle in the largest vein in my neck. I remember expressing my concern—that a friend had been given one and it hurt...a lot. His answer was terse. "Mrs. George, you are one sick lady. We need to pump some powerful antibiotics into your body *fast*. This is really our best option." I recall responding with a simple, "what*ever*." This communication with the ER attending was my last. During the intervening weeks, my body endured two spinal taps, two CT Scans, three EEG's, many other tests, needle punctures, and procedures to help me survive—while my family and friends waited.

On my birthday, November 20th, my family was told to say their goodbyes. Nothing more could be done. Prayer chains and cross-country connections were informed of my 10% chance of survival. My mother never left my bedside in all those days— weeping, praying, believing, and bargaining. My sons wrestled with their imminent loss, unable to accept defeat, while my husband juggled his job, the doctors, mounting medical bills, a floundering catering business, and two traumatized teens with truancy issues and slipping grades. All the while,

I lay positively still.

But I wasn't, not really. Somewhere in my comatose state, I had been visiting with God. I now tell people, in teasing, that I didn't actually *see* God, but I most certainly felt his presence. I must have been in the outskirts of heaven—in the suburbs I suppose. The brightest, most pure light imaginable beckoned me, and I was drawn toward the strongest, most genuine feeling of love that has ever been bestowed me on this earth.

Returning to the real world, I felt as if a long arm reached into my surroundings and yanked me out—being literally extracted, with all the force of childbirth, away from this most enchanting place. Suddenly, there was pain, tears, fear, and overwhelming feelings of violation and vulnerability. The memory of where I'd been was palpable and hauntingly magical. I begged to go back with a fervent desire to forsake my family and friends, to remain on the other side. The indescribable beauty will stay with me always.

Once awake, the days ebbed and flowed as I dipped in and out of actual consciousness. My brain was not yet truly functional and hallucinations played havoc with my thoughts. I married Elvis, slept in an airplane hangar, and was convinced my doctor was an accomplice in an elaborate plot to kill me. Thankfully, as the minutes turned to hours, and hours into days, I became more lucid and was able to be present and embrace life again, but not fully. The infection had done its damage, and I could no longer hear. I can tell you firsthand that being suddenly deaf is about as still as it gets.

The reality of the many challenges ahead had not really settled in until a visit from yet another doctor took place. It was the podiatrist's chance to share, with his charts and graphs and through written notes. The hideous infection had also taken its toll on my extremities and for the first time, I was shown my feet. They were quite a ghastly pair—crusty, black as coal from heel-to-toe. A severe case of gangrene had set in early on, worrying my Mom half to death. The doctor suggested I prepare for surgery and possible amputation. Then he left.

There is really nothing so still as a hospital room after bad news has been delivered. I watched as the second hand on the wall clock continued to tick at a steady rate.

It was not told to be still.

Foot surgery came. The damaged tissue was scraped and the gangrene removed along with four of my toes on my left foot. A glass-half-full kind of gal, I prefer to concentrate on the six that remain. To this day, I wait to perch atop my first pair of post-surgery high heels.

On a recent trip to the Florida Keys I did have all six toes polished—adorned with flower stickers—so wearing sandals was not only possible but attractive. A bit of a bold move, I admit, but it worked. Few people noticed my shortened appendages. Today, I am toying with the idea of getting a tattoo—of a little pig, carrying a sign with an arrow saying "off to market."

Rehab and physical therapy came 10 days after surgery and lasted nearly a year. I longed for strength in my hands and arms to return and the ability to activate the use of my cell phone and laptop. Only then would I be able to access my friends and family through the written word and research the truth about my illness—most especially the possibility and extent of my recovery—facts that my family and doctors were just as pleased I didn't know.

One of the very first items on the physical therapist's agenda, after relearning to eat on my own and accomplishing the arduous task of sitting upright on the edge of my bed, was an excursion to the bathroom. I welcomed the removal of the catheter and certainly hoped the adult diapers I'd been wearing were also prepared to leave. What I could not have known was how much one uses the auditory sense when in a lavatory. We all take for granted hearing the familiar plop of an excretion hitting the water, alerting us as to its arrival at the expected destination; the sound of a stream of urine which lessens in intensity as one is finished. It's amazing how much we utilize hearing rather than feeling. I had to learn to apply the act of looking to see if the toilet actually flushed or the faucet turned off, rather than trusting my ears.

The sensation of deafness is best described or demonstrated by putting ear plugs in one's ears and a pillowcase with two Casper-like cutouts around the eyes. Life is only that which is seen through the holes. No peripheral sound, nothing to the left, nothing to the right—only an abyss behind.

What a world lay beyond the capture of my ear drums. An air conditioner cycling, a fan running, a phone ringing, a fire alarm screeching, a television volume too loud or low were all forever lost to me. Handy tools such as a flashlight to shed a beacon on an unheard motion, the tremor of a vibrating cell phone beating against the table, the smell of food announcing mealtime, and closed captioning television all became fast friends. My eyes became more valuable than ever.

I walked the rehabilitation center hallways one step at a time and found that physical and occupational therapists are truly God's angels with skin on...they applaud the tiniest movement and encourage one more step, one more action toward full recovery. Our bodies are arguably a most incredible creation... damaged, broken, and weak; they heal, mend, and recover. They can sit, stand, walk, and move after being prostrate for weeks on end.

I eventually stopped being angry with God. I asked with regularity why he allowed me to survive if I couldn't even walk or hear. What kind of miracle was I anyway? I found the answer in my stillness. It ushered in a period of time with me and my family that bordered on miraculous. Time spent together sharing triumphs and failures, hopes and fear, laughter and tears, the value of touch and sight, and the memories that remain. The act of running my fingers through my boys' locks of hair; their hands cradled in mine just before visiting hours ended; arms that helped to lift and sometimes carry me when my body failed; smiles of encouragement and approval—some so necessary during the bleakest times—the relief on my kids' faces upon believing that Mom was actually here to stay.

Christmas that year was celebrated with cards, gifts, emails, and Facebook posts from friends and relatives from points south, north, east, and west. A tiny tree mounted on a desk and a wreath on the door of my room were the only signs of the season, but having my family gather in my room on Christmas eve to open gifts (some that I had begun to collect before I was stricken) and partake of a holiday meal in the dining room with my fellow recoveries were unforgettable moments. It was my first time sitting upright at a table and all of our prayers were given with renewed energy and sincerity, thanking God for His Son, my survival, and the future—with whatever challenges and blessings it held.

Now, I use my stillness as a gift—taking time to watch others, witnessing their blessings and my own more clearly. I treasure each glance from those I love and have learned to read lips. How precious the words are formed by my youngest—specifically for my comprehension. I am reaping more joy from other senses, like slipping into a steamy bubble bath and soaking until tepid, my head cradled on a soft down pillow or in the fur coat of our dog, Wynonna. I've noticed being deaf accentuates my sense of smell. Flowers, particularly lilacs and gardenias, overtake a gentle breeze, and the scent of a wood-burning fireplace is as powerful as the deep glow of embers. I no longer hear the crunch of snow beneath my shoes but can feel it shift and give way as the cold penetrates to chill what's left of my feet—and I am home a lot more.

I've had to relinquish practicing as a caterer but partnered with a young chef whom I am able to bless by sharing my knowledge while still keeping my hand in the business. In my spare time I've resurrected an old passion—turning my creative skills in another direction. I am now writing. It's the quiet, personal act of putting my thoughts on paper and sharing them with the world that now excites me so.

I *am* STILL and thankfully I *know* God…and what He has done for me.

A Mayflower descendant, Great Grand Niece of Pearl S. Buck and child of restaurateurs, Jerri Lee George was born in Miami Beach, Florida. Spending summers on Cape Cod as a child she carried a love of New England, along with cooking and writing, forward in life—not necessarily in that order. Following hurricanes Katrina and Wilma in 2005, Jerri moved to Colorado where she owned and operated Catering by George until stricken with Bacterial Meningitis in 2009. Now deaf, as a side effect of the illness, and a proud mother of two sons, Ethan and Zachary, Jerri resides in Denver, works as consultant to Vision Catering, LPA; is founder of ThereButForTheGrace.org, a non-profit helping others to overcome financial crises due to illness or accident; and is currently summoning her naturally-inherited ability for writing in order to complete the next chapter of her life. She is working on

Cater$avvy, *a book about catering secrets, and* Seaduced, *her first novel set in post WWII Miami Beach and Cape Cod.*

I AM THAT GIRL

Christi Milroy

Sitting across the table, I couldn't believe what I was hearing. Our normal card game had come to an abrupt halt as we sat and listened to Traci tell us that she was in a healing group for post-abortive women. As she shared her heart, I tried to stay focused on what she was saying, but the words seemed to float into a faint murmuring in the background while my mind began racing through millions of thoughts. *How could she sit there and just bluntly state that she'd had an abortion? She didn't even know me very well. Should I share that I'd had an abortion as well? No way! She may feel the need to share but I certainly do not. I am fine...after all I haven't even thought about my abortion, or should I say abortions, for quite some time. Why would she bring this up? Why now? And why am I now thinking about those dreadful days...those dreadful years?*

At the age of 16, as a sophomore in high school, I moved out on my own. To this day the reasons that my parents allowed it are beyond me. I would like to blame my parents for allowing me, a mere child, to live on my own. I would like to hold them responsible—to see their decision as the beginning of my destruction—but the honest truth is that I was already living a life of rebellion and self-destruction. I had been engaging in sexual activity and partying from the age of 12, trying to mask the wounds of sexual abuse from a tender age.

Living on my own allowed me free reign to do whatever I wanted, and I did. I found myself engaging in every destructive activity I could get my hands on. I hooked up with a guy not long after I moved out on my own, eventually moving in with him. He was manipulative, controlling, and abusive; even better, he was a drug dealer. He knew exactly how to cause pain and then how to numb it. I became a great chameleon, presenting myself as having it altogether while I fell apart more and more inside.

When we found out I was pregnant, he drove me to the clinic

to "take care of it." He was happy to pay; after all, it would be a mere penny in comparison to the cost of the alternative. I was scared and panicked. *How would I care for a child when I was still in high school myself? How would I? How could I? I just couldn't!* The drive home was silent. He didn't know what to say. I didn't know what to say. I felt completely numb inside—as though a part of my soul had been ripped out of me.

My life seemed to spiral deeper into darkness after that day. Trying even harder to mask the pain, I continued in a vicious cycle of drugs, abuse, and excuses. As a senior in high school, while others were enjoying the freedom of being teenagers and looking forward to graduation, I spent a week in a courtroom because of domestic violence and dreaded what would come next. I underwent a brutal weeklong trial, testifying against the man I'd been living with. Not only was this experience one that most high school seniors would not have been involved with, but most grown women haven't had to deal with such an ordeal either. Six months following the trial, I was back with my abuser.

After high school, at the age of 18, I became a stripper (not an exotic dancer…there isn't anything exotic about it). The job seemed to be a perfect fit, as it not only supported my vices, but it also made my life seem normal. No longer an outcast for the life I'd been living, I was now working amongst women who were living lives just like mine. My boyfriend had furthered his career as well, stepping into selling drugs that I never imagined I would ever try.

Somewhere in the midst of the madness I found myself pregnant again by the same father. It was a simple answer for him. We would take care of it just as we had before. This time, however, it wasn't as simple for me. I knew all too well the pain it had caused the first time. I was older and wiser and definitely knew better. Why had I allowed this to happen again? Knowing that I had been using drugs like LSD, weed, speed, cocaine, and crystal meth, on top of drinking, I couldn't even imagine what kind of damage I had done to my child.

The nurse tried to console me but it wasn't working. I knew better this time. I knew it was not just a blob of tissue like they told me the first time. I knew it wasn't just a simple procedure. I knew the statement, "I would never have to worry or think about it again," was a lie. I knew the pain would not just last for a few days. I knew… Yet, I aborted my second child anyway.

As he pressed the gun to my forehead, it all seemed like a dream. How had I gotten here? How had I allowed my life to come to this point? Was I to die here…now? Fear and panic filled me. The feeling was all too familiar. I had lived a lifetime with this man in a period of six years. At that moment, I realized just how much I hated my life. I survived that day, but the gun he put to my head was the final straw. Somewhere in me I found the strength to leave him.

Only a year after leaving him, I found myself in another relationship but still broken and so very desperate to be loved that I convinced myself he was something he wasn't. Before I knew it, I was pregnant again. He assured me he would be by my side, marry me, and we would be a family. Thankfully, they were all lies. For if he had told me the truth, the real truth, that he had no intention of sticking around, that he would never even see the day his son was born, or for that matter, ever look him in the eye, I would have likely aborted my son, Devin.

Devin was my wakeup call. That little bundle of joy was all it took to convince me it was time to grow up and start making better choices. A mom now, my focus was on my son and my desire to show him the love that I seemed so desperate to find. The turbulent currents of my life seemed to drift away. With his birth, I walked away from the lifestyle I had previously known. His birth gave me the courage to do that.

Eventually, I fell in love with a man who truly loved and cared for me, and we were blessed with another child to love. Finally, I was able to rest. I had walked away from that life and the self-destruction; I stuffed it all away for no one to ever see. As the years passed, the life I had lived faded into memories, but my mother's arms still longed to hold my unborn babies. My heart ached; my life felt incomplete. The decisions of my past would haunt me forever, even as I tried to pretend they'd never happened.

Months later, sitting at the same table where Traci initially decided to confide in us about her abortion, I found myself once again forced to recall those memories that I had tried so hard to forget. As she conveyed to us the healing she had received and the newfound desire to not only share with others her experience, but see other women healed as she had been, I felt angry. *How dare she bring this up again! It was great that she had been healed, but I didn't want to hear it. After all, I was okay. I had moved past those days, past my sexual abuse, my drug use, and my abortions. I had changed. I had walked away from that life and decided not to look back.*

As I listened to her tell me the staggering statistics, that 43% of women of childbearing age have had an abortion, I felt as though she were speaking directly to me. *She must think…who cares if that is what she thinks…I will just let her know that, yes, I had an abortion (no way would I admit to two), but that I am okay, and she can go on talking to someone else about it.*

I did end up telling her that I'd had an abortion. And yes, I only admitted to one. I told her I was FINE and I DIDN'T NEED HELP—her help or anyone else's. And I let her know that others who'd had abortions were fine too—just like me—I was sure of it. I understood her need to have a cause and be a part of it, but I told her she'd have to find someone else to get involved. I was not the ONE. I didn't need anything from her.

Over time, we joined a church and began attending, but initially my interests in church were for my boys, not for myself. Fearful that I would lose my boys to the same decisions I had made, I wanted them to know God, so they would hopefully make better choices.

One Sunday morning, my husband and I got into an argument over the time it took for us to get ready for church and how we would have to decide to be extremely late for service or not go at all. Frustrated, I decided to go to the church just down the street from our house, knowing we wouldn't make it to the one we had been regularly attending. As we walked through the doors, I saw Traci sitting at a table with a couple of other ladies. She noticed me right away. Her smile spread from ear to ear. She was visibly happy that I had come, and although she and I had become closer since those initial uncomfortable conversations at the dining room table, I wasn't quite sure why she was so pleased that I was there.

As I sat in the service, I learned that it was Sanctity of Life

Sunday, and that of all weekends, this was the weekend to remember the importance of human life. They played a video about a bible study. It was the healing group that Traci had previously talked to us about on those evenings I had tried so hard to forget. To my surprise, the pastor talked openly about abortion and the heartache women suffer because of abortion. I couldn't believe what I was hearing. I felt so overwhelmed, so confused, so hurt. I couldn't hide the shame and guilt I had stuffed for so long. It seemed to rush out of me like a faucet that had been turned on full blast. All I could do was cry.

Lord, I am scared. I don't know that I can do this. I don't want to experience all of those feelings again. I don't want to remember all of the gory details of my life's past. If I do, I don't know that I can handle it. I can suffer the decisions of my past; in fact, I deserve to suffer for aborting my children. What is the point? LORD, PLEASE DON'T MAKE ME DO THIS. I walked in the door to that first meeting praying the whole way, asking Him to tell me that some way, somehow, this was not for me. I am not really sure how I found the strength, but I made it through the door.

That day was the start of the rest of my life. I fought and struggled for the next eight weeks working through those painful memories. I learned how dangerous it is to live in silence; the wounds from my youth would never be forgotten, and the shame and guilt had held me in bondage. I learned the power of truth and the real effects of post-abortion trauma in my life. I discovered that anger is natural and that anger can be expressed in healthy ways. I came to understand how to forgive and that by forgiving, I am not forgetting.

Most of all, I realized that I had already been forgiven. It was not my duty to forgive myself but to accept the forgiveness already given me. God paid the ultimate price. He sent his son, Jesus Christ, to die on the cross for me so that I could live in freedom. He exchanged my sins for His grace—His unmerited favor. I learned the difference between healthy grief and destructive sorrow, how to address past wounds by embracing my pain and rejecting the shame, and how healing is a process from the inside out. The battle was hard but it was worth it. I met my God, my Pursuer, my Comforter…my Healer.

"You have searched me, Lord, and you know me. You know when I sit and when I rise; you perceive my thoughts from afar. You discern my going out and my lying down; you are familiar with all my ways. Before a word is on my tongue you, Lord, know it completely. You hem me in behind and before, and you lay your hand upon me...For you created my inmost being; you knit me together in my mother's womb. I praise you because I am fearfully and wonderfully made; your works are wonderful, I know that full well. My frame was not hidden from you when I was made in the secret place, when I was woven together in the depths of the earth. Your eyes saw my unformed body; all the days ordained for me were written in your book before one of them came to be." Psalm 139:1-5, 13-16 NIV

You were there Father. You were there the whole time. You never left my side. You saw my days before I was even created... and You still chose me. You pursued me. I know now it was You who gave me the strength when I needed it most. You ripped me from the darkness I was living in and have shown me how to live with joy. *"You redeemed me from the pit and crowned me with love and compassion; you have renewed my youth, and forgiven all my sins."* (Psalm 103) Thank you Father.

So, YES, I REALLY AM THAT GIRL, and...
- I am free
- I am loved
- I am forgiven
- I am good enough
- I am not ashamed
- I am a child of God
- I am not who I used to be
- I am cherished in His eyes
- I am not defined by my past
- I am broken but made whole through Christ
- I am invited to sit at the table with my heavenly Father
...and you are too!

Christi Milroy is a proud wife and mother of two beautiful boys, Devin and Ryon, and has two dogs (otherwise known as "the poopers"),

Brownie and Max. She has worked in mortgage lending for over 16 years. She is currently walking in freedom and passionate about seeing other women free from the guilt and shame of abortion and bondage to which it holds us. She has just completed her certification to become a Surrendering the Secret bible study leader. For more information and to connect to a group near you, you can call Christi directly at 303-915-3739 or visit SurrenderingTheSecret.com.

LETTING GO IS
SETTING ME FREE

Lisa Shultz

As a little kid, I remember holding on to my mom's hand tightly as we crossed the street. But I quickly grew into an independent pre-teen and teenager since my siblings were all grown and out of the house by the time I was eight. I felt a bit like an only child due to the wide age gap between me and my next oldest brother, and I wanted to be as grown up as they were. Letting go of my mother's hand was easy because I could venture further into the independence I yearned for.

My parents divorced at a time when parents rarely did. I did not see my dad much during middle school and high school, and my mom began to work to rebuild her life. Even with these changes in my family life, I still felt supported by my parents and quickly learned to be comfortable "being alone." Instead of feeling bad about my situation, I embraced it and enjoyed the feeling of independence. Letting go of an intact family was easier because of all the experiences I was able to have on my own.

During my sophomore year in high school, I applied for a mini-exchange program with my German class. During the summer I was 16, I went to Berlin with a few other classmates for a month. Most of our day was unstructured. With one of my classmates, I explored the city on foot and via the public transportation system. A month of uninhibited exploration of a major city without an adult took me to a new level of independence. I got very good at using maps and schedules and became proficient in all the ways to get around a city (and a foreign one at that). I barely knew the language, yet still managed quite well.

By the time I got home, I felt more independent than before and decided to apply to college out of state. My mom had always told me to live on my own for a while before I got married so that I would know how to take care of bills and learn how to support myself. She'd married at 16 and never had a stage of independence until she got divorced 30 years later. I took her advice and got my own apartment after graduation from college. I worked for several years before getting married.

In my youth, letting go was exciting because the world was an adventure to explore. I felt exhilarated to spread my wings and fly away from my home nest. But as an adult, I sometimes did not feel that thrill with letting go because it hurt. As time passed, letting go became more and more difficult.

I realized it was extremely important for me to have a partner in my life to share our days and experiences together—that was how I saw my marriage. I found myself holding on to that concept tightly even when my marriage began to deteriorate. I held on to the belief that we had married for better or for worse. Although it became worse, I gripped even harder. As a result, when he declared it was over and he was leaving, I fought it. I did not want to get a divorce despite the fact that he was unkind and unloving to me.

My heart broke during the unraveling of my marriage and subsequent divorce, and the big world seemed daunting to navigate alone with two children. Suddenly, I was out there as a single mom, whether I wanted it or not. And I soon discovered that letting go was going to be a skill I would need to practice throughout my entire life. Letting go with my ex-husband had been difficult, but the letting go I had to learn to do with my girls was even more challenging.

Many intact families get to enjoy their kids at home all the time, but when my kids were very young, I had to start letting them go long before parents normally do because of the time they spent with their dad and step-mom. Sometimes it was painful to be without them. I envied families that did not have to be separated during their kids' younger years.

As a result of this new way of living, I missed out on monumental milestones in my children's lives. For instance, when one of my daughters lost a tooth while at her dad's house, I felt sad. The tooth fairy visited them there and my tooth fairy duties had to wait until they happened to lose a tooth at my house.

My daughters soon began traveling and took the trips my ex-husband and I had planned for our family, except that the girls went on these trips with their dad and step-mom instead of with me. They came home from faraway places with experiences and memories I would never share with them. I learned to let go of another layer of my vision of motherhood and family life.

I was sometimes alone for a major holiday that was important to me. This was especially difficult, as children often make a holiday—such as Christmas and Easter—special with their excitement to open their stockings and presents or hunt for Easter eggs. Filling those empty days with something else was a real test in letting go.

When my oldest daughter, at twelve years old, decided to live in Paris with her dad for six months and then spent a whole year studying abroad in Italy at fifteen, people asked me how I could bear it. I simply answered that I'd had practice. I'd become accustomed to a fifty-fifty schedule split and learned to adjust to the many trips they took with their father.

During those times when I was completely alone, without my daughters, our family life felt broken—I felt broken. I was thankful for my beloved dog Sally, who remained by my side until she died many years later. She was my constant companion through those very difficult years of adjustment.

Adjusting to the "shoulds" in my life was another lesson in letting go. For instance, I thought the justice system *should* give a certain verdict or that my husband *should* behave a particular way. Neither complied with what I thought "should" happen. Sometimes they behaved in the exact opposite way and no amount of support from family and friends and attorneys changed it.

Processing and letting go of these "should have happened" or "should not have happened" events was difficult. The lack of justice made no sense in my mind and made me sometimes wonder if I was the crazy one. I even remember once feeling like I'd been set up by a child advocate during my divorce. He'd asked me for a list of things that were especially important to me, such as meaningful holidays. Then, after I provided the list, he asked me to pick the one that meant the most to me. So I did. Shortly afterward, he ruled that I would not be allowed to see my kids on that special day. I sobbed from the deepest part of my heart. How could I trust others if they asked for what I most desired and then made sure I lost it? I really had to learn to let go during that time and also learn to trust again.

67

Being forced to let go of our family of four after the divorce, I made the choice to utilize my alone time to make new friends and start a new business. This was probably the first time that I *consciously* realized how "letting go" opened new doors and opportunities. These new friends, as well as the time to deepen my existing friendships, led me to richer, more meaningful relationships than I had ever experienced before.

I also began to explore new ways to make money—more ways than I had ever envisioned with my degree from college or my stay-at-home-mom days. I learned new skills and explored untapped desires, such as writing books. I realized that letting go of a marriage that dampened my spirit was freeing. I could create a new me and be whatever I wanted.

When I was alone, I used that time to redefine myself. I did that continuously; it is still ongoing. I had time to explore who I was, what was most important to me, and express my true talents and strengths. I began to allow myself to dream and create. I adopted an attitude of not wanting regrets later in life. So with that attitude, I took bold acts of courage in many areas of my life. Some flopped. (I prefer that word instead of failed.) And of course, a flop is not a flop if you learn and grow from it. I can happily report that I did learn and grow. I have decided to learn and grow until the day of my last breath!

As I began to explore new relationships and new careers, I found myself getting attached and holding on tightly to some of these new directions. With each new endeavor, I convinced myself that this was "the one." So, I was a bit surprised and disappointed when "the one" seemed to slip away or I released it consciously after discovering it no longer served me. I continued to redefine myself, what I wanted to be and which relationships would add to my life, while allowing myself the freedom to be, do, or become my highest potential.

Admittedly, even though I attempted to make lemonade out of lemons through self-development and self-rediscovery when I was by myself, I still had times of loneliness and sadness. I had several years of playing excessive tennis to cope with that loneliness. For quite some time following my divorce, I played every league game and tournament I could find to fill space. I then moved on to being incredibly busy and became a workaholic.

Over time I gradually let go of these coping mechanisms, completely laying down my tennis racquet and simplifying my business life significantly so that many days had white space on my calendar with no obligations or appointments.

My mom's advice entered in again as she told me that a relationship with a man is ideally the icing on the cake or the cherry on top and not the cake itself. It was my responsibility to establish myself as a delicious cake that became magnificent with a bit of frosting to top it off by adding a guy. So, I let go of ideals and misconceptions that I was incomplete without a relationship and allowed myself to first become a great "cake" alone.

I've discovered that when I let someone or something go, they've returned in new and often better ways, if they were meant to come back at all. I have a wonderful friendship with a former boyfriend that will likely stretch into the rest of our days. My daughters appreciate me more when they leave and come back to visit and hang out with me. My oldest daughter even said recently that she didn't get enough of me growing up. She wants to figure out how to spend more quality time with me even though she is attending college.

I in turn am hanging out more with my mom and dad these days too. They are in their 80's, and we still enjoy each other's company. I feel fortunate to have been an independent kid and still have the opportunity to spend time with my parents today. Experiencing this time with them makes me realize that my kids will explore the world and still want to come home to their mom too. So I focus on creating a home they'll love to visit and will welcome them each time they return.

Another element of letting go in my life is the quantity of "stuff" I own. In today's society, it seems common to gather more and more stuff to fill any available space we live in. In my case, when I moved to Denver in 1996, my husband and I bought a large house and proceeded to fill every room, closet, and storage space in it. When he left, he took very little and I filled those gaps again fairly quickly.

Over time, this large-sized house and the stuff it contained felt overwhelming—so much to care for, clean, and organize. For one person, it felt heavy to continue to manage on my own. So I set a plan in place to sell the house upon my youngest daughter's graduation from high school. In order to downsize and simplify my life, I've had the daunting task of eliminating more than half of what I own. I knew I would need at least a year to do it, so I began little-by-little to sort through every space, clearing it away gradually.

I could only do a small part of my home at a time because letting go of so much too fast felt stressful. At times when I opened a box that had emotionally-charged things in it, such as wedding items, I had to take it very slow and allow myself to feel the emotions and memories tied to the items so I could make a decision about what to do with them and also heal my feelings around each item.

Gradually, as I let things go to others who could use or enjoy them, I have felt lighter. Carrying so much stuff around my living space had become a pressure I am slowly releasing. Sometimes, like peeling the layers of an onion, a month or so had to pass before I could take the next layer out and examine and disperse those things.

Letting go has involved big lessons in learning to live with uncertainty and change. When I've entered new territory or experimented with a new direction, I've had to develop the courage to step into the unknown. This new venture might hold success or it might hold a new learning experience that I could never have imagined. So letting go of what is safe and known and moving into new and uncharted worlds has taken a leap of faith and a willingness to let go of my comfort zone.

Happily, my courage has served me well. Each new door I've walked through has been an adventure. Each door brings new friends, new growth, and lessons that I may take with me even if I exit from that door and go through another one.

Letting go of anger when things did not go the way I hoped and letting go of bitterness that came from my perceived wrongs was a challenge, but letting in happiness and peace instead are the biggest blessings in my life today. It is a matter of what I allow my thoughts to rest upon. What do I quickly dismiss and what do I embrace? I have chosen to redirect my mind when it lingers on a past hurt. There is so much to be grateful for now that it would be foolish of me to waste moments in remorse, regret, or self-pity.

It took me awhile to heal my heart and sweep out the bitterness cobwebs to return to a place of positive anticipation. As I continue to let go of emotions that do not serve me so that I may live my highest purpose today, I am liberated. I choose freedom. I choose letting go of the people, things, and even memories that do not serve me with positive energy today.

Letting go of unfulfilled dreams is the biggest test of making lemonade out of lemons. But I countered that by being creative to design a new dream and carry on. I was always aware that children observe and internalize what they watch their parents do, so I just kept figuring out how to make something good out of the disappointments in my life. And I still do so today. As a result, my life now is different than I ever thought it would be, but it is amazing nonetheless. I am grateful and appreciative for all I have and who I have become. As both my children will be out of state at college in the fall of 2012, and I will be moved into a new home in a new town, I have a new adventure to embrace and experience.

Each day, my mind gives me options about what to dwell upon. I train my brain like I train my muscles for a sport I love. With diligence in guarding my inner freedom, I practice thoughts of prosperity, health, and happiness. I dismiss other non-serving thoughts as quickly as possible and go out and seize the day. Letting go is truly setting me free to live my best life today. I am excited about the future and thankful that I can let go of what holds me back from being all I can be and reaching my full potential.

Lisa Shultz loves to write books, coach, and pursue entrepreneurial endeavors. After a recent move to Breckenridge Colorado, she is embracing a new living environment, friends, and adventures as she explores having an "empty nest" with her two daughters attending college out of state. As she approaches her 50th birthday in 2013, she is excited to see the world and explore the next chapter of her life. Follow her journey on her blog, www.LisaJShultz.com.

THE CALLING OF
MY SACRED VOICE

Beverly Sullivan

For most of my life, I was sick with the Good Girl Syndrome. Sound familiar?

Symptoms include saying yes when we mean no, repressing our feelings, not speaking up for ourselves or setting clear-cut boundaries, and being inauthentic, along with people pleasing.

This Good Girl behavior of holding my tongue literally made me ill. Unspoken words and unexpressed feelings built up like toxic waste, causing physical and emotional symptoms. When I visited my internist in the late '90s, she diagnosed peri-menopause. As the symptoms continued to worsen, I endured, holding my tongue and not questioning her authority.

It wasn't until a year later that a new doctor diagnosed Graves' disease, an auto-immune disease of the thyroid (the 5th chakra—the throat/voice), and my diseased thyroid gland was irradiated. After riding a roller coaster of emotions for months, I felt tremendous relief. But I was also bereft, realizing that by keeping my mouth shut I had done irreparable harm to my mind and body. On a deeply spiritual level, I recognized that my voice was dying to be heard. I pondered my reflexive voice-silencing pattern. Why was it so hard to speak up?

For me, it began as a child. I had a speech impediment, and kids teased and called me names, creating deep shame and fear to speak at all. In the movie, "The King's Speech," King George VI displayed the naked terror of having to speak in public with a speech impediment—my exact experience. Why speak out when it resulted in humiliation? The silencing of my voice became a habitual pattern that diminished my self-respect.

Additionally, I was raised in an environment where children were neither seen nor heard. My parents, who grew up in the culture of the early 1900s, were not able to express their own feelings or needs. Healthy communications and clear-cut boundaries were non-existent. I never knew I had crossed a line until it was too late. Just like in the popular TV show title of the '60s, "Father Knows Best," my father was the voice of authority in our family of eight children.

One life-altering episode from my childhood clearly stands out in my mind. It was suppertime, and mashed potatoes were served. I hated their lumpy texture and bland taste with a passion. While I picked at the food on my plate, I expressed my honest feelings and said, "I don't like mashed potatoes."

Suddenly, with great disgust, my father grabbed my fork, filled it with mashed potatoes and shoved them down my throat. I gagged, choked back my words, and burst into tears. Shame, humiliation, and anger ran through me like electric currents as tears streamed down my face. All I could think was, "What did I do wrong?" No one said a word about the incident during or after dinner, and I was afraid to ever talk about what had happened that night. By identifying with the family credo about not airing "dirty laundry," I shoved my feelings deep inside my body and began to lose a connection with myself. It was as if a part of me began to die.

That experience taught me powerful lessons I've embraced for most of my life: don't question authority, don't feel or express your feelings, and don't say what you are thinking. Above all else, avoid conflict at all costs.

After being force-fed that night, I initiated Operation Good Girl, realizing it was the safest course of action to get my needs met. Unconsciously, I began to adopt my parents' behaviors in my quest for love and acceptance. I was an obedient child, eager for approval, and thus began my people-pleasing behaviors in earnest. Taking risks felt unsafe, so I became hesitant to be the authentic whole of me. Personally, I felt watered down.

Powerfully adding to that was the religion of my childhood, which told me I was imperfect and flawed. I recall sitting in catechism class listening with rapt attention as the priest said we were made in the image and likeness of God. In the next breath, he reminded us we were sinners at birth. I sat there silent and stunned. Like a helpless deer caught in the headlights, fear gripped my gut. My young mind felt unsettled, confused, and deeply saddened. How could God possibly love any of us if we were imperfect sinners?

Because on some level I believed this conflicting religious message that had been shoved down my throat, I experienced the feeling of spiritual bankruptcy and disconnected from God and myself. An undercurrent of unworthiness seeped into my subconscious mind like a polluted river, and I unconsciously moved away from my inherent spiritual nature. Self-love and self-esteem became huge issues for me. I worked to be a Good Girl for God by silencing my voice in a fruitless attempt to win His love and favor, just like I'd done with my parents.

Gratefully, in later years I began to question the unhealthy religious teachings I'd been force-fed. My muddled mind raced and raged with myriad thoughts about God and my identity. If I were made in God's image and likeness, how could I possibly be imperfect? If God gave me a voice, why was it wrong to use it? What was the real truth about this soul called Beverly and this thing called life?

Feeling like a six-cylinder car running on four, I knew I was overdue for a spiritual tune-up and starved for answers to questions that plagued me. In 2003, this inner hunger led me to explore the metaphysical Science of Mind teachings of Ernest Holmes.

Science of Mind espouses oneness, wholeness, perfection, and completeness. "God is what you are," Holmes wrote. "There is no judgment, no condemnation and no criticism in God. God created man after His own nature, out of Himself. Thus, the wholeness you are after is already within you."

Upon hearing those life-affirming principles, I felt like I was awakening from a long, deep sleep. I allowed them to saturate my being. When I began to fully digest Holmes' message, I gleaned a deeper meaning: the voice that for years had been longingly calling out to be heard was my *sacred voice*. And by honoring it, I connected to the inherent sacredness of my soul. Writer Anne Hill says in her book, *Dancing Animal Woman*, "finding my voice was finding my soul." Raising my voice from the dead felt like I was resurrecting my soul.

While immersing myself deeper into Holmes' soul-nourishing teachings, I realized a profound truth about myself, God, and life. I was born whole, perfect, and complete. I did not need to change; I simply needed to realign my beliefs and to see myself and life from this healthy perspective. By employing this spiritual floss to remove the old beliefs and by embodying these nurturing life principles, I strengthened my spiritual muscles. I was ready to co-create the life I desired and deserved.

Armed with this empowering knowledge, I inaugurated a new way of being in the world. I looked more honestly at all my relationships. Soon I realized it was time to end the unhealthy partnership with my boyfriend of eight years. It felt like I was wearing clothes that were too tight; there was no room to grow. I was experiencing intense adult growing pains. When we agreed to part ways, both of us knew we had been mirrors for each other, reflections of our unresolved childhood issues. I was deeply saddened by the loss, but the greater truth of me now knew it was time to move in the direction of my spiritual authenticity.

After the breakup, my tender spirit needed nourishing. I intensified my Science of Mind studies, happily investing time and money in classes and workshops. It was exhilarating to be with people on the same spiritual path. As I absorbed more of the life-sustaining teachings, I slowly began to speak up for myself, learning how to say no and to set more healthy boundaries. In essence, the fear of not using my voice had become greater than the fear of using it. When I allowed myself to be vulnerable in front of others, sometimes even airing "dirty laundry," something unexpected happened: others heard me and began to feel safe to expose their own vulnerabilities. We were able to share on a spiritual and emotional level, and for the first time in my life I realized I was not alone in my struggles.

I began the year 2011 by setting an intention to fully listen to and allow my sacred voice to be heard more frequently to reinforce my new beliefs. Naturally the grinning universe was happy to honor this by presenting me with numerous opportunities disguised as "challenges" to test my resolve.

One challenge was when an acquaintance asked to live with me temporarily. My Good Girl said yes without hesitation. Oops, I thought, I may have just set myself up for upset. As weeks passed, I became more uncomfortable about her staying with me since we had not set any initial boundaries. I realized we needed to talk and requested that she meet with me. After asking the Divine for guidance the morning we were to speak, I noticed a squirrel dance effortlessly across a nearby power line. On a deep soul level I understood the animal wisdom: take the leap of faith.

That same day I needed further inspiration, so I randomly opened my *Simple Abundance* book. The words that spilled onto the page made me laugh. They addressed setting personal boundaries and using one's voice. I knew then exactly what to say and how to say it. When I spoke to my guest, I expressed my honest feelings with clarity and compassion. Because my voice was coming from a strong, deep, holy place, she was receptive to listening and we cleared the air. I felt triumphant in speaking my truth.

As the year progressed, there were more challenges that required me to speak up. Three specific incidents stand out as pivotal in my journey to honor my sacred voice. The first episode involved a dear friend. We were sitting outdoors at her home when she said to me, "I am thinking about having our mutual male friend move in with me." I listened to her reasoning, and when the timing was right I interjected my honest thoughts on the subject, allowing my truth and authentic voice to be heard. She expressed her gratitude for my candor and thanked me for helping her hear her own truth.

In previous years, I would never have dared take the risk to express what I was thinking. The fear of arousing ire in another was too great. The new, real me gave myself permission to be seen and heard. It now felt safe to do so.

Opportunity knocked again in the form of an abusive client. The plan was to organize her kitchen. I offered numerous viable options to get the job done, but she was totally uncooperative. My Good Girl reminded me that this woman was dealing with severe health challenges. The habitual pattern of stuffing my feelings and silencing my voice temporarily resurfaced. My mind was going in circles. Suddenly, a voice inside my head said, "Trust your feelings, honor your sacred voice, and speak your truth." In the depths of my heart I realized I could not revert back to the old way of being in the world.

In the past I would have said nothing, stuffed my feelings, and suffered the pain of abandoning myself. I would have experienced inner anger and intense disappointment. I could no longer cause myself such suffering. I had worked too hard to move away from my harmful Good Girl behaviors. All the years of personal struggle to use my voice came down to this defining moment.

Though I felt intense fear, with great courage, conviction, and compassion, I walked over and stood in front of my client. I remember gazing intently into her eyes and saying, "The behavior you exhibited was abusive and unacceptable. I do not deserve this emotional abuse nor will I tolerate it." She agreed she had been out of line and responded with a sincere apology. She told me she recognized the courage it took to express my honest feelings. To me, those words were worth the anguish this situation had caused me. I headed home after the organizing session with my self-respect intact. I wept copious tears of joy at my resolve to honor my 2011 intention.

The final challenging opportunity came via a doctor I consulted. The initial appointment did not go well, as his actions were disrespectful. Again, I experienced the old patterns of voice silencing and conflict avoidance. I saw with great clarity how ingrained the old behavior was. That awareness alone was my saving grace.

I vowed to return one last time and confront him with my authentic feelings around his unacceptable behavior. I was extremely nervous the day of the appointment, but the fear of not using my voice propelled me into action. Upon entering his office, I was conducted to the exam room. I pulled up two chairs facing each other and awaited his arrival *and* our face-to-face talk. No longer fearful about using my voice, I expressed my heartfelt feelings. Afterward, he apologized and then thanked me. I departed the office never to return.

By embracing my fear, I stepped into my power and felt completely vindicated. In the deepest part of my being I realized this incident enabled me to rectify all the times I had allowed so-called authority figures to emotionally abuse and disrespect me.

I turned each challenge I faced into a victory. I was becoming real to myself and others. I expressed my authentic feelings. I was seen and heard. I tasted pride, integrity, wholeness, and freedom. I was realizing the dream for my life. It had been a long, arduous journey to reclaim my disowned voice, but at long last I severed the stranglehold of my Good Girl. I blessed her for the life-enriching lessons she'd taught me. With tremendous gratitude, I then sent her packing.

Rachel Simmons, author of *The Curse of the Good Girl*, summed up my lifelong struggle and the resulting deleterious consequences. She wrote, "Without permission to express herself unconditionally, she did not possess critical skills to manage her emotional experience. The cost of her attempt not to know her inner life took a toll on her physical health. Women are subjected to multiple health problems because of cultural indoctrination and messages not to speak up."

After all the years of struggle, I realize I just want to be free to be the All of Me. Don't we all yearn to be free, to be ourselves, to be seen and heard, to be whole, and to be loved exactly as we are? Our *Sacred Voices* are calling from our inner depths, waiting to be given permission to express our unique selves with authenticity and conviction. As with any yearning, action is required that demands compassionate effort to bring it to birth. That's why it's called a "labor of love."

As an ardent and willing student enrolled in this earth school, my becoming aware of the calling of my Sacred Voice, and then honoring it, has led to a life transformation. I experience a connectedness to myself and Spirit when I grant permission to this spiritual being called Beverly to authentically use her Sacred Voice. I then awaken to my deeper truth and align with my inherent wholeness as a person who is made in the image and likeness of The Creator. As a result, I enjoy the freedom that is my divine birthright.

Freedom! I would not be enjoying the freedom of "voicing" these thoughts and feelings today were it not for all the earth angels who lovingly labored with me to give birth to my dreams. I am deeply grateful to my twin sister, Ariella; my friend, Shannon; and my lifelong friend, Vicky. If they had not compassionately listened to my Sacred Voice and encouraged me to speak my truth, the writing of this chapter would not have happened—the dream for my life would have gone unrealized. I profoundly appreciate their willingness to see the truth of me. It is my fervent prayer that every person reading my story sees the truth in themselves and love themselves into greater freedom and wholeness by answering the Holy Call of their Sacred Voice.

Known by her clients as a compassionate, non-judgmental, lighthearted professional organizer, Bev Sullivan has been helping others break free from the imprisonment of home and office "Clutter" since 1996 in metro Denver/Boulder. She believes clutter robs people of peace of mind and is devoted to showing people this is not a tradeoff worth making. She absolutely believes in the transformative and healing benefit of getting organized. She conducts organizing workshops and speaks to groups on organizing topics, including The Sacred Act of Organizing. She lives in Denver and can be reached via her website, BevSullivansOrganizeNow. com or her cell @720-353-9476 (call or text). She is a singer, songwriter, writer, poet, and with the help of her five great nephews and nieces, a bubble and bubble gum blowing aficionado.

SPOKEN SECRET

J. Eve

I wonder where and who I'd be today had I never disclosed. For seven years, I didn't have the ability to express anything about what I had suffered. From the time I was eight until fifteen, remembering the abuse I'd endured at about eight years old felt more like a figment of my imagination than a secret I kept hidden. Sometimes, this fragment felt like a vivid nightmare, at other times like a lie I was itching to tell. But the possibility that it was a real experience simply didn't make sense. Why would my family member, someone I idolized and deeply trusted, expose me to such horrifying sexual acts? The protective mechanisms of my mind repressed the images, scents, and emotions for a long time, but gradually, slowly, they rose up and entered my awareness.

The beginning of remembering took place while I was journaling on an ordinary spring day, sitting on the porch steps of the house I'd lived in my entire life. My abuser walked to his car and made a goofy face at me that sparked a thought—a memory— which translated into a written disclosure to my journal that I believed nobody would ever read. Within hours, my mother discovered my journal and saw my secret. No investigating, no prying, no discovering the crime in action, she simply stumbled upon my journal as so many snooping mothers do, only to discover a sentence that would change our futures indefinitely: *"I wonder if anyone will ever find out about what happened between Sean and me."*

Though we were all devastated, each member of my family adopted a different mentality to make sense of what had happened. My father minimized the abuse, categorized it as sibling bullying, and said I needed to let the past be the past because "shit happens." My brother didn't allow himself to process any of it because he simply didn't know how or what his place was in this drama.

My mother asked me questions to which I had no answers; it was as if I'd known for years, yet I quite literally couldn't remember enough to respond. Her tone was urgent; she was furious. I stood before her emotionless. Despite remembering the abuse enough to write that one sentence, I remembered nothing more.

Instead of teaming up with my distraught, protective mother, I warned Sean that my parents knew. Years later, I would miss this brief moment of feeling I had an advocate. Yet at the time, I wanted to protect him and me. Even though I wasn't yet clear what I was shielding, this felt like our secret. Maybe he could think up something to say to them to make this okay.

Within hours—or days—my abuser was confronted. The intensity of these events caused my memory to fail me. It felt like everything happened so fast and then, just like that, was over. He admitted to it right away and that night he wrote me an apology. Wanting her family to put all of this behind us, my mother encouraged me to forgive and reconcile with my abuser. I forgave him, or at least that's what I told him. I had no idea what it meant to forgive someone who says they love you but is responsible for much of your own needless suffering.

What happens to a child's sense of self when they grow up believing they are guilty of acts so terrible they don't have names? For years I talked to different therapists, searched for books that reflected my experience, and consulted friends to help me make sense of what had happened. In my second to last semester of college, I took a course to become a certified sexual assault counselor. It was during this class that I gained tremendous perspective on my experience.

When I first heard the term "grooming," I realized I'd been groomed. My abuser created a game conducive to getting what he wanted. He knew he had my complete trust and adoration long before the abuse started. I learned about power differentials and finally came to terms with the fact that the abuse didn't happen between the two of us. In actuality, my abuser was aware of what he was doing and fully capable of understanding his power over me. Conversely, I didn't know what was happening and didn't have the language to stop him or seek help.

Every time the class met I felt a little lighter as I accepted that the abuse had not been my fault. Midway through the course I disclosed. After I spoke, several other classmates did so as well.

Later, Hope told me, "I just couldn't let you feel like you were alone for one second." It was incredible that many of these women had, just like me, been drawn to this advocacy work after having been violated. I was stunned that it had taken so long for all of us to come forward, but mostly I was horrified by the numbers in the room and utterly moved by the contagiousness of my courage.

I've learned that disclosing is a critical piece of recovery from sexual abuse. Yet disclosing to my journal, and eventually to my family (not by choice), was not enough to begin the healing process. For years after the disclosure, I minimized the abuse because I felt pressured by my family to move past it. They wanted to leave this awful part of our family history behind and not let it change our family dynamics. They feared the consequences of people finding out what had gone on in our house. The judgments about how this would reflect on their parenting were overwhelming, but mostly they worried about what this could mean for my abuser's future.

As we'd believed ourselves to be prior to the disclosure, we continued to portray the life of a wholesome family unit that vacationed and celebrated holidays together. We gave each other advice and smiled for pictures, continuing to project the image of a loving, connected family. One year we traveled to St. Thomas over Christmas. The photos from this trip of my mom and abuser wearing matching pink shirts, their tanned skin causing their teeth to look especially white and perfect, does not reflect the underlying, unspoken tension bubbling beneath the surface during that week. For a brief moment, in the midst of a peaceful and "ordinary" trip, my mom shattered the culture of denial and minimization, saying, "The two of them cannot sleep in the same room!" I was annoyed at how insensitively she expressed her concern, and I felt extremely uncomfortable—it seemed her emotion was misdirected because we all knew I was no longer at risk around him.

I created a checklist of factors that can lessen one's odds of being messed up in the aftermath of abuse—I received checks in three. The family believes you. *Check.* The abuser admits to it. *Check.* The abuser apologizes and tries to make amends. *Check.*

I thought I was fortunate for all those checkmarks that signified I had family support to heal. These factors were not enough, however, because they alone couldn't heal me or the rest of my family, and those checks had all occurred during one week of communication. After the disclosure, confrontation, and apology, I was left with the consequences. Recovery is ongoing.

At first, I wasn't sure how the abuse had impacted me. My mother's initial hysterical reaction made me wonder why I had no tears. Was I really OK? I wondered whether life would just go on like nothing had happened. For the most part, it did. Nobody in my family ever brought it up—as if all that needed to be said had been said, as if the entire reality of what had happened could be safely sealed into the past without touching our forward-looking lives. Nobody asked me how I felt or if I wanted to talk about it.

Truthfully, I wasn't ready to talk right away. I still didn't have words or emotions for what I'd experienced. The memories came back slowly. Asking my abuser questions about what had happened helped me put the missing pieces back together. Despite his willingness to answer my questions, however, these exchanges were always electronic and maintained the culture of family denial. I slid notes under his door, we emailed from across the house, but when face-to-face, we pretended the abuse had never happened.

I learned that not talking about it and wishing it away wouldn't change the past or the collateral damage that persisted. I had many close, honest relationships, but the abuse presented a challenge for me. I didn't know how to share my situation with others. It was on my mind and I wanted to talk about it, but I knew I wasn't supposed to bring it up within my family, and I didn't know how to communicate these intense feelings with my friends. What would they think of my family? Would they be judgmental? *Was this my secret to tell?*

I had clearly received the unspoken memo that my family did not want to talk about it. They felt guilty that they'd failed to protect their little girl, ashamed that their perfect family image was forever stained, and they remained clueless as to how they needed to support me. As unimaginable as it seemed to bring the abuse up in conversation, I was reminded of it every single day—when my roommate asked me to take a survey for her class about my first sexual experiences, when my self-defense teacher talked about child abuse, even dissociating during sex, which was directly caused by the abuse. There was no way to tell my family I was hurting and wanted to talk about it, or that it was affecting my sex life. I followed their lead and didn't bring it up.

Once I went away to college in 2008, I found the space I needed to start processing the abuse. My coursework overlapped with my introspection, and I decided to write about the disclosure and my family's reaction for my final English paper. It was therapeutic to compile my journal entries documenting those tense moments around the dinner table when everyone in my family was thinking, yet not speaking, about what had happened, along with my written attempts to initiate our family's healing process.

I sent emails to mend familial relationships and to prevent permanent damage to our family. I provided lists of resources and books for my parents so they could process what had happened and give it the attention it deserved. I needed them to learn how to support me. I wrote back and forth to my brothers. Playing the role of peacemaker, I reminded them that we wanted to be close siblings.

I refused to be the reason my family fell apart. I too wanted to maintain and be a part of the image of a close family. Until recently, I still felt it was my responsibility to make sure the entire family healed, and I insisted my abuser return to therapy since he'd only ever attended one or two sessions.

After documenting my struggle for my class, I figured that simply clicking "attach" and "send" in an email was a feasible way to share my mixed-up emotions with my family. Still, I was apologetic as I shared the essay—I felt guilty for sending information that might upset them. I didn't want to alarm them or disturb the fragile equilibrium of our relationships that were contingent upon me being untroubled by the events of the past. I made sure to tell them everything was fine.

Each family member reacted differently. My father maintained his initial attitude, reminding me that life goes on. My brother said he was glad I was getting in touch with a wider variety of emotions, as simply forgiving my abuser didn't seem healthy. Though I'm certain they learned a lot, my paper didn't change the culture of silence between us. In the end, I was the one who benefited from this exercise. It helped me find my voice and express to my family what I was dealing with.

I wonder how I would have coped had I been able to talk openly about my feelings with my family prior to leaving for college. Maybe I wouldn't have felt compelled to share my story with others and seek outside support and validation. Not getting the support I needed, however, I found a community where I could express myself. I had a story that needed to be told and a voice to tell it, so I became an outspoken survivor in spite of my family's attempt to silence this shameful family secret—*this was and is my story to tell.*

The newfound independence I experienced in college and the support of a mature, sensitive, patient, loving partner helped me erase the messages I'd internalized from my family. I was beautiful and resilient and could be proud of my strength. I deserved to have meaningful sex. I was sick of feeling invisible to my family and ready to feel independent and strong. I was an activist at heart who'd always been committed to helping people.

I realized I could do something positive with this awful part of my past, and I didn't need approval from my family, though I would still struggle to get it for years to come. As scary as it was to be vulnerable in front of strangers, classmates, and new friends, it felt right to talk about it. With mic in hand, I participated in "Take Back the Night," an event uniting the campus to raise awareness about sexual violence. The people attending these events wanted to hear my story, in contrast to my family who'd never even asked for any details. As I experienced my first round of applause and received my first emails detailing how my story moved someone, I felt proud. No longer did the abuse have to be a source of shame, guilt, and sadness.

I learned how widespread sexual violence is—it is one of the most underreported crimes because of the complex pressures from families, communities, and perpetrators to stay silent. This confirmed my belief that breaking the silence would inspire other survivors to come forward. In speaking out, I became part of a community of survivors. I was no longer isolated by my family. I had found an outlet to channel my mixed emotions about reconciling with my abuser and remaining a part of my unsupportive family.

As I embraced my new identity as an outspoken leader on my college campus, the pain of my family's abandonment had less power over me. My mentors, professors, and friends made up my created family, and they couldn't have been more proud of how I was thriving.

I continue to seek new forums to share my story so that I can make sexual violence less of a taboo. This issue is rampant, plaguing young girls and women all around the world. I became a speaker for the Rape, Abuse, Incest National Network and am working on a book to let every survivor know she is not alone.

It is my hope that one day my family will learn how to be there for me, but my testament proves that it is possible to survive and thrive without them. I want to use my experiences to teach others how best to support someone who has been through trauma. The details of my story may be unique, but the patterns of being silenced and isolated are universal.

I will no longer be silenced by my family's fear of the repercussions. Silence perpetuates suffering. Silence was in the room as I was molested, during the months when my innocence was taken from me. Silence was in my house as I suffered alone, feeling guilty, responsible, and confused. Silence was forced upon me so that my family's lives would not be impacted by the past. Silence has stolen the voices of women all around the world as they suffer alone because so few people can safely and confidently come forward.

Someday my family might recognize the strength and courage I possess. If not, I will surround myself with those who admire my integrity, values, and my healing. Those are the people who matter the most. I'm confident that in time the abuse won't feel like the center of my world—it will fuel my passion but won't hold me back. I won't ever stop telling my story. My commitment to prevent child abuse and advocate for those abused will be a part of me forever—a part of me I love.

J. Eve is 23 years old and graduated from Trinity College in 2011 with a degree in Human Rights. She wants to move to Colorado from the East Coast to enjoy the sun, mountains, and community. Her career ambitions include advocating for abused women, criminal justice, youth leadership and development, and sex education. She loves learning to cook, meeting inspiring people, and spending time with her partner and friends. During challenging times she looks to Gloria Steinem, Eve Ensler and Oprah Winfrey for strength and plans to follow in their footsteps as courageous, fierce feminists! Please contact her at JocEve89@gmail.com, she wants to hear from you!

BOTOX:
NOT JUST FOR WRINKLES

Sharon Hampton

My dance with dystonia began over 17 years ago when my neurologist diagnosed me with cervical dystonia. It all started with the *Twist*—a slight, yet uncontrollable pulling of my head to the left side. Dystonia falls in the family of movement disorders such as Parkinson's disease and tremors. I was told that it could be brought on due to a genetic predisposition or trauma to the body. Having experienced tremors in my hands since early childhood, the genetic explanation seemed reasonable. Remember doing the *Jerk?* Now I am truly dating myself. The jerk for me was the dystonic tremor I experienced in my upper body.

Once properly diagnosed, my neurologist went on to explain that the treatment of choice was botulinum toxin, Botox, administered through injections into the muscles of my upper back and neck. Today, most everyone has some idea of what Botox is good for; but on that day, before Botox had been approved by the FDA for such use, what ran through my mind were bent food cans, food poisoning, and botulism. And on that day, I chose to take a risk with the hope that a small amount of botulinum toxin might treat my symptoms. My treatments began then and would continue every three months for over fourteen years.

As a wife, a mother of three young sons, a student working towards my undergraduate degree in education and expressive art, and an early education teacher, I simply looked upon all of this as my *pain in the neck* and kept going. I went along fairly well for a while explaining to others the mysterious condition I experienced, joining a support group, gathering information where I could, and working to take care of my family and myself. It was not until I returned to Texas to visit family in 1995 that I came to realize the deep connection between my mother's physical makeup and my own.

While visiting my sister, during a conversation with my young niece, she shared with me a cassette tape made by my

89

mother before she passed away from cancer a few years earlier. My mother had shared copies of the tape with my niece, who had listened to one and felt it could be helpful for me. She thought I might better understand my mother's medical history—the challenges she'd faced and how her journey had unfolded for her.

Through listening to the tape, I learned that my mother was also once told she had a movement disorder, "something like Parkinson's," and at the time would have to rely on medication to ease her symptoms. She went on to explain that she soon discovered having a drink also eased her symptoms for a while, until the next day when another drink became necessary. I grew up with a mother who endured a never-discussed medical condition masked by medications and alcohol, who I now know simply wanted to be understood.

My relationship with my mother was always challenging, sometimes destructive, and continually unpredictable. I grew up wanting to be nothing like her. However, one of the sweetest gifts she and I ever experienced together was during her time of transition. She lived with the diagnosis of pancreatic cancer for only a few months, and what a blessing it was for me to be there with her and witness her leaving this earthly condition and moving beyond.

I remember this time as one of her most graceful. She was so petite to begin with and as her small frame grew smaller and smaller, she appeared even stronger to me and so full of faith. Her laughter remained as beautiful and infectious as ever. Her aura and last breaths brought comfort to me, reassuring me that life goes on. Life is never-ending. As her organs failed and her body gave way to a life beyond, my healing journey began.

Staying long enough to help my sister organize the house following my mother's funeral, I finally flew back to Colorado on Christmas Eve to be with my husband and sons who were four, five, and ten years old at the time. In light of how I felt after the recent loss of my last parent, it was almost surreal coming back to my children, especially at that time of year. As a child, I was grieving. Yet, as a parent I returned home to be a part of the wonder of the holiday with my own children.

The accumulative effects of all of the changes I had experienced over the past few years—including the loss of my dad to cancer the day before our youngest son was born, the loss of my grandparents following my dad, and most recently my mom—were working to get my attention. Initially, it felt easier to try and be happy for my family than to deal with the depth of grief that accompanied such loss. Then, as life often allows, other stresses arose, as though to say, "Listen child." In beginning to pay attention, it started to sink in that I was *sinking in* too.

I needed help. I returned to church and sought counsel. I participated in a support group and later decided to return to school and focus more on religious philosophy. I was seeking God, trusting that I would find peace there. Instead, what I found was a belief system based on everyone else's beliefs.

I thought I had done all I was supposed to do. I followed the rules. I was a good Christian and thought I knew what I believed. I tried to live as I thought I should in order to find the peace of God. Yet, nothing was working in my life as I thought it should. My childhood was running back to me, and I was beginning to see how I had been running away from it. I was very confused, in pain, and extremely disappointed in God.

The following school year, 1998-99, I taught early education in Jefferson County schools. That April, twelve students and one teacher lost their lives at Columbine High School. It was the most incomprehensible event, and I knew that my views of God and life and my belief system were only creating more confusion within. As a mother of three sons who would all graduate from Columbine, and being a teacher myself, I struggled to make sense of things and did not want to give into the uncertainty I was feeling.

That same year, while driving home one night from an education class with my co-teacher, we passed by a dome-shaped building, and she simply said to me, "That's a good church." Given some time, I started attending what I now know to be Mile Hi Church. I found the Sunday services to be very uplifting and the messages to be extremely thought-provoking, peaceful, and inclusive in a way I had not experienced before.

Mile Hi embraces people from all walks of life, varying faiths, and lifestyles. I felt it validated thoughts and feelings I'd had as a young child. I started taking classes and attending workshops to more fully understand the philosophy behind their teachings.

Given time, I wanted to share all of this with my family, my sister in particular, and it was during a "What Will Set You Free" workshop we attended together that a much deeper healing began to unfold. So began my *waltz* with Spirit God as my partner. A smooth waltz involves steps taken consciously. One-two-three, one-two-three—rhythmically encompassing both strong and weak elements, passionately and compassionately, ultimately flowing gently with a bit more grace.

It was during this time that I took a much closer look at my relationship with my mother. I had to feel all that I had pushed away for so long. It required me to redefine the terms good and bad. It required me to take a good long look at myself, inside and out, where I found more of the good, the bad, and given time, the hope. I grew to feel more confident and more trusting in a God whose will for me and for all was good.

By looking within, by more fully understanding my relationship with myself, I have come to a much greater understanding of my relationship with Spirit God. It has brought me to a place where I can openly and freely consider my relationship with life and all that it offers. I found that the God I sought was not out there, but rather all around me and in all of life. I came to trust more in the gifts as well as the challenges that came to me as opportunities to learn and grow. It is all a matter of choice as to the amount of light I allow into my life. For me, it did not happen overnight nor is it complete. So, this brings to mind two questions—how is all of this working for me and what does all of this have to do with Botox?

Getting back to the workshop offered at church, it was there that I wrote an affirmation for myself regarding my dystonia: *I am free to look in the right direction of my life in every given sacred moment, through every given sacred movement!* Yes! I have now meditated on that thought for over two-and-a-half years, fully believing that my body could heal and the chemical makeup of my brain involving neurotransmitters could improve. Along with changes that I have made in diet, such as removing gluten and most sugars; exercise, including physical therapy and biofeedback; and lifestyle changes that include practicing meditation and yoga, I am now botox free.

I no longer feel my body or my life pulling in one direction or the other. I have released certain ideas about my life and embraced others by taking them in hand, drawing them close, and taking one step at a time. As I no longer teach, I volunteer when I can. I ask for help when needed—I no longer attempt to keep going and do it all. By letting go of the idea that I have to control life, I realize that I am in control of my life through my thoughts, actions, and choices. In releasing one aspect of my life, space is created for the enhancement of other aspects of life. Pleasure can be found within the experience of them all.

Once I accepted myself as all that I am, dystonia became the danseuse. So I continue to take one step at a time, finding comfort in the knowing that in quiet moments of solitude, I have found the peace of Spirit God, and even in pain there can be joy. Joy lies in the gift of choice. I choose to believe, to practice, to have faith in purpose, and to take full responsibility for my happiness and healing.

I am the student who can now sense and literally feel solid ground under my feet. I am grateful for the journey and the understanding that comes from knowing a good and loving Spirit God who, I now know, has always been there. I have taken dystonia and rewritten it to look more like this:

D   Divine love and light
Y   Yes! To life and the journey
S   Spirit God
T   Trust in all goodness
O   Open heart, open mind
N   Nutrition of body and mind
I   Intelligent mind
A   Awareness

I am grateful for the teachings of others such as Ernest Holmes, Bernie Siegel, M.D., Dan Millman, and Jill Bolte Taylor, Ph.D., to name just a few, for they all teach that the body is capable of healing. I believe we are on the forefront of understanding to what degree and what role we play in the process.

Dr. Joe Dispenza teaches that every thought we have creates a certain chemical reaction within our bodies. Our bodies are in constant motion and change as a reflection of these chemical reactions. There is an internal intelligence that heals. We witness it every time a cut heals. By tapping into this intelligence—that which is within and giving our bodies, minds, and spirits what is needed—healings can occur on various levels, even in places where we never thought possible.

The American Academy of Neurology publication *Neurology Now* continues to support medical findings that the brain is not rigid or inflexible, but rather experiences plasticity. It is possible to alter the chemical makeup within the brain as demonstrated at Baylor Medical Center in Houston, Texas. It is possible to utilize our brains to help sooth physical pain. Studies published over the past several years have shown that (simply the) "anticipation of pain relief can lead to a lessening of discomfort through the release of opiates produced by the brain." It is amazing to me to ponder the power of the mind, the power of thought, and how perfectly our bodies are created, even if there should be a time when it feels differently.

I am also very grateful for all that my mother taught me. Sometimes it comes down to simply having healthy resources to choose from. Back in the sixties, my mother had only a few options. My mother, Vivian, was petite, yet powerful, and by 1974 she had stopped drinking and moved into a place of greater faith. When I think of her today, I see her as my greatest teacher. The only voice or sound that I hear is her warm, infectious laughter.

Laughter, as we know, is very good medicine. It creates endorphins, which are the body's natural pain killers. Laughter is like aerobic exercise, internal jogging that massages internal organs by enhancing the blood supply and increasing their efficiency. Laughter simply feels good. Understanding the benefits of laughter led me to become certified in laughter yoga.

Less than a year following my father's passing, Vivian and I found a quiet moment and time alone to share in great laughter over the one love letter my father wrote to her as a young woman. What a sweet gift to share in that together.

I share this story to honor her path so that she might be heard and to recognize a deep generational connection between the divine feminine mother and child. There were a few other things that Vivian shared on her cassette tape, being her faith in a good and loving God and her knowing that earth Angels do indeed exist. We sometimes find them in the faces of those around us and at other times experience them when we are all alone. Sometimes, through a warm and comforting embrace, we are shown a deeper understanding that we are never alone, that we are always loved, and that all is well.

Last week, a new affirmation came to mind: *I am now free to move in the right direction of my life, in every given sacred moment through love and light, in joy, with ease and grace.* And, so it is.

Sharon Hampton is a retired early education teacher and a student of life and love. She lives with her husband in Littleton, Colorado, near their three sons and grandchildren. Sharon served as the support group leader for the Dystonia Medical Research Foundation in Denver for two years and is a certified Laughter Yoga Instructor. Sharon enjoys writing, glasswork, photography, and playing in the great outdoors of Colorado. As this is written, Sharon continues taking philosophy classes at Mile Hi Church and includes dancing as part of her daily practice. If you would like to contact Sharon, she can be reached at shamp05@earthlink.net.

I HAVE A POWERFUL VOICE

Kim Conrad

I was born with a powerful voice, talking in sentences before I was a year old. In school, I was a high achiever, very quick and insightful, which was disconcerting for some and enjoyable for others. I experienced being picked on and beaten up in school and physically attacked several times in my life. No matter who I was or what I did, I repeatedly felt I was not good enough. Rarely feeling heard or understood, I often felt invisible and not welcome in many areas of my young life. Life just didn't feel safe. Yet I continued, again and again, to push through, to stand up once more and speak out. I chose to continually see my life through the context of learning, growth, and success, thus unveiling the keys to my own transformation.

I believe in making the best of what happens, turning vinegar into wine, which gets better with age. I ask, "What lessons can I perceive that give me the power to create a life that's more than I've ever imagined? How can the lessons I've learned be passed on to others? How much fun, magic, and miracles are possible as I recreate me?"

An enormous challenge and opportunity came along a few years ago that was greater than anything I had ever anticipated or previously known. I learned, and am still learning, what it requires of me to make it through, to come out more whole than I've ever been, to have my life and my voice more congruent, more natural, more powerful, and more fully me than ever before.

On May 9, 2007 in Washington, D.C., a letter accepting my artistic life's work into the archives of women artists at the National Museum of Women in the Arts was sent to my home in Broomfield, Colorado. At 7:30 a.m. that same morning in Denver, Colorado, a one-ton, commercial F350 truck moving at about 40-50 M.P.H. rear-ended my stopped half-ton truck.

I heard the screech and felt the slam. It was extremely hard, jolting, and shocking. I was dazed. I could move but felt intense neck pain. Then an unusual thing happened. I had a sense that this accident would lead to profound changes in my life. This knowledge came through my fogginess and enveloped my entire body. It was so powerful and important I could feel it flowing into every cell. It has since grown into a platform for perspectives that continue to nurture and promote my recovery. It helped to once again provide a foundation for creating joy from sorrow, wine from vinegar, and to bring a voice back from silence. Little did I know how hard this journey would be or how long it would last.

I was able to walk and communicate enough to exchange information with the other driver. The truck was owned by a contracting company that was insured. For that, I was grateful. The police arrived. The pain, nausea, and dizziness were getting worse. When the ambulance arrived, I was curled up on the sidewalk, ice pack on my shoulder, nauseous, dizzy, and on my cell calling a friend for help and support. I was scared and shaky. After being taken to a hospital, where they found no broken bones, they pronounced me fine and sent me home.

The next day I was in the office of a chiropractor well known for successfully treating athletes with serious injuries. I didn't have a personal physician to oversee my care and couldn't think clearly enough to find one. I would have loved a supportive person at home to help me navigate the years to come, but that was not the case. As with many of us, we navigate these unfamiliar medical, legal, and financial waters by ourselves, finding support wherever we can. In the process, we find out how strong and capable we are and become great marathon runners. We willingly confront the challenges, harnessing the power of adversity through unstoppable determination, an indomitable will, nurturing choice, and never giving in to giving up, even when it means good cries along with good laughs to keep us going.

The chiropractor gave me a soft neck brace that kept me company for about four months. From the beginning, I had severe pain in my head, neck, shoulders, back, and hips. During the unfolding of the first few weeks, signs of brain injury increased markedly as my ability to function decreased. I could no longer talk, read, or write, nor make sense much of the time. I could not look at a computer screen for more than a minute without getting nauseous. Paintings came off the walls as my ability for visual processing couldn't handle the lines on the walls; curtains were drawn to keep things as dark as possible. All sensory input was overwhelming—even the heat coming on in the house, running water in a sink, or the flushing of a toilet.

When my brain was overwhelmed, my body shook and I was often unable to remain standing. I would lie down on the floor wherever I was, curl up in tremors, and hold my head until I recovered enough to get up and go to bed. When out in public, I often had to find a quiet, dark corner and do the same, even if it meant curling up in the corner of a cold bathroom floor. I sought out whatever was available to me to move forward. I never realized how much noise there is in the world or how much power it can have over us when we're no longer capable of filtering it out.

The only place I felt a sense of peace, calm, and recovery was in a completely dark and silent room. Ice on my head became my survival friend. I felt better and laughed when I stuck my head in the freezer. I became comfortable with being uncomfortable. I learned literally to *"Make up my mind!"* and when I did, my body and life followed. I literally *"made up"* a new me with nutritious thoughts, foods, feelings, meditation, yoga, exercise designed for each new level of capability, and a powerful therapeutic team that believed in my vision for a better future.

Focused breathing exercises have not only cleared the air for a brighter day; they have exponentially enhanced my healing. An ongoing practice of forgiveness of me and others has actually released more of my energy for faster healing. A daily practice of gratitude is a sweet and nourishing act that keeps me focused on my present, setting me free of my past, so I can create more things to be grateful for. In the beginning it was simply, "I am grateful I can breathe; I can take one step; I can open my eyes." I choose to keep moving forward even when I feel like quitting. I keep the drive of my dreams greater than any adversity.

Rewriting my conditioned perceptions of what mistakes and failure are has been invaluable to encourage and sustain my recovery. Now, mis-takes are simply outcomes that turned out different from my expectations. Letting go of expectations helps release limitations, giving birth to all kinds of limitless possibilities. What if all mis-takes were chances to see the world anew, opening doors to new possibilities I never imagined existed, that I can now take advantage of because I can see and receive them? As for failure, I now perceive it as the brainchild of false and pre-conceived limitation. I am choosing instead to follow in Edison's footsteps and set my creativity free to live a life where failure is but a blip on the radar screen. As Edison said after inventing his light bulb, "I haven't failed. Why would I ever give up? I now know 1000 ways that don't work."

From these shifts in perception and healing, my sense of worthiness and self-love is again flowing and becoming a more fulfilling way of life. I continue to learn in more and more ways that I have a powerful and beneficial voice; that my value, or anyone's sense of value, does not depend on our outer reality. It is something we create. When we are guided by our heart, which is now documented as the strongest generator of both electrical and magnetic fields in the body, we literally have the capacity to create and recreate ourselves by choice. I am finding this to be true the more I learn and grow, propelled by the momentum coming from how I respond to the challenges before me.

Reweaving me and finding my voice again has increased my courage to stand up for myself and create the life I desire. It has been both the accomplishments and the willingness to make and learn from my mis-takes that continue to make this transformation possible, that have given me instrumental wisdom through the experiences of pain, joy, and more. Indeed, challenge gives us the opportunity to discover in many ways who we are and who we wish to be.

Things have gradually improved over the last five years with my continual and persistent choices for a new world inside and out. I am learning to listen to my body and give it what it needs, especially sufficient rest so my body has a chance to heal. I am now beginning to again enjoy sound, light, movement, and other sensory input. It was two years before I was able to read a book. It had to have large print, lots of space, a simple font, short chapters, and then I had to cover the opposite page to be able to read at all, since my brain could not handle the tsunami of visual information from both pages. It was the opening of another door. I still look forward to being able to do things like listen to music, watch a movie, go to a party, ride a bike, and dance again. I continue to improve and *celebrate* every chance I get!

A business of mine for more than 20 years, my primary source of income, involved selling at trade shows. I went from being "one of the best and most caring sales people" (as friends have shared), to some kind of unexpected weird person whose behavior was in stark contrast to the other participants at the shows. I had that out-of-place, brain-injured intensity, and deer-in-the-headlights look. Like someone who's had a stroke, I often thought I was making sense when what I was speaking was nonsense. Shocked customers ran away, most likely thinking I was crazy. A friend said that before the accident I talked so fast she couldn't keep up with me; after the accident I talked so slow she couldn't remember what I'd last said.

I am relearning my previously wonderful social interaction and communication skills. I look like a grown woman, yet have been learning the relationship lessons of a child all over again. As my brain cells recover and reconnect, lights are coming on. All functional areas are improving, including memory and my abilities to focus, stay on task, complete conversations, perform normal sensory processing, executive functioning, and successfully engage in social interaction. Along the way, I have learned to find ways to laugh—to understand that having fun with my circumstances is healing for me and lightens up my situation for others. An example: I wear protective headphones on top of customized ear filters to help me function while my brain continues to heal and fully restore my ability to process sound. When people inquire, I respond, "I'm winning the Princess Leia Imitation Contest!" They grin and say, "You have my vote!"

When you have a brain injury, the faculties you use to be aware of yourself and the world are damaged, so you can't assess how injured you really are. Quite often, you are not conscious of what you are or are not doing. Staff and friends became allies as I asked them for their caringly candid perceptions of me and my behavior. I continue to use this invaluable feedback as a learning tool and an important gauge for self-evolution. I have let go of what I perceive myself to be in favor of what I've chosen to become. I continually focus on my choices rather than on my circumstances.

Life is different after. What if after can be better than before? Some doctors and people have more limited perspectives about more traditional recoveries, especially about age, since I am now 56. When tradition doesn't work, why be traditional? Albert Einstein said: "You cannot solve a problem from the same consciousness that created it. You must learn to see the world anew." Indeed, *"I came from a womb with a very different view and I've been out of the box ever since!"*

Instead of trying to go back to who I was, which is not possible, I revel in this freedom to choose and create who I want to be today. *Now* is where my success is achievable both today and tomorrow. Challenge and choice is an opportunity for greatness. More and more, I am *loving* this opportunity!

My first sign of a better me was when I started typing faster and with greater ease than ever before. The fact that I can actually write this chapter brings tears of exultation and smiles of delight. We are all on this journey called life. It's when I am aware of my progress, both great and small, that I become capable of "getting better" in varying aspects of my life.

Taking one step at a time, I began from where I was in each moment. Especially in the beginning, choosing baby steps rather than judging my circumstances and progress enabled me to continue to recover by making wise use of my fragile energy and cognitive capacity. I found that this turned out to be the best head start program for getting a-head!

Each of us *is* a powerful voice just by the nature of our existence. The power of who we are underneath everything is the voice that speaks into the world *as* and *through* each of us. We each have a contribution to make, a part to play, or we would not be here. Small things add up to great things, individually and together. Even the contribution of simply being *present* can be of such great value.

Someone sitting by my side and supporting me was just what I needed when I was learning to count five one dollar bills again. No conversation needed, just the caring presence of another. No contribution or part is of lesser or greater value than any other. When we listen to what we *love*, what calls to us, we are guided to fulfill our powerful voice, to fulfill our role(s) in this play called life.

It seems to me that I and the world have both sustained concussions. I've learned that it is possible for anyone to realize their potential and use the powerful voice they have within. These lessons have taught me that not only *I*, but *we*, can be greater than we've ever been when we design through love, perseverance, and collaborative choice. We can exponentially unveil our potential and the powerful voice of each of us in all areas of our lives. It's important to believe in ourselves no matter what and know that *we are not* our circumstances.

We are who we *think* we are, *feel* we are, and who we *choose* to create ourselves to be. The power for a better world begins today. It *is* possible. It *is* happening. I believe in me. I believe in you. I believe in us. Take your next steps now. I am. Why wait? Choose to create a life you love today. *You* have a powerful voice. Unleash it and use it. When *you* do, we *all* have a more powerful voice.

Kim Conrad, M.A. is the founder of Being For... You and the creator of the "I Have a Powerful Voice!" Experience described as "Super-Powerful!" She is a veteran of stage and an award-winning author. Combining her creative talents with her Masters in Psychology, as well as her 25 years' experience as a successful entrepreneur, she brings to life the voices of individuals, corporations, and organizations, unleashing the power of their spirit and increasing both their effectiveness and success. Through her acclaimed work with BoldLeaders.org, presenting her writings at the International Global Healing Conference with Desmond Tutu, as emcee and facilitator at the Festival of Enlightenment, and other engagements, Kim continues to fulfill her passion of facilitating, speaking to and inspiring audiences worldwide. To connect with Kim, visit her website: www.BeingFor.com.

BEYOND THE ARENA

Devon Combs

"Dev-Dev, come home," my 12-year-old sister wails into the pay phone as I stand in the gas station parking lot of a small mountain town. My parents have the police out looking for me — I'm on a suicidal mission to end the pain that devours me. A faint voice inside my head tells me to pull the car over and call home. I don't know what to say as I put the quarters in and dial the home number. My mom answers and I recall nothing she says. I am numb. Then another voice comes through the phone and my senses stir.

It's my younger sister, Darien, and I hear her crying. More shocking, I feel her pain coming through the phone. She cries that she doesn't want to lose me, and I believe her words. Her young voice strikes through my self-hatred and loathing, and I listen. She is telling me to come home. She speaks to the part of me that I long ago shut out. I tell her okay — I promise to return. I get in the car and head back down the mountain, away from a mountain ledge I had imprinted in my dark brain — the one I knew would do the trick to end the pain.

I walk straight into the house and slink downstairs to my bedroom where I slam the door and bury my face in the pillow. I have no words for anyone. In fact, I have nothing for anyone. I am dead inside.

Moments later, I hear a knock on my door followed by two men's voices announcing that they are the police and they're coming in. I have no fight left in me, and I know why they are here. I know why my parents had to make the toughest call of their life — to have their daughter arrested in their own home because she is a threat to herself. I barely sit up and do not make eye contact. They promptly handcuff me and walk me upstairs past my parents who are waiting by the front door. My mom and dad have tears in their eyes. From what I can imagine, they're experiencing the greatest scare of their lives, not knowing what's happening to me. I have disappointed everyone. I'm relieved the cops are taking me away. I need help and have no idea where to start.

Weeks before, I had come home from living abroad in New Zealand, which was supposed to have been my fresh start. I truly believed that if I travelled far enough away I could escape the bulimia and self-hatred that consumed me in college. Ignoring the intuitive thoughts that urged me to seek treatment, I found myself halfway around the world, at an all-time low, with no support system of friends and family. I realized I'd been wrong. I couldn't escape me.

New Zealand had been my last attempt to outrun my addiction. I had previously dropped out of two colleges because I couldn't make it to class. My days were consumed with frequent trips to the cafeteria where I loaded to-go boxes with more food than college football players consume in a day. The daily pattern played out as I raced back to the dorm room, binged and purged, drank heavily at night to forget my day, and woke up in places I still shudder to remember. It was not the college experience I had dreamed about.

Living at my parents' house again, I hardly recognized myself from the bright, outgoing, horse-loving girl who felt on top of the world when she left high school. That identity had been flushed down the toilet along with more calories that I can count. I had no sense of who I was anymore. Days before I decided to end my life, I had taken scissors to my beautiful long blond hair and given myself a dreadful mullet-pixie cut. My exterior reflected my interior. I was operating at the lowest vibration I'd ever experienced—shame so deep that suicide sounded like a logical way to end the pain. I had hit rock bottom.

Post-handcuffs, I spent time in two different psychiatric wards in Denver. I needed the 24-hour supervision, yet I knew substance abuse recovery classes and anti-depressants were a temporary fix. They didn't get to my core issues.

My parents would not allow me to live at home again, which turned out to be a blessing. I had to seek alternatives. I admitted I had a problem and was willing to accept that in order to recover, I needed a huge shift in the way I had been living. I searched the

Internet and my intuition nudged me once again as I landed on a particular page. Yes, this was where I needed to be—at a holistic eating disorder treatment center, Mirasol, in Tucson, Arizona—where I needed to travel to get back on my feet.

I arrived in the heat of the desert and for the first time in my life, I began the journey inward. The center had holistic modalities for healing, such as art therapy, acupuncture, inner child work, and Reiki. These were unfamiliar concepts to me, yet I was willing to try anything as long as it kept me out of the psych ward.

The modality that literally brought me back to life was their equine therapy program. All the patients loaded into a van and drove to the therapist's ranch where the "therapy" horses were boarded. As a horsewoman my entire life, I was excited to be around horses again, but I had no idea that this day would mark the beginning of my life's purpose.

At the ranch, it was my turn to go in the arena where Jack, the horse, stood. I entered, determined to prove my horse knowledge and experience in front of the rest of the group. After all, I had grown up with horses and competed in three-day eventing. Strutting up to Jack with my hand out, he turned his head away from me and began to walk the other way. I was embarrassed and confused. I was an experienced horsewoman and used to being in control. Jack didn't give a damn about any of that. Being a prey animal, Jack instantly sensed my energy as a predator coming toward him with an agenda. Through reading my vibrational field with his heightened sensitivity, he also picked up on something I had mastered hiding over the years—my incongruence. I was skilled in the art of acting like I was fine when on the inside I was a mess. Jack's feedback showed me that I had to get honest inside and out. I had a lot to learn from this horse.

From the outside of the arena the equine therapist, Marla Kuhn, suggested I stop my actions and breathe to get grounded. She guided me through a series of breath work where I felt my body anchor into the dirt arena. With the desert sun beating on my face and my palms outstretched to the universe, a melting feeling washed over my brain. Something started to shift. My inner critic's voice was nowhere to be heard, and I was aware of a connection to my body, a completely foreign sensation. For the first time in a long time I didn't try to make things happen, try to change the way I felt, try to change the way I looked, or try to make everyone like me. I gave myself permission to just stand still and breathe.

Simultaneously, Jack walked straight up to me from the far side of the arena. I caught myself, tempted to put out my hand for him to sniff as I had for so many years with horses whenever they approached. Yet, Marla encouraged me to simply be aware of Jack's presence and continue to take the long, slow, and deep grounding breaths that my body hungered for.

Jack put his face inches from my chest and stood still with me. His four hooves did not move an inch while he breathed into my heart area. A flood of my suppressed emotions washed over my body and through my brain. There were no words, just a connection that I had been craving my whole life...with no agenda and no expectations. Heaving, as the tears streamed down my face, I noticed that Jack did not move or run away. He stayed present and continued taking deep breaths with his eyes soft. I was astonished that the weight of my emotions had not scared him away or made him run for the hills. He stood with me in my pain. Slowly but surely, I too embraced the present moment without running for the hills...or the cafeteria.

I connected with Jack in a way that made my heart dance. The dark clouds of my eating disorder began to part. I came home—into my heart—and released tears and fears and joy that had been locked up deep inside my body. I had not been able to access these emotions through any prior methods.

With Jack, my ego had to back off in order that my feminine power could come through. What a life-changing concept! I was able to open up with this gentle giant in a way I had never felt comfortable doing with family, friends, boyfriends, teachers, or therapists. I saw how self-destructive my mindset had become when I relied on external, artificial things to make me feel good about myself. After stuffing down my feelings, yearnings, and desires for so many years my body, mind, and soul cried out for help. In that moment, Jack helped me open, and instantly, I felt myself on solid ground. I found my footing in the world as I stood in that arena.

I was astonished to witness the profound shift in others who worked with the horses that same day. Their body language changed, their confidence rose, and they carried their heads higher. I looked on with hope and was blown away by the powerful healing these animals brought all of us.

I knew life had given me a huge wakeup call through my eating disorder. It was the red flag I needed in order to forge past the artificial bullshit and live authentically. Horses had come into my life at an early age to be my companions on my journey. They stuck by me through hell and had always been there for me to draw strength from their wisdom, spirit, and power. My energy vibration was raised in the presence of these magnificent creatures. My soul danced, my body came alive, and my feelings were honored. When the student is ready, the teacher appears. My teacher just happened to eat hay and had a mane and tail.

I returned to Mirasol radiating love—not only for horses but also for myself. I felt clearheaded and excited, having discovered a new way to interact with the equine world. On the bus ride home, I knew I had found my true calling. A light bulb went off, and the thoughts running through my head gave me hope. I had a sense of possibility that someday I could do this and help others, especially women who struggle with eating disorders. I had a vision, a mission, and a soul's desire to share the spirit and wisdom of horses, which truly changes lives. Funny, how all along my connection had been with horses. I just didn't know it would lead to my calling.

When I returned to Colorado from Mirasol, I saw life through a new lens. I embraced being a woman. I invited the intuitive gifts I could rely on from within as opposed to always seeking external answers and validation. Horses taught me that I was best when I was myself and that there was no shame in crying or being vulnerable. As an oldest child, I'd always tried to be the strong one, showing no tears but only strength. Through working with a four-legged teacher, I learned to also embrace the feminine power in me, which is soft and intuitive and compassionate. My true power emerged from within once I allowed it to breathe and stopped blocking it with resistance because I was afraid.

In Colorado, I started working with a life coach, Deb Roffe, to support me in my forward growth. Deb helped me recognize when my inner critic was leading my life and how to get around my self-sabotaging beliefs to keep moving forward. I was determined. I had a mission that went far beyond my life. No longer was it simply about "me, myself, and I." With all my heart, I knew that I was destined to make a difference in women's lives through horses. I realized that trying to please everyone else by throwing out my gifts is what led my soul to revolt. My eating disorder literally took me to a mountain ledge in order that I would wake up and realize I was not aligned with my calling.

In 2008, Deb forwarded an email to me about a woman in Boulder who was teaching a course on how to create a career with horses. I attended the introductory call about the course and even before the hour was over I knew with all my heart and soul that this was what I had been seeking. My intuition went nuts. This time, I was able to honor my inner knowing.

Unlike the classes I'd studied in college, I knew this "horse course" was a fit. It was the learning and experience I had been yearning for, way beyond a traditional academic education. This education resonated with my soul. Thus, my next teacher appeared—Melisa Pearce, CEO of Touched by A Horse™ Certification Program. During the next 18 months I became certified in the Equine Gestalt Coaching Method™ and learned how to create a business by partnering with horses to coach women who struggle with eating disorders. At my graduation, I was empowered, passionate, and eager to use my life experiences to make a difference in other people's lives.

Today my business, Beyond the Arena™, is my "dream come true." With horses as my partners, we help women access their inner wisdom in the arena and take their "aha" moments beyond the arena into their everyday lives.

Sitting in the back of a police car with handcuffs on, I never would have believed that I deserved joy. Yet, my eating disorder could not fight or prevent my life purpose and calling. By the grace of God and a horse named Jack, I learned how to channel the enormous energy it took to turn constant self-loathing into something that feeds my soul and benefits the greater good. Striving to live authentically, serving others, and speaking my truth is freedom for me. And freedom is the best taste there is— much better than chocolate!

Devon Combs is the CEO of Beyond the Arena™, LLC, which is based in Larkspur, CO at a stunning horse ranch with an indoor arena. Devon is passionate about sharing the life-changing impact that horses have on people, through the Equine Gestalt Coaching Method™. Her joy in life comes from offering women hope and tools for eating disorder recovery and beyond. She offers retreats, workshops and individual coaching sessions at the horse ranch and over the phone. For more information on Beyond the Arena's services, please visit www.beyondthearena.com.

Self Discovery

EMBRACING ALL OF ME

~~~

Sabrina Fritts

For as long as I could remember, I had lived a painful duality. On the outside, I was a strong, confident, intelligent, and attractive woman. Inside, I was tormented, ashamed, and empty. I felt unworthy. It takes a lot of effort to live so inauthentically, to maintain such a façade! I presented only the positive aspects of myself to the outside world, while suffering inside, afraid that people would see me for who I truly was.

Fear of discovery fed my controlling personality. I believed everything would be fine as long as I focused all my attention on orchestrating my world and securing external approval. This compulsion to control everything affected my relationships with others. Determined to receive approval for everything I did, I manipulated others' behavior to suit my needs, always alert for opportunities to prove myself.

It was my extreme attention to detail that led to a successful and rewarding human resources career, with great benefits and compensation, all without a college degree. I unknowingly manifested my personal belief that with hard work and determination I could accomplish anything I put my mind to. My life was one many identify with, including the stress, anxiety, and fear. This "typical" life, which I'd been well prepared for, came complete with a steady paycheck. I was happy on the surface, but deep down I desperately hoped there could be more to life.

An overwhelmed working mother of three, I assisted my husband in the build-out of his tattoo studio. At this particularly stressful period of my life, I found myself proclaiming, "There HAS to be something more than this!" In that moment, I decided to pursue those "glimpses of spiritual awakening" I'd experienced earlier in my life—those times when suddenly I KNEW—I knew I wasn't alone, and I knew there was something much bigger out there than I'd ever imagined.

By this time, I had rejected my religious upbringing. In fact, I

115

pushed strongly against organized religion for many years before I learned to accept that there are many paths to Source. I avoid using the word "God" even now, after dealing with a lot of false programming around a bearded old man in the heavens who judged everything and always found me lacking.

With my newfound determination to pursue spirituality and my two closest friends by my side, we began attending meditation and yoga classes together. I dusted off the recommended self-help books I had previously purchased and actually read them. Using a deck of angel oracle cards I had been given, I began developing my intuition and became open to receiving guidance and validation. I also started researching the healing properties of crystals and enjoyed collecting them.

Early in this new journey of self-care, my young son protested loudly as I left for class one day. He begged me to stay home. I felt the limited time I had with my children acutely, and in his case, I shared custody with his father. I didn't succumb to my maternal guilt, however. Instead, I looked into his eyes and acknowledged that I would miss him too, explaining that I had to do this for me. My time away was helping me become a better mom, the mother I wanted to be, needed to be—for him and my daughters.

I had grown accustomed to playing the role of the resentful, over-burdened mom, the one who does it all with little or no recognition. I was incapable of receiving help because I didn't believe I deserved it. The unacknowledged additional benefit of taking care of everyone else was that I "didn't have time" to look at my own pain.

I began to enjoy this time as I nurtured myself and explored my spirituality. I even found some relief from the everyday stress. One Saturday afternoon, I drove from my Colorado mountain community into "town" to visit a crystal shop. My two daughters were in the car with me when another car forced us off the mountain highway into a rollover accident.

I remember seeing the accident as it was about to happen, feeling powerless to alter the events now set inexorably in motion. Suddenly, I had the overwhelming feeling that I might become responsible for the deaths of my girls. I knew I could not—would not—stay if anything happened to either of them. I recalled what I'd recently read about angels—that they will intervene on

116

our behalf if it is not our time. So I found myself repeating the mantra, "Help us get through this; help us get through this; help us get through this." And suddenly we rolled upright onto all four tires. I jumped out of the car and breathed what felt like the freshest air I had ever inhaled, enveloped by the bluest sky I ever remember seeing. In that moment, my "typical" life was over. With the rolling of my car, something shifted and expanded within me. No longer would I be able to see the world in the same way—there was a "broader more" to everything.

Aside from bumps and bruises, we were virtually unhurt. Two weeks after the accident, I attended a metaphysical fair in Denver. A woman was scheduled to present a class on how to communicate with our angels, and it seemed just what I needed to learn. I'd also decided I wanted a personal reading and asked to be guided to the most appropriate person. I walked through the maze of vendors in the crowded pathways until I came upon a booth offering readings that included a drawing of one's personal angels. This was the reading for me! Coincidentally, it was with the woman who would be presenting—the very reason I was there.

During the reading, she connected with my angels and began to discuss my recent accident and the "quick trip" I'd taken. She seemed surprised that I didn't understand what she was talking about. Apparently, when the car was upside down, my head hit the ceiling and came down hard on my shoulder. At that moment, she said my soul left and was given sixteen important things to do in this life. I couldn't believe what I heard. I was already struggling with my personal to-do list, and now my angels were giving me another one!

I was told eight of those assignments that day. The angels were hesitant to give me the eighth, since they were unsure if I would understand—they instructed that I was to live a "typical/not-so-typical" life. They told me the remainder would be revealed when I was ready. In addition to these eight tasks, they informed her that I needed to have a Reconnection. I'd never heard of this before, and she told me to jot down "Dr. Eric Pearl." She said I needed to see him and have this work done. It would cost $333. The angel communicator said I was in limbo, that my soul wasn't sure where it belonged, and that this would help me. Then they clarified: Eric Pearl wouldn't be the one to do it. I should find a practitioner personally trained by him.

Something inside me lit up. I had no idea what this work was about, but I had knowingness that it was right for me. I went home, Googled his name, and found that he traveled the world teaching people to do this healing work. I ordered his book and found a practitioner.

My husband thought I had lost my mind. I wasn't sure I hadn't. I was about to pay good money and the person wouldn't even touch me! This wasn't a massage, but rather "energy-based" work. I couldn't explain why, but somehow I knew doing this was important for my journey. As it turned out, the money came easily—which always seems to happen when I'm doing something for my highest good. So I scheduled my Reconnection. As I lay on the massage table, fully clothed with eyes closed, I made a silent request. "All right, I'm here as you recommended. Do whatever."

At the beginning of the session, I felt a lot of energy in my head as it expanded in a way I'd never experienced before. I could feel and "see" a light moving across my face, back and forth in different locations, as if someone were holding a flashlight and tracing lines on me. Then I felt my head begin to move on the leather table. My head was being repositioned without my control, as if someone were holding it and tilting it toward the head of the table—projecting my chin toward the ceiling—even though the practitioner wasn't touching me. I quietly protested, "Wait one minute! I'm not going to lie on this table in that position. It will hurt too much." I was afraid that this might cause the all-too-familiar neck and shoulder pain I regularly experienced. I immediately took back control of my head and placed it in a comfortable position, directing my awareness back to my experience.

Suddenly, my head started to move again. I stopped it and moved it back. I found myself in a tug-of-war, something or someone tilting my head up while I countered by moving it back. Then it dawned on me: here I was, Miss Control Freak, trying to take over a sacred, once-in-a-lifetime experience, even after stating "Do whatever." I almost burst out laughing. Silently I acknowledged, "You got me, you can have this. All I ask is please, no pain." Of course, my head tilted up, chin to the ceiling, and there it remained for the duration of the first session. I experienced no pain.

Afterwards, I noticed a reduction in stress, not needing to control every little thing. I was learning to allow and trust. I noticed I was now manifesting more rapidly, including the elimination of some things I no longer wanted in my life. It was Dr. Wayne Dyer who had introduced me to the teachings of Abraham-Hicks, and that is when things really started to turn around. Consciously playing with the Law of Attraction, I began the process of forgiving others and myself. I began to let go of that which I had outgrown and started clearing the clutter from my home and mind.

My intuition also became heightened, and one day I heard very clearly, "Eric Pearl is in town next weekend." I looked at my calendar and remembered he would be teaching in Denver in July. "That's nice," I thought, and went back to working at the computer. I did not see myself as a healer, and I definitely didn't want to learn to wave my hands around people. I already had a stable career. Besides, who would take me seriously?

Of course, when you are meant to do something, the messages become louder and more persistent until you pay attention. I arrived in the office one morning and opened an email from a friend who lived in another state. She indicated that in her morning meditation she'd received the message, "Sabrina, The Reconnection, Level III" and asked if I understood. I explained that a local seminar would be taking place that weekend, but I didn't plan to attend. She would not let me off the hook with my typical excuse of "no time or money." I acquiesced and invited my girlfriend, who'd also had her Reconnection, and we registered the day before the seminar. It was an impulsive act way outside of my comfort zone on so many levels!

Despite my inhibition and uncertainty leading into the seminar, after the weekend of training, I was hooked. I offered healing sessions outside of work and often at the office. I played and had fun, allowing myself to be childlike and loving it. A few months later, I attended my Level III training so I could facilitate The Reconnection™ for others.

My heart called me to leave my mainstream career so that I could dedicate my life to helping others. My rational mind couldn't fathom why I would willingly give up a steady income and benefits. After all, I was helping to support my family and had created what I previously considered to be an ideal working situation, one in which I worked from home four days a week. Being able to go into the office only once a week allowed me more time with my family.

On one of my "office" days, my boss, the Chief Financial Officer, informed me that the Chief Executive Officer wanted me back in the office full-time. Apparently, the fact that I was performing well in my job, while being present at the office merely one day a week, threatened the status quo at this male-dominated civil engineering firm. Other employees now wanted what I had: a flexible schedule with the option of working from home. Silly me, I thought, they should have it! This was my invitation to freedom. I suggested that the CFO hire my replacement and allow me to train them before I ended my employment.

I was unsure what to do next. I took over the management of my husband's tattoo studio, something I could do from home, so he could focus on his art. Once I concentrated on his business and got comfortable with my life, the business prospered. The bank balance rose and business tripled that year, easily replacing my income.

As I facilitated healings for others, I received healing as well. My life evolved in all areas, and my passion and enthusiasm compelled me to share this life-altering work with others. I thoroughly enjoyed this healing journey, becoming a Teaching Assistant, volunteering at seminars, and teaching others to do this work. This little girl from Kansas was beginning to travel extensively, including trips to Italy and Amsterdam. Still needing to excel at everything I did, I advanced to Associate Instructor and became an integral part of moving the work forward globally. Yet, I soon realized that even a healing organization is not immune to the pitfalls of corporate dysfunction.

In early 2011, I became aware that if something was not authentic, it would naturally and effortlessly fall away, as long as I was willing to release it. Promoting an organization that continued to operate under old fear-based business practices was no longer authentic for me. As painful as it was, I had to let go. Again, I walked away from a role that had been fulfilling in so many ways and was also a source of financial stability.

As a result, my life is no longer "typical" by any means. I am now focusing on new paths that assist others in finding more joy, ease, and abundance in their everyday lives. And I do it best when I am authentic, when I show up and reveal my true feelings—the good, the bad, and the ugly—and when I allow others to know that I don't always do life perfectly. In letting others know the real me, I joyfully and more deeply connect with them. In sharing my real-life stories—whether on a stage or in one-on-one situations—I invite others to find and connect with their inner strength, compassion, and true empowerment. In embracing all, there is great joy to be had, which is much simpler than we ever thought—life isn't hard and doesn't have to be.

I trust that as I continue to honor my authentic self and accept every facet of my being—including those not-so-pretty parts—I will experience all of life's blessings. Already, I have joyfully discovered that sharing my vulnerability is a sign of strength, not weakness, and thankfully not so scary after all. I continue to discover that every time I am willing to detach from the person I thought I was supposed to be, I am pleasantly surprised at the version of myself I did not even know was possible.

Sabrina Fritts is an intuitive life coach, healer, and teacher. She nurtures her soul by living with her family in the mountains of Colorado. She is passionate about sharing her personal experiences and expertise in living authentically for the sake of helping others expand and allow more joy and ease in their daily lives. Today, Sabrina is pleased to offer spiritual coaching and individual healing sessions, both in-person and from a distance. She teaches self-empowerment seminars and co-hosts a radio show, "Authenticity Rising," on Transformation Talk Radio. Find out more at www.Simply-Sabrina.com.

THE LIFE OF MY DREAMS

Tara Nolan

Can my life and livelihood intersect to create fun and abundance? Writing this chapter, it seems funny that I even ask this question as I remember different instances of karma, the universe unfolding, or whatever any of us may call it. Looking back it becomes clear how the unexpected turns in our life path, at times unwanted, actually manifest new opportunities. It seems we must *need* to keep relearning this faith as we go through life.

When I was a senior in high school, my mom picked me up one Saturday afternoon and instead of going home, we—my brothers, my mom, and I—went to an airshow. I went along sullenly (I was a teenager after all). In my mind, as the oldest of six kids, I already spent a great deal of my time babysitting for our large family, and I had been looking forward to an afternoon to myself. What I really enjoyed doing, especially on a Saturday afternoon, was escaping to the barn to play with my horses. Why would I be interested in an airshow? I had never wanted to be an astronaut growing up. Instead, I dreamed of being a veterinarian and taking care of puppies and horses. But, when I saw the Thunderbirds perform—the Air Force's F-16 demonstration team—it set my heart racing.

As I walked around the different static displays, I came across a female pilot and I excitedly asked her what it was like to fly a fighter jet. She replied, "I don't know, they don't let women fly them." I was stunned. This was the very first time I encountered a roadblock to a goal. This was not something I could fix by working harder, and it set my competitive type-A personality into motion.

I surprised everyone by going from an uninterested airshow attendee to deciding that I would apply for the Air Force Academy. No one believed me. My parents had been hippies—my mom had even attended Woodstock. My parents didn't take me seriously at first, and I actually had to start filling out the lengthy applications by myself.

My mom did prepare me by taking me shopping for a business suit to wear to my entrance interview. After I got accepted to the Academy, my mom figured out how to fly us out to Colorado for the orientation. In fact, she recently shared that this had been a big financial leap of faith at the time and she'd gone to the bank to extend her credit in order to make the trip.

On this trip, she shared two experiences she had while I was attending the orientation at the Academy that fall into the category of the unexpected. First, my mom went to eat at the Waffle House next to our hotel and the waitress told her, "Why you're Jean Nolan from West Virginia!" My mom had taken care of her in the emergency room and this woman remembered her. What a coincidence!

Second, when the Academy's commandant, Brigadier General Redden, spoke to the parents the following day, he asked, "What kind of men come to the Academy?" He answered that it was traditionally-oriented young men. Then the general asked, "What kind of women come to the Academy?" and his answer was, "Your non-traditional and in fact fairly liberal young women." My mom knew I was in the right place.

I went to the Air Force Academy, and my graduating class included the first group of women to be allowed to fly fighters. I was so thrilled the law changed that it didn't occur to me I might not get a pilot slot. But, it was also a year of massive budget cuts. Only 20 percent of my class got pilot training slots instead of the normal 100 percent.

No matter what, we knew our direction would be in the military as new officers. All of us were excited to do something besides study and march in formation and have military inspections. I was ready to start working in the "real" Air Force. I was given my career field assignment, logistics, and I can honestly say that I kept an open mind because I had no idea what logistics was all about. Logistics is really a problem-solving position where you are given a task such as, "We need to get twenty people prepared and ready to spend ninety days in the Middle East, and they leave in six days." In reality, this was right up my alley after growing up as the oldest child of six siblings. I knew how to organize, entertain, and direct a crew of kids. Adults are a snap to deal with in comparison.

The rub for me, however, was that I still wanted to be a pilot (although being a logistics officer would open a door for me almost 15 years later). I'm not sure if I wanted to fly as much as I wanted to have the best job available in the Air Force from the perspective of a type-A competitive person who had seen the movie Top Gun. I mean, as an 18-year-old woman, why else would I even be in the military? If I wasn't going to have the chance to be in charge of a fighter squadron, why be there?

More determined than ever, I set off to get a pilot slot. Rather than ask, "Can I?" I probed the question, "How can I?" Four years later, I was selected to go to pilot training from my logistics career field. When I became an aircraft commander flying the C-130 it was almost a two-fold experience, falling into the category of not exactly what I wanted. The C-130 is a large airplane that can hold eighty people or carry one big army tank in the back. The back door on this plane can open up in flight so army troops can jump out or equipment can be dropped into locations that do not have a runway available for landing. The plane was definitely designed for people who can pee standing up, and I can tell you the women came up with some unique solutions. When focused on the mission and capabilities of the aircraft, I enjoyed hopping around Iraq and Afghanistan delivering supplies and bringing guys home but I cannot honestly say I liked flying in and of itself.

Decision time for the unexpected arrived again as I approached the end of my ten-year military commitment as a pilot, almost fifteen years since I first entered the service. The Academy was willing to send me to get a Ph.D., but my C-130 career field was not willing to release me for school. My supervisors counseled me to not leave the Air Force so close to my eligibility for retirement. At this impending fifteen-year mark, I only had five years remaining to leave the Air Force with full retirement pay. I remembered back to when I had been a cadet and thought to myself, *"I don't ever want to be in the military solely for the security of a paycheck."*

In the military, one's job is training, going where you're told and doing your job to the best of your ability. Your job is to always to be and do your best. The measure of your success is in how good you are at what you do with no dollar sign attached. How well you enjoyed what you were assigned to do was up to you—I was very good at making the best of any situation I found myself in.

For example, I was sent on a trip to Spain with two days' notice for an undefined length of time. I found out later that it was intended to be a punishment for, shall we say, not playing well with others. This ended up being an awesome trip both professionally and personally. I got to learn a new aspect of the Air Force mission that combined flying with my previous logistics training. And, I got to visit the Spanish Riding School and meet a local family who allowed me to ride their beautiful white stallion.

This riding experience brought back memories of my childhood dreams and how I'd always loved riding and spending time with my horses. As a result, I reconnected to my lifelong dream. My passion had always been my horses. I had invested in dressage horses and wanted time to compete and ride them. I wanted to find out if I had the skill to ride Grand Prix dressage.

If I stayed in the military, my life would go back to deploying to the Middle East and my personal life would be completely on the backburner again. I knew I would have to give up my dream to pursue dressage. I also knew I'd already put off my riding goals for many years, so I was a lot older than most who pursue that dream. If I put it off again at this point I would probably not be physically capable to accomplish my competitive goals in another six years.

I also had to admit that what I thought about when I was flying long legs to and from the combat zone was how I'd much prefer to be on my horse rather than on the flight deck. The idea of racking up more hours in an airplane was not really my dream. I always enjoyed accomplishing the mission but building hours didn't grab me the way thoughts of riding my horses did.

This forced me to make a tough decision. I had to choose between what I should do—what I was expected to do—as compared to what I truly wanted to do. Serving in the military was important to me and part of who I am, but I did not feel that spending another six years in a flying squadron was the best use of my time and talents. I wrestled with feeling selfish as I contrasted what I really wanted to do alongside what the military wanted from me. Being in the military had ingrained in me a strong sense of duty and ethics, but I also wanted to go in a direction that allowed me more independence and choice in my daily life. Deep inside, I felt that whatever any of us do with our lives, the majority of our one lifetime must be a passionate experience, yet I felt guilty for wanting this kind of joy in mine. I struggled with having to choose either my sense of "service before self" and "duty to my country" or my deep knowing that I have one life on this planet and I desire to live it with passion.

It was at this point that the idea germinated in my mind, "Can I contribute to my community and country in a positive way and enjoy myself at the same time?" I'm not sure at what point I had adopted the notion that if I was enjoying myself, it somehow didn't count as valuable work. I knew I did not want to go into a work situation because I felt that I had no other choice. People who labor under this false assumption are the worst to work with energetically. I started to explore other options much like a young college student might. Since I had graduated from a military academy, choice and self-determination were some new toys to play with, and I was eager to answer the question, "What do I want to be when I grow up?"

On the day I became eligible to end my commitment, I put in my request. I filed my separation papers from the Air Force. As scary as it was to turn my life upside down at 40 years old and consider going in a whole new direction, I knew I had to do it. Somehow, I believed there would be a way to have it all—a meaningful career that served others, financial independence, my dreams of riding once again, and fun.

As I explored the unknown realm of being a civilian, however, I had a hard time deciding what to pursue. I knew I could apply for a corporate job and start making good money, but was afraid I'd end up working long hours and not be able to pursue my riding once again. I considered teaching riding lessons but knew I wouldn't be able to afford the same lifestyle I currently enjoyed. There had to be something else that would allow me to make money, have time to ride my horses, and enjoy contributing in a positive way to my community. While I was waiting for the universe to let me know what that thing would be, things started to happen, more slowly than I would have liked, but in an unpredictable way.

I separated from active duty and started my own financial

planning business, becoming the entrepreneur I'd always wanted to be, but found it challenging. I knew this was the right field — combining my interest and life skills in investing with my education and training in logistics, and I knew I could help others strategize and plan for their futures. I had looked at other options, including franchises, but nothing combined my particular skills, training, and interests in the same way the financial arena did. The hard part was that I was used to following clearly-defined guidelines and checklists to get from point A to point B. Being an entrepreneur meant I had to develop many new soft skills — building relationships to build my business and networking in order to create those relationships.

Although initially challenging, leaving the Air Force allowed me to create and have my entrepreneurial life and to get involved with my passion of riding once again. And then something completely unexpected and wonderful happened. I was selected for a new Air Force reserve job in Hawaii because of my logistics background that would not have happened if I was still on active duty. I was promoted, able to plan my travel, and contribute to the Air Force using my skills in this new position. It was fantastic to be able to maintain my connection to the Air Force and not have to throw away my career. This reserve position gave me the ability to merge both my values together — I no longer had to choose between service to my country and living my passions. It continues to allow me to be in a unique and flexible role that also contributes to the retirement I will be able to draw after I turn 65.

Additionally, in my gap time, I started to work on a book about learning to ride horses and was able to publish it. The book was inspired because my true calling is teaching what I've learned and making things simpler for others. I saw the relationships between learning to fly and learning to ride. Both require knowledge of basics before one can begin fine-tuning. The mechanics must be understood before the art can be applied. I love teaching, in general, and have great fun teaching people to ride and connect with their horses.

There is the old saying that when you are ready your teacher will arrive. I connected with a business coach and honed in on the missing skillsets I needed to run my business successfully. Today everything is taking hold, and I'm learning to move amongst the different activities that are a part of my life. My business, pursuit of Grand Prix riding, and Air Force reserve time have integrated my passions with my values to create a life that is woven together beautifully. Every day brings me joy even when I have momentary instances of panic, wondering just what I've gotten myself into. I truly have found that work can be fun, enjoyable, and prosperous all at the same time. It is possible to have the fun, positive life of your dreams!

Tara Nolan is a renaissance woman—author, military pilot, teacher, rider and entrepreneur. Tara lives what she writes. While flying the C-130 around the world, she found a horse to ride in nearly every country where she was deployed. Tara has taken her passion for education and is creating a system of learning geared toward adult women who want to learn to ride horses, beginning with her book, Out of the Saddle: 9 Steps to Improve Your Horseback Riding. *Tara has created a unique process for empowering her clients as they create powerful financial plans to cover the gap between now and where they really want to be.*

WHAT'S IN A JOB?

Susie Schaefer

It was a typical early spring morning, just before seven o'clock. I strolled across the parking lot with briefcase and lunchbox in hand, ready to start my usual eleven-hour day. The air was crisp and cool, with a hint of winter wafting in the breeze, but no longer cold enough for a heavy coat. I stepped through the doors and greeted the opening shift employees as I made my way to my office and turned on the computer, stashing my briefcase and putting my lunch away in the break room refrigerator. After a few minutes, my computer was ready to go and I opened my email to see what was in store for the day ahead.

There it was...the email we all dreaded. Not a personal phone call, not a carefully crafted letter, but an email confirming the inevitable, that over 2,500 of us nationwide would lose our jobs in a couple of weeks. After all our hard work, long hours, and dedication to our profession as human resource managers, there it was in black and white. That was it. Done. The end. An ending that turned into the beginning of my nearly decade-long journey to find another career...

It wasn't the first career hurdle I'd encountered, as my husband and I had only moved to the small rural community of Sterling, Colorado, four years earlier. At that time, our plan was to leave the Denver metro area and establish roots in a quiet town in order to plan for retirement over the next 15 years. It wasn't a difficult decision to leave the city. We both loved the country atmosphere and the tall fields of corn blowing in the summer breeze. We even took the winters in stride with a few brutally cold days and the occasional blizzard.

Although my husband was able to transfer and keep his position with the state, I had to dig deep and find work that would bring in enough money to keep us afloat—a difficult proposition in an area with few high-paying jobs. In moving away from the Denver area, I left behind my cushy corporate job at a national broadband call center where I had enjoyed an income greater than my husband's. What would be in store for me in Sterling?

Initially, I landed a job at a small call center as a customer service representative but had to take a 75% pay cut from my Denver salary. What a reality check! It was the first time since graduating from college that I made minimum wage. Plus, it was not exactly a glamorous job either. It entailed spending virtually every shift listening to banking customers vent their frustrations because their account was overdrawn or they had bounced a check. It was tough, no doubt, but probably one of the best lessons in customer service I had received in years. I guess you could say it was a lesson for me in humility.

That was the end of summer 2004. Fortunately, we bought a great house and were both working, but our debt was out of control due to what we had accumulated based on my previous salary. We ended up cashing out my 401K and using it to pay off creditors. We were feeling a bit desperate and were praying for a better job to come along for me…and voila! In the spring of 2005, I applied for a position with a home improvement retailer that was opening a new store in our area. My husband and I drove to Denver for the three-hour interview and testing process. A couple weeks later, I was offered a job with a salary in the range of my previous Denver income, plus benefits and quarterly bonuses. I accepted on the spot and when I hung up the phone, I broke down in tears. What a relief! *Whew*, I was back in the saddle!

Three years later, in the spring of 2008, we received the email from our corporate office. It was a crushing blow, as I had just found my stride in working the long hours and juggling the stressful demands of the job. I was finally in a groove after breaking in several store managers and constantly staffing a store with ever-changing sales requirements. At the same time, receiving that email was a huge relief. We had a close-knit group of managers amongst the stores in our district, and we had heard rumblings about a potential layoff, but it hadn't been confirmed… until that communication.

So, what should I do now? There weren't many corporate jobs in rural Colorado and certainly even fewer positions in the field of human resources. I immediately started to search and applied everywhere. Finally, I heard about a position as the business manager of the local country club and golf course. The club had recently changed ownership, and they were looking for "new blood." With my background in human resources and a degree in hotel and restaurant management, it seemed a perfect fit. After two interviews, I negotiated my salary, accepted the offer, and started work right away.

I soon discovered that the general manager had his hands full with the pro shop and golf course, which left me to manage the business office, restaurant and bar, banquet facilities, as well as handle all the monthly billing, accounts payable/receivable, and inventory. It was a HUGE job, so I found myself hiring part-time staff and delegating as much as possible. In addition, we had several golf tournaments and events during the course of the summer to promote the club's new ownership and recruit members.

Just as we were gearing up for the big Labor Day tournament, I learned that members and guests had been sexually harassing the female wait staff. I reported this to the general manager, who assured me he would take care of the situation. We had a successful tournament, and the following week I was called in for a meeting with the board of directors—not uncommon, since we met on a fairly regular basis. It was then that I learned they were "letting me go." I had no question as to why. I knew I had challenged the "good ole boys," and now I was going to pay for it. I have to say, that was very difficult for me. In my heart, I knew I'd made the right call but never thought I'd be fired for it. And then, the realization set in…I had lost TWO jobs in less than six months. It was a blow to my self-esteem and my confidence.

I let myself have a little pity party and then decided that feeling sorry for myself was unproductive. It was time to move on. One day, I happened to be in the bank and heard about a part-time opening. I went home and immediately applied. Within about a week, I was hired and excited to be working in a place full of energy and social camaraderie. However, although the position was "fun," I was back to making a meager wage that didn't even come close to my previous salary.

Keep in mind, it was now September 2008, quickly approaching the stock market crash of October 2008, and there I was working at a bank! It was that next month when I received a 401k statement from my previous employer. I had to figure out what to do with my retirement account. I instructed them to send the check to my Edward Jones broker, and that's when it happened...the crash! I met with my broker, and the first thing I asked was, "How much did I lose?" "Nothing," he said. The check hadn't yet been deposited into any account, so I was safe, but it had been a very close call.

After several hours and looking at every possible option, we came to the conclusion that it would be in my best interest to cash out the retirement account and take the hit on taxes rather than potentially lose what retirement money I had saved. Our calculations showed that the account would be enough to pay off my car and give us a bit of cash flow. (We later realized how incredibly lucky we were that we didn't reinvest the money—we would have lost nearly 50% to the declining stock market.)

I spent the next year-and-a-half working at the bank, always looking for another position, but never finding anything that was a step in the right direction. At that time, the bank was in the process of creating a "sales" environment—even the tellers had sales requirements. Now, don't get me wrong, the corporate world revolves around sales, but it was getting out of control. We constantly had customers complain that they were being "sold to" instead of being able to simply take care of their business needs. The environment became threatening, and pretty soon everyone was walking on eggshells. I knew I had to find something else and get out, but a new manager beat me to the punch and let me go due to "insufficient sales."

Based on the information I was given and my background in human resources, I knew I could fight them in court, but I just couldn't bring myself to do it. I had just come out of a long drawn-out legal battle with the country club, and it had been emotionally draining. Although I won my case against them for reporting sexual harassment and received a nice settlement, it had been a difficult process—something I would not recommend unless absolutely necessary. With the support of my husband, it seemed like a good idea at the time.

Once again, I was unemployed. All this time, my husband was incredibly supportive and really understood how difficult this "status" was for me. My confidence was shattered, and I questioned my ability to be professionally productive. I'd had four jobs in the six years we'd lived in Sterling, and I felt like a failure. My husband knew I had planned a trip to California with my two best friends, so he said, "go for it," knowing that I needed to recharge my batteries.

The trip to California could be a story in itself. Initially, we planned to fly to Los Angeles, then drive up the coast to Napa, do a little wine tasting, and head our separate ways. During the trip, our plan was to gather ideas for a book that the three of us would write—a kind of "perspective" on life from each of us. Well, let me just say that the trip started out great, but time got away from us and disagreements ensued. After a strained last couple of days, we parted, not knowing where our relationships would stand once we got home.

Feeling alone and insecure, I headed home, giving me time to reflect on the importance of my relationships; not only with my two best friends, but with others in my life as well. I decided it was time to make amends, regardless of the cost, because those deep relationships are few and far between. It was not a time for regrets, but a time for repair. Not only did the three of us mend the fences, but we found that our relationships had survived and were stronger than ever by coming to an understanding about what was important to each of us. That was the true test of friends...lifelong ones at that.

The month before our girls' trip, I had read in the paper about a CASA (Court Appointed Special Advocates) group that was looking for someone to work part time to manage the program in northeastern Colorado. I didn't know much about managing a non-profit but figured I could learn just about anything at that point. Learning more about the program, I realized I really wanted to do something that had meaning and served the community. After two interviews, I was hired, believe it or not, due to my DIVERSE CAREER path. How do you like that? My perceived "failures" were actually an *advantage*! They liked that I had experience in human resources, management, recruiting, marketing, fundraising, working with volunteers, and that I was self-directed. What an amazingly perfect position for me! I was ecstatic.

Over the course of the next year, we grew the program from

a handful of volunteers to 19 unpaid volunteers that served 40 abused and neglected children. In October 2011, we were astonished to hear that Colorado CASA, the umbrella organization for our program, had decided to close all the rural programs due to funding. It was quite a blow to the volunteers and advisory committee after all their hard work and progress.

Well, I have to say, this gave me a lot of determination. I met with the Chief Judge, and with his support, decided to put together a steering committee and create an independent non-profit CASA organization to serve our Northeastern Colorado communities. While we're still in the planning stages, it is evident that we have a tremendous amount of community support and the program is very much needed. I never would have thought that my eclectic career would take me to such a place of caring for others and wanting to contribute to my community…and to making a real difference.

Throughout these ups and downs and career highs and lows, I was fortunate to be continually active in the community, which kept me busy between jobs and in touch with my network. I was on the Northeastern Junior College Board of Trustees, had a leadership position as President of Colorado Business Women of Sterling, and served on the City of Sterling Personnel Board. I knew that keeping my contacts in my line of sight and continually networking would eventually help me either find my next position or at least keep me in front of the movers and shakers. And it did!

As a true test of why networking and community service is so popular during these economic times, I was at our local radio station in January to do a live on-air interview for an upcoming fundraiser. After the interview, the program director and account representative told me that they had a position open and wanted me to apply. Needless to say, I was hired a few weeks later and felt as if I had truly found my niche. Between writing, sales, live remotes, and production, the fulfillment of a career position has finally come to fruition.

It turns out my meandering career was actually a lesson in gathering skills and experience, leading to the culmination of a decade's work. Through it all, I never let it get to me "too much." Even when things looked questionable, they worked out. I knew that, no matter what, I had to overcome my fears and keep my chin up, 'cause the next great thing was just around the corner... or in the next job.

Susie Schaefer attended college at California State Polytechnic University of Pomona and moved to Colorado in 1992, where she lived in Vail for several years. In 1997, Susie relocated to Denver and met her husband Tim. Susie is a member of the Northeastern Junior College Foundation Board of Trustees, Colorado Business Women of Sterling, and has a home-based business with Arbonne International. Susie currently works for Northcast Colorado Broadcasting and is a business consultant in her spare time. Susie is actively working on the CASA project in Northeastern Colorado and hopes to continue advocating for abused and neglected children.

WHAT'S IN A NAME?

Rita Kyker

I grew up in a New York Italian-Irish Catholic family where my mother's and aunt's names are the same as mine. What's interesting though is that my family never called me "Rita" because my father nicknamed me "Rinky-Dink" as a young child and it stuck. My parents didn't want any school or official papers written with the same name as my mother's so I was always "Rita Mary" on paper and "Rink" in casual conversations. I didn't mind even though I still liked my original name. Little did I know that I would come to *love* my original name even more as I got older once I found out what the name "Rita" really means.

In the late 1970's when I finished high school, women were just beginning to branch out into the traditional male-dominated fields. Since I always hated the way I had been brought up, with girls and women doing all the cooking and cleaning and the men doing the mechanical stuff, I became one of the women who wanted to branch out into the male world. At that time, I never saw myself as a woman who wanted to stay home and raise a family. Far from it! So with my mechanical-math mind, the curious adventurous side of me went against the traditional female norms and I decided to study aviation. I remember as a child that I used to lie on the ground and stare up at the sky watching airplanes fly so high and wondering how they were able to do that. Having never forgotten that, I proceeded to find out.

After high school, I went to college to study Aeronautical Engineering with an Air Force ROTC scholarship, which meant I was committed to servicing four years as an active duty Air Force officer. During the last year of college, I met a man who I thought I loved. We had a lot of similar interests and backgrounds so it felt comfortable. He knew I was going into the military (he wasn't military), but he asked me to marry him anyway and I said yes. I remember having this warped sense of insecurity that I should have a husband because I thought people would take me more seriously as an officer and leader. I was a non-conforming female simply by being in the aviation field, yet I didn't want to stand out *too* much and latched on to some of those old traditional norms of conformity I forgot I hated.

When we got married, I received my orders to go to Alaska where the adventure really began. We both loved the outdoors and wanted to explore something new in our lives, so Alaska was the perfect place! Little did we know what lie ahead. The signs were obvious in the beginning but I didn't see them—as is usually the case. His angry outbursts, the constant health issues he had, and the embarrassing encounters he had with our friends. He started to verbally criticize me about little things. Then it happened! We had a verbal argument in the car on the way to the store one day and he snapped! He got so angry that he punched me hard in the leg! It came from nowhere, and the throbbing in my leg kept me from thinking rationally at first.

When we got to the store, he went in by himself while I stayed in the car to stew about what had just occurred. I couldn't let him get away with punching me, so I decided to just leave him there and took off with the car. Hours later, when he got home from walking the seven miles to our house, no words were spoken. My fear subsided because I'd stood my ground that time. Unfortunately, things got worse with time. He eventually pulled a gun on me once and then turned around and pointed it at himself. Yes, this was anyone's worse fear—he was an abuser!

We were isolated from family and only had a few friends because most people couldn't relate to me having a civilian husband and him having an officer for a wife. He had serious physical issues to deal with. His pain was hard for him to handle most of the time, and I used that as his excuse and took his verbal and physical abuse. I felt sorry for him. I began feeling guilty for having brought him all the way up to Alaska away from his own family and friends. It began the downward spiral of the life of a battered woman: guilt, low self-esteem, loss of weight, problems with my job, physical illness, and the feeling of isolation.

Wait a minute—I, an officer in the Air Force and a woman who overcame obstacles to get into the Air Force with an aeronautical engineering degree, being abused—how had I let it happen? How could this be? Well, with a look back at my strict Catholic upbringing, I unreasonably felt that since "I'd made my bed, I had to lie in it," meaning I was stuck with what I had created. I also felt that since I've overcome so much already, I could overcome this too. I just didn't realize my self-esteem was being eaten away—literally.

The stress of hiding it all manifested into stomach problems so severe I had to have stomach surgery. I had a really strong negative image of myself. I was always embarrassed to go out in public with my husband for fear of him overreacting to something. I compensated by being overly nice to others and never rocked the boat in any situation. I buried myself in books and got my master's degree, taking night classes. I tried to do my best at work, but my performance suffered because I had little confidence in myself. I even fell in love with the wilderness of Alaska probably because I was in a wilderness of my own.

The hardest thing I had to endure was feeling like I had absolutely nowhere to turn. I didn't want to tell my parents because I was ashamed and didn't want them to worry. I didn't want to tell my friends because most of them were from work and I didn't want people at work to know my personal situation. I was embarrassed. Perhaps I still thought I loved him and I didn't want anyone to think poorly of him. I also felt as though it was entirely my fault.

What could I do? Where could I go? I remembered that a friend of mine needed support for family issues years before and several of her friends directed her to the abused-women-in-crisis shelter. Could I do that for myself? I was desperate and researched shelters in Anchorage but as luck would have it, my military unit had a community service project which just happened to be— helping the abused-women-in-crisis shelter. Yes, my commanders were volunteer counselors at the shelter! *How could I ever let my commanders know about my personal problem? After all, I was an officer in the Air Force. I couldn't have personal problems!* That's what my sad, warped mind thought. So I continued my life as a lonely, battered woman.

After three years in Alaska, I finally got orders to go to New Mexico. Ahh…a new start! The dry weather would be better for his health and I could start a new job with new people. When we got there, however, he couldn't find a job because the base wasn't located in or near a big city. The frustration and depression began to set in, and at times, he was like a caged animal. I received word that I had been selected to attend a two-month course in Alabama where I was going to learn about the strategies of war and how to be a better officer and leader. I was very excited because it was an honor to have been selected and because it would get me away from him for two months.

Shortly after telling him, I remember being in the living room and playing chess with him. He won the first two of three games. I wasn't as competitive as he was, so I knew it made him feel great to win. But when *I* won the third game, his ugly side surfaced. He began to throw chess pieces all over the room and said some nasty things to me. It seemed as if it happened in slow motion. The pieces were thrown one at a time, barely missing me. I didn't make a move and was numb from the sudden shock of his outburst. As I watched this scene unfold, I remember praying the pieces wouldn't hit my precious crystal airplane collection on a shelf on the wall. I was so dazed and saddened by this outburst that I didn't even care if he hit me. The objects were all that mattered to me.

Then he began mumbling words as he whipped the pieces across the room. He said something to affect that "women can't strategize and shouldn't be able to win in chess." As I sat there hearing these words, all I thought about was how out of touch he was with my life and the path I was heading toward. The two-month course I was about to attend was all about just that—strategizing! This was it—the last straw.

The reality from that one single episode shook me awake. I realized I needed to get him out of my life. I was going away for two months and knew it would be a great time to think about how I could execute a safe plan to divorce him. Since he wasn't working yet, he decided to go back to his family in Oregon for the two months I'd be gone. Relief washed over me because I didn't want to feel responsible for him while I was gone. I was the sole provider at this time. Part of me was hoping I would miss him while I was gone and wouldn't go ahead with planning the divorce, but I guess my willpower was *finally* stronger than it had ever been and I didn't miss him at all.

When I returned from my training, he returned a changed man. During the time away, he got very close to God. He apparently did some serious praying and wanted to change things for the better. *Now what should I do?* The guilt started to creep in again, but the training must have strengthened my resolve. I was able to talk to him and tell him I didn't want to stay with him anymore. We agreed to get some counseling, but I had to admit in the sessions that I just didn't love him anymore. Still feeling sorry for him, I never admitted in counseling that he ever abused me. I just wanted to be rid of him so I could start living a life without fear of verbal or physical abuse.

By this point, I had finally told my parents. They didn't know all the details but were very supportive and wanted to come out and help me. I assured them I was OK and had to handle this on my own. I do believe God was involved in the entire process because everything went smoothly and peacefully and we divorced shortly after.

I was one of the fortunate women able to get away from my abuser. I had my own job/career to help me feel positive about myself and a great family to support me. With all the hard training and mental challenges I had in the military and aviation world, I never encountered anything more challenging than enduring that relationship. Because I had so much emotion invested, it was extremely hard to end my marriage. I even went off to serve in the Gulf War and still didn't feel as much pain and guilt as I did in breaking up with him.

So what does my name "Rita" have to do with all of this? Years ago, my mother told me our name means "pearl" in Greek. It was just one of those gee-wiz nice-to-know things she shared with me. No big deal. Well, after having gone through the abuse, for some reason, that little tidbit of information resurfaced. It came as no surprise when I researched all about pearls, to rediscover that my name meant "pearl."

I have always loved pearls more than other gems, so I reflected on what a pearl really is and how beautiful they are. The process of how a pearl becomes a pearl is a very interesting, amazing, and natural event. It all begins with a foreign substance, like a pebble or grain of sand, getting inside an oyster. The foreign object is an irritant to the oyster much like when we get a splinter. The oyster's natural reaction is to cover up the irritant to protect itself. This protective reaction begins a biological process of producing a substance called "nacre." As long as the irritant stays inside its body, the oyster will continue to secrete nacre around it, layer upon layer. Over time the irritant will be completely encased by the nacre coatings and the result is a beautiful, iridescent gem called a pearl.

So, you see, I was the irritant in the ugly mess of an oyster. I came out of the process as a beautiful person that others are able to love. When I was in the turmoil, I never felt lovable because my self-esteem was shattered. When I slowly started to realize the abuse was not what I had to live with, it was like the layers of nacre on the pebble giving it strength. I felt strong and beautiful when I was finally on my own—like a pearl ready to come out of the oyster. I even fell in love again, remarried, and have a child now.

I'm not saying my life is perfect and that there aren't other challenges I've faced, but that was my first and biggest one yet. If I can go through the process like a pebble becoming a pearl, then I can overcome anything. I am Rita—a Pearl!

Rita Kyker is currently a secondary math teacher living in Denver, Colorado with her 15-year-old son. Her background includes seven years as an Air Force officer with over 1000 hours in the E-3A AWACs (Airborne Warning and Control) aircraft and a Desert Storm veteran. She grew up in New York, both upstate and Long Island, where most of her family still lives today. She enjoys traveling around the world and wants to reach out to other abused women, especially in the military, hoping that her story can help others. Email Rita at rkyker16@gmail. com.

LOVABLE ME!

Tami McGirr

My world came to a screeching halt as the physician on the other end of the telephone told me my diagnosis. In a monotone voice, he stated that I had the start of a brain aneurism. All of a sudden I noticed how alone I was, sitting in the hotel room at a local water park resort in Arizona. I thought, "I should be outside, enjoying my friends' company and playing in the pool or being whisked down a refreshing water slide." Instead, everything in front of me started to move in slow motion.

Just a minute before, I had been struggling to hear the voice on the phone because of all the commotion outside my hotel room. Now, all I could hear was the monotone of my doctor. He told me I could live with this condition for anywhere from six months to thirty years. I told him, "I'll take thirty years." He said I didn't have a choice. I replied, "Yes I do." I was not sure where my response came from. It just seemed to pop right out of my mouth without any forethought.

As I hung up the phone, I sat back on the fresh pile of pillows at the head of the bed. They reminded me of hospital pillows—they felt cool and stiff. I had spent the better part of the last three months in and out of hospitals, going through test after test, trying to explain the recent bout of migraine headaches I had been experiencing. I was lost in thought as I sat there. *At only 33 years old, how could this be happening to me?*

The next business day, I called my doctor's office to schedule an appointment with him to discuss the results in greater detail and talk about treatment options. The first available time was several days later. I spent the next few days thinking about my life. *Had I done everything I wanted? Had I become everything I wanted to be? How had I impacted the lives of my friends and family?* I struggled greatly with these questions, and the answers were not at all agreeable to me.

The more I discovered how dismayed I was with my life, the

145

further back I searched. I kept trying to figure out the last time I had felt loveable. I realized that maybe I'd never felt loving connections with most of the people in my life. I directed my thoughts to the one pressing question that kept playing over and over in my head. *Who would be affected if I were to succumb to the brain aneurysm?* Eventually, that question led to an even darker one. *If I didn't matter to anyone, why was I fighting so hard to live?* I knew I did not want to die, but I did not feel as though I was really living or ever had.

At two o'clock of the morning before my doctor's appointment, I woke up. Suddenly, I had a thought that jolted me straight out of bed. I had made a giant discovery. I wanted to live! I didn't, however, want to stumble around like I had been doing for the last 33 years. I wanted to *really* live my life. This horrifying medical condition was not going to be my impending fate but rather the second chance for how I would live from now on.

In order to move forward with renewed hope, I felt it was important to completely re-evaluate my past. I needed to discover how I ended up just as emotionally inadequate as everyone else around me. So, still consumed with my reflections, I came to the conclusion that I had walked away from my childhood not feeling loveable.

I had not experienced a bad childhood—there was no abuse or any major devastating events. But, by no means did I feel any strong, loving connections toward most of the people in my family. As a result, I did not feel as though I mattered to anyone. It was as if I was a ghost living beside the others, but they did not notice me or what I was doing.

I also saw a reoccurring pattern in my adult life regarding dating. The men I had chosen to date were not capable of participating in deeper, more meaningful relationships. Over and over, I had allowed myself to get involved with men who were emotionally limited and unavailable. This left me feeling even more unwanted. These superficial relationships solidified my life's theme of feeling unlovable.

No doubt, I had played a hand in this feeling of being "unlovable" my entire life. I kept seeking out those people who were filled with the same insecurities I had. That was part of the initial attraction that I didn't notice or understand until much later in the relationship. In the beginning, each one seemed charming and caring. Then, once the terms of the relationship were established, they would tuck their emotions away, never to be seen again. Each man's lack of emotional capabilities began to shine through, and I would find myself completely consumed by these men, not maintaining my own persona. The feelings of "unwanted and unlovable" would return to haunt me, even though I believed I was in a committed, loving relationship.

I did not go back to sleep that night. For the first time in a long while, it was not because of a migraine, as it had been over the past several months. That night, I started to answer the questions I had been recently asking myself. I moved from my bed to the balcony and curled up on a lounge chair outside. The night air was soothing and warm. As I stared up into the desert night sky, I felt a strange peace come over me. I somehow knew I was on the right path. For the first time in years, I noticed the massive number of stars in the sky. At that moment I felt very much alive!

I was able to meet with my doctor the next day. He explained my condition in greater detail. Then he gave me three treatment options. I did not like my first two: radiation or brain surgery. The remaining option was to prevent all triggers for a migraine. He told me that even the smallest headache could be fatal for me. I would have to become very proactive in reducing exposure to potential triggers. In my case, the biggest triggers were my hormones. They were completely out of control, so I was scheduled for an immediate hysterectomy. I learned I would need to make other radical lifestyle changes as well. The arts of biofeedback and meditation would become necessary and useful tools in my life. I also had to eliminate several foods from my diet, which felt like a great sacrifice.

As I drove home from the doctor's office, it occurred to me that the biggest changes I would need to make were related to the relationships I had with other people. If I was going to live, I was really going to live! I would no longer accept superficial relationships with anyone in my new life. I was going to deepen relationships that mattered. For instance, I had a niece and a nephew who lived in Colorado. I wanted to get to know them better and for them to know me as well. The relationships with them became very important for me to cultivate.

147

The first call I made was to my mom. In the past, our relationship had not always been ideal. However, I did know she was one of the few people who had always loved me. I gave her the news of my medical condition. Since I had been doing so much self-reflection and evaluation of my feelings about being unlovable, it was difficult to ask my mom to come to Arizona and support me during my surgery. Somehow, I stumbled through the request and she agreed to come. I felt relieved. I really looked forward to having someone around who was going to be supportive. I rejoiced in the thought that I would not be alone for the surgery.

The day of surgery, my mom and I went to the hospital. It was great having her there. She helped ease my concerns about the surgery. Afterward, when I awoke, I instantly felt better. My head felt clearer and I did not have that feeling of another looming migraine. Over the next few days, while recovering in the hospital, I was able to finally enjoy the mother-daughter time I had been hoping for. I explained to my mom how I wanted to utilize this second opportunity at life that I had been given—I wanted to live life to the fullest. To me, this meant that anyone who wanted to be in my life would *need* to want and love me as much as I wanted them. Otherwise, they would not be invited to share in my life.

My mom agreed that these changes were necessary. "Life is too short not to live it with great zeal," she told me. Family connections were going to be at the top of my new list of priorities. To do that, my mom suggested I move back to Colorado where all my family lived. I thought her idea was a great one. Two weeks after my surgery, I did just that. I loaded up the moving truck and drove back home to Colorado.

In the process of moving home and lifting furniture so soon after surgery, however, I ended up with a hernia. As a result, my second week back in Colorado was spent in the hospital recuperating from another surgery. The upside was that this recuperation allowed me the time to visit with family members. I made plans to go out and do fun things with my niece and nephew once I was completely healed. I was so excited that I would be involved with their world.

I am now a large fixture in my niece and nephew's life; we

see each other quite often. After going through these trials, I have come to believe that everything happens for a reason. Being diagnosed with a brain aneurism will not be my focus or the reason to mope about things I cannot do or have. Rather, it has become the drive for me to live my life to the fullest.

Three years have passed since I moved back to Colorado. While my life is truly great, it is also a struggle at times. The old behavioral patterns have been hard to break. I did find myself in another romantic relationship with a man who was emotionally limited. While it took me the better part of two years, I eventually realized he was not capable of changing. Even though he never appreciated me for all my glory, he did help me discover one of my greatest strengths…my freedom. I no longer have to depend upon him or anyone else to feel wanted. I can provide that feeling for myself.

I have learned I do not have to settle for that type of relationship ever again. I deserve better, and I am fully capable of starting a new relationship with a man who already knows how to be emotionally responsible. I know I will not settle for anything less.

Having a 'bucket list" may seem cliché, but I have one. I am very proud to say I am actively crossing items off that list, which is just one example of how I am living my new life. I have also incorporated several other examples of my new zest for life into my day-to-day routine. I meditate each morning before getting out of bed. And as I prepare for my day I ask myself, "What amazing gift from the universe am I going to receive today?" I take breaks at work just to go outside and sit in the sunshine for a few minutes. At the end of the day, before I fall asleep, I say how thankful I am for that day's gift.

Over the last few years I have been able to strengthen my relationships with other family members. But most importantly, I have discovered I can only be responsible to strengthen my half of *any* relationship. The other half is up to the other person. Today, I feel that I am very lovable and wanted. I may not always be loved exactly how I want to be by the people in my family or others in my life, but today I am loved *all the time* by someone who matters *most of all*…me.

Tami McGirr is a friend, sister, daughter, and an amazing aunt. She makes friends with every four-legged creature that crosses her path. Tami was raised in Colorado and has lived in Wyoming, Oklahoma, and Arizona. She believes in giving back to the community and serves as a victim's advocate for her local police department. One day soon, she will be a family therapist where she hopes to be able to empower others to love their lives, too! To contact Tami, email her at: tmcgirr@msn.com.

EMPOWERING YOURSELF FIRST

Helen Brougham

It was my intention to be an empowering role model for my children throughout their lives. The ideal of raising a family on our own farm made my heart sing. In actuality, bringing up four small children while working hard on a farm was an extremely busy and demanding life for my husband and me. Little did I know that as time went on, my life would become increasingly challenging—to the point where I would become ill and desperately need help. Thankfully that help did come at a point in my life when I needed it most—in the form of an ad in our local paper.

The moment I was told by the doctor I was pregnant my mum alert button went on and stayed on. All of a sudden it became extremely important to consider what food to eat, to decide there would be no more alcohol, and to learn more about being pregnant. It was important to determine when I should see the doctor or set an appointment to see a midwife. Day-to-day living included thoughts about what I should be on the lookout for that might signal something was wrong with my growing baby. Of course, it was important to be careful not to fall over. As my belly expanded, my thoughts grew to include what pram to buy. All these considerations became stronger and moved me to an intuitive, high-alert status as a mum-to-be.

I could see my husband changing as well. His alert buttons went on as he thought about becoming a dad and seeing me pregnant with our first child. With my mum's body and mind shifting, so did his mind move to the many changes already happening and to all the impending changes that would become new experiences and bring on unknown, yet anticipated, new stress.

One by one, over the next six years, our four children entered the world, each beautifully unique. Life on a farm with four small children, however, gave little time to contemplate their

151

individuality. Living on a farm with my husband was a busy life. Each morning my husband and I woke up early and went outside to milk our two cows. Life on a farm means time is not restricted or scheduled by the clock. Rather, it is dictated by where the sun is in the sky at any particular time of day. Mornings meant tending to the animals in order to provide for our family's sustenance throughout the day.

On the farm, seeding is done in winter, when it is wet, windy, and cold. Working as a farmer's wife meant I drove the truck out to the paddock at seeding time while my husband was in the paddock on the tractor. Often, the children sat in the tractor where it was safe and warm while the seeding was completed.

On the warm summer days, I took the children out into the paddock so they could have a run around it and play on the stone heaps. It brought such joy as I watched them experience the breeze on their faces and enjoy the sunshine.

There was always work to do on the farm, whether it meant lifting bags of oats and bales of hay around on the ute or driving the ute into the paddock to feed the sheep. I was constantly torn between wanting to become an empowering mum bringing up happy children and needing to be a farmer's wife working our farm to survive.

I did not realise at the time what pressure I put on myself in trying to maintain balance and in meeting all my self-imposed expectations. Not only was there a level of stress in wanting to be a mum, but the strain that went with trying to be a *good* mum was extreme. It was important that I teach my children to have good manners and that I encourage them to get on with each other and communicate well. It was also extremely important that I ensure they didn't get hurt—especially living on a farm—and that I foster an atmosphere of happy, peaceful, and loving children.

It was always easier to stay home instead of getting everyone ready and organised to go out. The children were very comfortable at home, but I knew they needed to be in the community with other people and to have social experiences. Striving to do it all, shopping with them or keeping them quiet in church became an art of its own as I sought to bring along small toys they could play with quietly or books to read and distract them to stay quiet.

As a mum, what I was most concerned about was whether I'd taught my children enough to handle the outside world on their own. I couldn't go to school with them and tell them how to handle any situation that came up. I couldn't be there to tell them how to act in new situations. I understood that my children would learn from these experiences. By playing, being in class with the teacher and finding out what the teacher expected or how the teacher wanted them to behave, they would learn to adjust their behaviour according to their situations. I only hoped that the love, caring, and support we provided in their early years would be adequate to see them through.

Often, the situations they encountered in school were quite different from what they experienced at home. For instance, not coming from a family that yelled, when they encountered situations where children yelled at them, they became upset and didn't understand. They also brought that behaviour home. Often, one of my children came back from school and then yelled at me. When any of them arrived home and was obviously unhappy, I took the time to sit with them and find out what had happened that day. Then, I'd wait for them to tell me. I'd ask why they were yelling at me and remind them that we didn't do this in our home. I'd explain that we liked to talk so others could truly hear. I noticed that all these habits came home and were tested out to see which ones were okay. Other experiences came home with them too—not being liked by everybody or not being included in schoolyard play—and it was equally important for me to invite conversation, tune in, listen, and help them navigate their feelings.

As it became increasingly challenging to be present to the needs of each of my four children with individual ages, personalities, thoughts, and situations in everyday life, I became more overwhelmed. I often questioned myself about whether I handled a situation correctly or had gotten it wrong. I wondered whether I was a bad mum and often felt guilty for my decisions. I also noticed I developed a confused, foggy head and felt guilty for that too. I know now that my constant guilty feelings related to my worry over what others would think about my decisions or how they would judge my children. I eventually learned that what I chose to do with my children only affected us, and if it worked out well, that was all that mattered, but that took some time and pain to realise. It took me a long time to get to the point, but eventually, I stopped telling people what I did or why I did it.

As time passed, I began to realise that I did not like the way I felt most of the time because it was so different from how I'd felt before having children. Prior to children, life had been peaceful, loving, quiet, and all around easy and relaxed. As my sense of overwhelm grew, I acknowledged that I felt quite the opposite and thought something must be wrong with me. Even though I understood that children have up and down days and solving those issues and showing our children how to manage disagreements and misunderstandings is a part of day-to-day life, I became more anxious.

On top of my increasing stress, I suffered a huge trauma when my two beautiful grandparents died eight days apart at 80 and 81 years of age, two years after my last child was born. My children missed seeing them every week, and so did I. Although we were all extremely sad, I believed it was important that normal life continue with the children going to school and me being available to listen to them and stay tuned in to how they were feeling. In the midst of trying to keep everything stable, however, I was suffering.

In 1992—four years after the death of my grandparents and a year after my youngest child began school—I finally acknowledged that something was wrong with me. I was more foggy-headed than ever before and I simply didn't feel well. I was exhausted all the time too. I wanted to feel better so I went to the doctor, thinking I must be sick. I felt overwhelmed, tired all the time, impatient, and I found it difficult to concentrate. After examining me and running tests, the doctor announced that no, there was nothing wrong with me. My symptoms were simply the result of the stress I was under.

What does one do with such a pronouncement? Life needed to continue. The children still needed me to be present to them. The farm had to be tended. I didn't see an answer for this malaise. Then, one day—a month after I had been diagnosed with "being under a great deal of stress"—I saw an ad in our local paper. It was an offer for a Remedial Massage session. I did not know what

Remedial Massage was, but I knew I needed to try it. I needed to do something, and I felt an urging to give this a go.

I had a one-hour massage and when I came out from it, I felt completely different. The confusion and fog in my head was gone and I felt light and at peace. Even the pain in my body was gone. That massage changed my life. I believe it even saved my life. I felt a sense of calm that I had not felt in years. I felt a release of all the tension I had been holding in my body, and I felt renewed. What I know now is that I had been grieving, fatigued, and suffering with muscle pain from working so hard. I had also been carrying the emotional trauma of grief in my body.

From that experience and the feeling that I had connected with a *new* version of my *old* self, I decided if all I had to do was have a massage to feel this amazing, I wanted all mums to feel this wonderful. I knew that I could not be the only mum out there who experienced overwhelm, anxiety, and exhaustion as a result of trying to be a good parent. I could not be the only one who felt as if I was *coping* through life rather than *living* it.

Three months later, with a mixture of excitement and trepidation, I left for Adelaide to learn to become a professional Remedial Massage therapist. I got on a bus, and for the first time, spent two weeks away from my children, husband, and my life on the farm. I look back in amazement at how everything fell into place so beautifully once I got clear about my direction. Since the children were all in school by then, my husband got the kids off to school each day and picked them up from the bus stop at night. He cooked food and made lunches for everyone. I rang them at night and spoke to my husband and each of the children. The farm work got done while the children were at school. Everything and everyone got taken care of, and I found the path for my own healing and the missing piece to how I could support my family more fully. I also knew I wanted to be able to support others.

Two weeks after I'd taken that first bus ride, I came home with my newly purchased massage table to start my own professional massage business in the exact place where I had experienced my first amazing massage. One week after I arrived home, I rented a room in the health house I'd first visited. I massaged four days each week and reserved weekends for time with my family. Subsequently, I returned to Adelaide many times to learn additional techniques.

In the process, I also learned more about myself and confronted my own childhood issues. The more I learned and healed, the more present I was able to be with my clients. As I changed my behaviour, by becoming more relaxed and clear-thinking, I saw changes in my children too. They got along better with others and their misbehaviour lessened. They no longer needed to get our attention in negative ways. I and my husband always kept our cool, no matter what our children wanted to talk about and no matter how private the conversation needed to be. I was able to support him and the children by massaging them, which allowed their stress and any aches and pains to be released, and freed them to speak about their concerns.

Through massage, talking, and clearing the situations that came up for them, they were able to release the stress of their experiences. Usually, I only needed to allow the children to talk about what was happening. It was important to let them speak without pushing to make them tell me. Empowering meant I could give them room to express themselves. I could also connect back to my childhood and remember how I'd felt. Then, I knew what I could say and how to say it to support them.

In turn, they discovered that when they felt listened to, they often answered their own questions. They grew in self-confidence and knew how to push themselves in sports and how they could talk to and empower their peers. They supported friends who were dealing with difficult life situations and stood up to bullying. They began to appreciate their relationship with us as parents who treated them with respect.

As parents, we also got to enjoy their open, loving, and natural knowing. They experienced their friends' and their own abilities to be successful. They also began to appreciate being with people of all ages—younger children, parents, grandparents, and great-grandparents. They saw that every relationship is important.

Sometimes, they wondered why we did not push and yell at them to make them do well at school as their friends' parents did. We did not have to because we understood that they knew what they wanted and how to get there. We understood it was our role to help them and to enjoy the journey alongside them.

In 2000, we moved to Adelaide and I opened my second massage business. Since then, my children have all gone on to become successful, thriving adults. They practice what we learned together. We continue to listen to each other and take the time to *really* hear what is being said. My grandchildren are benefiting from all that we've learned and experienced, being raised in a supportive atmosphere of openness where they are free to express what's going on, no matter how painful or difficult. It's beautiful to watch their unfolding. It makes me know that my journey of discovery and empowerment will continue and pass into this next generation and beyond.

Helen Brougham is empowering women in everyday life, helping them step through life's challenges. She offers massage four days each week and coaches mums, dads, and children through personal and family leadership training courses. Helen continues to create programs to help mums have more grounded children. She also offers online coaching and blogs regularly. Helen is the author of Empowering You & Your Family. *To learn more about Helen, visit: http://www.HelenBrougham.com.au.*

Always Remember —
You are Worthy & Deserving.
To Honor Your Feelings.
& Speak Your Truth!
I wish you Trust &
Blessings, Nancy :)

TRUST: A NEW WAY
TO NAVIGATE

Nancy Rizzo

I stood outside on my patio with my arms firmly outstretched and open wide—my face pointed upwards towards the sunny, blue, warm Heavens—and asked, "I am ready to receive. I have no idea what that is, but I'm open to receive!" I didn't see any other options other than to reach up for help. In my head, I heard that beautiful, inspiring St. Francis song, "Make Me an Instrument," so I spoke just that, "Please make me an instrument." I then received a warm, sun-bathed sensation on my face, like a glimmer of safety and support.

Even though I was overwhelmed by the unknown, the depth of that warmth fueled me just enough to keep going forward. I felt that somehow my best interests were being looked after. In that unspoken conversation I sensed the divine that creates an intuitive, assured knowing. It was the beginning of my new navigational system of learning to trust and be open to receive the next chapter of my life. Of course, I didn't know at the time that this *was* the beginning of one of the best chapters in my life.

Previously in my life, everything had been merrily rolling along in the management position I so loved. I saw myself happily retiring from that career. No matter how many deadlines, how busy we were, or how hard the task, my hard-working staff and I got it all done and had fun doing it. But for some strange, mind-boggling reason, my professional life decided to take a whirlwind 360-degree turn and became so personally uncomfortable that the joy of working there came to a screeching halt. It was the first time I couldn't fix *it*, make *it* work, solve *it*, or keep *it* going. I literally felt this unbelievable, integrity-challenging situation chiseling away at my soul. Symbolically, I saw and felt a cement block being painfully cut away piece by piece.

For months, I tried to make my existence there work, but it continued to go wrong, and my attempts failed. I ignored the voice in my head that kept saying I did not belong there anymore while my insides continued to harden.

I should have known better, but eventually the emotional stress turned into physical symptoms, and I wound up on a treadmill glued to a chest-full of electrodes.

"What are you feeling?" the nurse asked.

"Like an elephant is standing on my chest." I answered.

With a puzzled look on her face, the nurse watched the screen as she increased my pace faster and faster and raised the incline steeper and steeper.

She then inquired, "Are you under any stress at work?"

"Tons!" I replied.

"That'll do it!" she said.

So, the mental stress of being catapulted out of life as I knew it by The Universe was causing me chest pain? I clearly see now that cliché, "there's a reason for everything," but had you told me during the chaos that this was all for that proverbial "meant to be" stuff, I would not have believed it for a second.

Gratefully, I'd always had the blessing of good health. For years, I'd worked diligently on my health after the devastating losses of my closest womenfolk warriors—my precious big sister and my beloved mother—who lost their battles with cancer just seven months apart. I had my nose in every book and was dedicated to proactive and preventative wellness. So, I steadfastly knew with certainty that I would never allow anyone or anything to challenge my health, not only for my sake, but for my family's sake.

"Everyone should have your heart!" the doctor happily exclaimed.

"Thank God. But what do I do about the chiseling feeling I'm still having in my chest?" I asked. I'm not sure what he replied, because in my own head I heard the answer loud and clear. It permeated through every part of me, and surprisingly it felt like my soul began to soften and heal with the word, "Quit!"

I went home in a surreal state. Quitting a job was not like me at all—never an option—not even conceivable. The thought of quitting was more like a heart-pounding, Hollywood suspense movie. I had no idea what would come after, but I knew for sure that I did not belong there anymore. Although I was riveted in that decisive moment, and truly nothing else mattered but escaping,

I was terrified. I was 100% sure and 100% terrified at the same time.

I managed to get my legs to carry me to work the next day because our client was waiting for a critical report. Of course I would do that, but the rest of the day was a nerve-wracking, emotionally painful blur. Finally after everyone had left for the day, my supportive, hero husband came to rescue me. On that cold, dark evening, we packed up and loaded my office into the car and never looked back. It surely must've been a legion of angels that orchestrated all of that for me, because the next day I shook my head and shuddered in disbelief. *Who was that girl and how the heck did she just do that?*

Quickly the shock turned into displacement. I knew very well that empty, confused feeling. I had felt it after my dear mother died. The next day, after being her daily dedicated caretaker, I headed up the stairs, but she wasn't there to take care of anymore. It was like being stuck in a time warp, feeling completely empty inside and clueless about what to do next.

This new displacement from being unemployed had me glued to my kitchen chair in a state of paralyzing fear. I felt semi-conscious, like being in white noise. For three months I sat in the chair. My son came home every day from school and asked, "Mom, are you still in that chair?" I couldn't move. I'm not sure what was worse—displacement or the horrible realization that "quitting" was the example I had just set for my children after all those years of our "we never quit" policy. Ah, yes—just a few more crushing emotions to further keep me stuck in the chair.

Then came the pivotal day that frightened me enough to get me up and out of that chair. In my usual state of staring off into space while fully awake, I saw a vision in my mind's eye. I was standing behind Alice in Wonderland, peering over her shoulder as she peered down the rabbit hole. While the rabbit hole grew bigger and bigger and blacker and blacker, my friend Alice and I began to teeter—and I knew I was going to fall in right behind her. It stopped my breath. I did not want to sink any deeper into despair. I had been there before, after I lost my sister and mother, and I knew that dark place of depression. That frightening place of despair scared me more than my fear to move forward. That's when I rose up from the chair. I thought, *Thank you, dear Divine*

Guidance, for the cartoon.

Soon after, a day of love-filled encouragement arrived and a long-awaited relief followed. On the morning of my birthday, I woke up to a card and an unwrapped copy of *The Secret*, which stood up bold and erect on the kitchen table. My two precious sons had left these for me. They wrote in my card: "You've been so many things to your boys over the years. You've shown us many things. Just when we thought there was nothing left for you to teach us, you taught us what true bravery is. To a mama who constantly surprises, we say thanks." My own children gave me the much-needed permission that quitting my job was okay. I have never received a greater birthday gift in my life.

The contrary notion that quitting my job had taken courage allowed me to pause for a moment with this new perspective that there was something else out there in store for me—something else I was supposed to do instead. This idea was my initial small step into my new navigational system of trusting—simply believing in that possibility and trusting that thought. I felt this awakening open my heart to accept that all would be okay and that I would be okay too.

That's how I arrived on my patio. In that cocooning space, I learned this magnificent new way to navigate through my life—using trust as my compass. I learned to listen to my inner voice—my intuition, my instinct. I had to quiet the often fearful and negative whirling chatter that usually went on up there in my head and stop dismissing the few affirming words I heard. That was the difference between my inner critic and my intuition.

I heard things like, "Contribute to humanity and not someone's bottom line. It's what you've been doing your whole life." *What do I do with that?* I wondered. Instead of dismissing these thoughts, I started processing what I heard. I had always been the go-to person, the eternal optimist, and my sister always said no one could make everything sound as hopeful as I could. She continually made me think I was making a difference in her life. Maybe I could be that person to others too.

My intuition became a navigational beacon for me on my journey. As my thoughts and ideas glimmered from an impossible mindset to a possible one, I learned to believe in possibility—not the all-or-nothing mindset of complete success or perfection—just the existence of each simple, hopeful possibility. That mindset became my new normal.

When my dear friend and mentor referred me to the possibility of life coaching, I had that intuitive, assured knowing that she was my divine messenger and this was my new path. I believed I could possibly even open my own practice! Coaching showed up in front of me, so it automatically became the next step. Every next opportunity and possibility that showed up thereafter became navigational directions for me on my journey to becoming a life coach.

At last I was connected to a purpose. This renewed energy and hopefulness motivated me to take steps in the direction toward that purpose. I followed my intuition to choose where I would obtain life coaching education and to decide that I would add wellness coaching to my practice. I also enrolled a business mentor to help me pioneer this new field.

I aligned myself with supportive people and the systems I needed to keep me and my fledgling business going. Many times, support systems seemed to just come to me on their own—or did I attract them? My divinely assigned coaching classmate and I clung to and coached each other throughout this uphill process. Even today, she and I never miss our weekly calls with each other. Our initial connection as class work "buddies" was random—or was it? For both of us, without a doubt, we were a match made in heaven.

I learned to commit to my life's purpose in my new coaching career and business. Truth be told, at times it was like a dedication to the unknown. Would I succeed or fail? What was I thinking? When I stopped using my new navigational system and followed should's, have to's, or the expectations and judgments of others, obstacles began to get in the way or stop me. Most of the time, those sidelines showed up in the form of limiting beliefs and led me to waste precious time and energy second-guessing myself, procrastinating, or losing clarity. Sometimes I questioned if I was being my authentic self, so I learned to only speak what I could deliver all of the time. At other times, I began to force situations or get into that racing-to-catch-the-train mentality. If I didn't get my new navigational system reengaged quickly enough, I got overwhelmed and stuck. I then had to get myself back to that believing and trusting mindset, sometimes via a trip out to the patio, where I pulled out my trusty compass and just did the next best thing—to begin again.

Continually, I chose to work on each task and challenge, one by one. When I considered the alternative of going back into the business world, my choice to keep moving forward with my work was crystal clear. This commitment brought about some very strange coincidences that I came to know and love as awesome validations.

There were so many unique and profound personal connections that my new clients and I shared. These were joyful realizations to me that we were meant to connect. There were times when a single phenomenon or sequence of unrelated events somehow came together and brought another success to my business. These validations became navigational guideposts on my journey that told me to keep going—that I was on the right path.

What I knew for sure was that the hard work was fully my job and my responsibility on this journey, and I trusted that my new navigational system would continue to show up and point me in the right direction. I lived by a formula I created to remind myself to keep going: "Do the work + Trust + Align myself + Be authentic = Abundance." Trust isn't one size fits all, and it's probably different for everyone. But when I listen to my intuition, continue to believe, stay committed, and navigate over and around anything that thinks it's going to stop me—even when I'm not quite sure what the end result will be—that's trust.

I safely arrived from that fork in the road, a bit tattered, but mostly awestruck and grateful—surely where I am supposed to be—working in my passion in joy. From my patio to "My Coaching Place," every trial and triumph along the way taught me how to trust. And having this new navigational system of trust in place, I know I could do it all over. It will never again be about the person or situation that shows up and challenges me— it will be about choosing what I want instead and pulling out my navigational system to get me there.

Nancy Rizzo is a Certified Life Coach and Certified New Life Story Wellness™ Coach. Nancy has created The Joy vs. Depletion System© and Life Tools from Your Tool Belt© to reach for each and every time, no matter what shows up to challenge you. She is a Speaker, Writer, Instructor, Group and Personal Coach who connects with heartstrings, insight, expertise, dedication and passion so you have exactly what you need to stay in Joy on Your Journey and be unstoppable! Childhood sweethearts, Nancy and her husband are blessed with a lovely family, forever friends, the two best magnificent sons, the two best spectacular daughters-to-be, and that legion of angels watching over all of them. Reach her at nancyrizzo@roadrunner.com, www.nancyrizzo.com, 716.812.0305, www.twitter.com/nancyrizzo www.facebook.com/NancyRizzoLifeCoach.

Loss

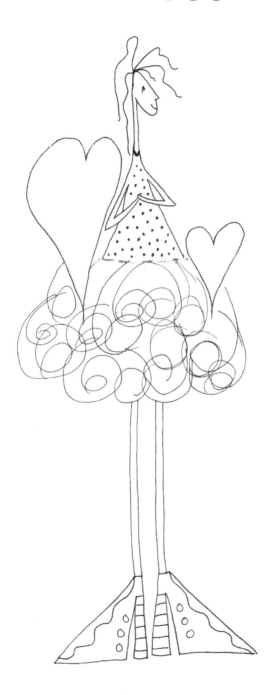

SET FREE

Tamlyn Evans Hill

6:30 a.m., Castle Rock, Colorado. Sound asleep in my bed. The ring of my cell phone startled me awake. Just days before, I had asked Mackenzie not to call so early. Didn't she get it? Reluctantly, I answered, abruptly awakened by my daughter's terrified voice. "Mom, I don't know where Dad is. He left at seven o'clock last night on his four-wheeler and never came home. I just know something is wrong."

How could this be? My ex-husband would never leave Mackenzie alone overnight. At 19, she still needed him. He just wouldn't have left her at the farm by herself in the middle of desolate Idaho. Surely, I must have missed something. "Slow down, breathe, and let's start from the beginning."

"Last night, Dad went out on the four-wheeler. He took off and didn't say where he was going. I called his cell at about eight o'clock to see if he broke down somewhere, if he needed me to come get him. He never answered his phone. I drove to our neighbors' houses to see if he was visiting, but no one had seen him. Eventually I went home, figuring he'd probably be there soon. I kept calling until about 11:30 last night. I left the porch light on for him, finally gave up, and went to bed. I thought for sure he'd be home when I woke up this morning.

"I got up at six this morning, like usual, to go for coffee. The outside light was still on, the four-wheeler was still gone, and Dad wasn't home. I drove to town, hoping he was having coffee at Castle's. All the regulars were there—Jim, Jack, Darrell, and Mike, but no Dad. I told Jen, the cashier, that Dad never came home last night and she told me to tell the guys. All I got out was, 'My Dad never came home,' and Jack and the guys flew out the gas station door to search for him. I am so scared Mom."

Panic ramping inside me; I did my best to convey calmness to my already frightened daughter. "OK honey, stay calm. The guys will find him. I want you to get in the car and head straight to the neighbors'. Do not go back to the farm. Call me as soon as you get there, OK?" I felt sick to my core as I hung up the phone. My hesitant fingers dialed Ron's number, and chills ran down my spine when his familiar voice message played.

I had just spoken to him yesterday. I was concerned about his conversation with our son Colin. Ron had been harsh with him, telling Colin that his recovery time from his upcoming neck fusion would give him extra time to focus and study harder. Disturbed by his lack of compassion, I had called Ron and asked him to lighten up. Willing to be his sounding board, I suggested he call me with his fears and not take them out on Colin.

I prayed that Ron was OK. Eight hundred miles away in Denver, I could not physically comfort my distraught daughter. Though Mackenzie was 19, trauma still triggered the challenges she'd lived with since her first year of life. Clinging to hope, suppressing my rising fear, I prayed that Ron lay injured, banged up from a fall perhaps, but still alive. He just had to be OK.

"Tam, it's Jack. We found Ron. There's been a terrible accident."

"Is he OK?"

"No, I'm really sorry…he didn't make it. He's dead."

Tears ripped through me. *How could that be? I just talked to him. He can't be dead.* "Jack, are you sure? What happened?"

"We found him in the alfalfa field, his four-wheeler dropped in a hole from when he dug up those pine trees he'd planted. It looks like Ron drove along the canal by the pivot, crossed the canal, and came in the gate by the trees.

"We can see the tracks as he rounded the corner past the gate. The grass was pretty tall along the fence; he must not have seen the hole. The front wheels of his four-wheeler dropped into the five-foot hole and his body was thrown forward. We found him face down in the grass. It looks like he never even moved. Tam, I'm so sorry."

Sorry? Oh my God. What do I do now? I am so far away. Mackenzie is in Idaho by herself. I have to call Colin and tell him. What the hell do I say? How do I tell him his father is dead?

"Mrs. Hill, this is Captain Miller. First, let me offer my condolences. I am at the scene where we found Mr. Hill. We found his vehicle and his body on the far end of your property. He was probably only going about three to five miles an hour when he hit the hole. It appears that he was standing as he rode. The impact threw him forward onto the ground. His feet were hooked on the handlebars when we found him. There was no indication that he tried to break his fall.

"We understand that your daughter is with your neighbors. We are sending a grief counselor and another officer to tell her. Again, Mrs. Hill, my condolences to you and your family."

The coroner estimated Ron's time of death to have been about eight o'clock the previous evening. He surmised that Ron had broken his neck when he hit the hole and suspected he died instantly. I felt the tiniest sense of relief come over me. *At least he had not suffered. And thank God Mackenzie had not been riding with him. Witnessing the accident would have been horrific. I know she was worried and frightened, but thank God she didn't find him last night.*

Falling into a sobbing heap on my bed, covers over my head, I tried to imagine what had happened. After talking with Ron about Colin, I imagined he needed to clear his head. He was still furious at the kid who had broken Colin's neck in the hockey accident a year earlier. He had expressed his frustration to me in our call the day before. He was worried about the upcoming surgery, angered that Colin had to endure a neck fusion due to a previous surgical error. Ron was far from calm when we hung up the phone.

Colin, oh how the hell do I tell him? He was counting on Ron being here for his surgery. "Colin, it's Mom. I have some really hard news to tell you honey, and I am so sorry that I have to tell you this. Dad went out on the four-wheeler last night and had a terrible accident. Honey, Dad is dead. I am so sorry."

Gasping sobs filled my ears, and my heart burst with tears. Reality taking hold, I could barely breathe.

"No, Mom. No!"

Ron, how could you be so careless? Colin needs you here for his surgery. Hell, I need you. Now I have to endure another surgery alone. How could you be so stupid?

"Mom, does Mackenzie know?"

Oh my God, Mackenzie. Even leaving Colorado early this afternoon, we won't arrive in Idaho until about two in the morning. I want to call her but don't know if the counselor has delivered the news yet. What do I do?

171

"Colin, get yourself packed and head to my house. Pack clothes for a week or two, and bring clothes for the funeral." *The funeral! I can't believe I'm saying such words to my son.* "I'll see you soon. I love you, honey."

It wasn't long before I heard from Mackenzie. "Mom, they found Dad. The police came and told me that Dad is dead. I tried to find him, Mom, I really did."

"Honey, I am so sorry. Colin and I are on our way. We'll be there as fast as we can."

As reality began to sink in, I reached out to friends and family. My dear minister friend drove an hour and a half to comfort us, bring food, and offer prayers for our family's safe journey to Idaho. I felt badly that she had driven all that way for 20 minutes of our time, but I felt the urgent need to get to Mackenzie.

The rhythmic pulse of the tires on the expansive Wyoming highway offered great comfort to my aching heart. Grateful that my son was driving, I took refuge in my memories.

Ron and I had been married for 20 years. Three years into our marriage, Colin was born, and Mackenzie arrived a short 18 months later. We lived just north of Denver and spent most of our summers at the farm in Idaho.

Mackenzie had taken a great deal of our attention in our early years. A well-baby check at four months old revealed a hole in her heart the size of a nickel. An "innovative" open-heart procedure had left her with a mild traumatic brain injury and moderate learning delays.

After Ron sold his companies in 2000, we moved our family to the farm. It wasn't long before I felt the isolation of the small town of 300, the loss of my friends, and the vacancy I experienced in our marriage. My growing need for connection took me to Vermont for a summer visit with my best friend. As the summer drew to a close, the thought of returning to Idaho paralyzed me. I rented a small house, drove to Idaho to get my things, and moved the kids and me to Vermont early that fall.

Vermont was our home for the next seven years. During that time, I found my voice, my strength, and my truth. College for Colin prompted our move back to Colorado. Although the time apart had mellowed our differences, Ron and I signed our divorce papers with tears in our eyes, knowing the contract had to end for our healing to begin. Even though our marriage was legally terminated, I was grateful to live closer to Ron, as he offered respite and partnership for Mackenzie's care.

Ron had an unmistakable intensity about him, a marshmallow encased in a thick crust. When we shared our quiet moments together, even after our divorce, I found the soft, tender heart that I had always loved so much. In intense work mode, however, he became unapproachable, opinionated, and gruff. The gale force wind that would overtake me at those times was formidable.

Colin's broken neck had drawn us closer together. In the hours that followed his hockey accident, we comforted each other as we faced his uncertain future. Colin's surgery, though unsuccessful in repairing his neck, had been the catalyst for our family healing.

Dim farmyard lights sprinkled the desolate country roads of Idaho over the two-hour drive between the highway and our town. Stillness blanketed Carey, Idaho. The humming florescent lights of the neighboring farms offered no comfort in the last three miles down the reservoir road. I offered a prayer to Mackenzie as we passed by the neighbors' house, hoping she was sleeping soundly. *I will see you in the morning my sweet girl.*

Shallow breathing, pounding heart, we rounded the last curve to the farm, no light to welcome us home. Palpable silence filled the air as we pulled in the long dirt driveway, past the pond Ron built and the new module home he had installed for the family that worked our land. Our dog Spike, who had accompanied Mackenzie to Idaho, sleepily met us as we entered the shop door.

I had been away for years, except for a recent visit in March, when I spent time there working on my first book. Ron had graciously offered the farm as my retreat hideaway while he stayed with the kids and the dog in Colorado. Although I had been there alone, the void now, in contrast, was profound. *How were we to go on without him?*

We unpacked the car and let ourselves into the house, each of us heading to our respective rooms. I entered the room I had once shared with Ron, fell onto the bed and hugged the pillow that had recently held his head. Everything was just how Ron had left it the day before—papers on the bedside table, laundry on the floor in the closet, shoes at the foot of the bed. I just wanted to believe he would be home at any minute, and yet I knew that I would never see his face again.

Just in case she woke up, I sent a text, "Mackenzie, we have arrived. It is 2:00 a.m. Call me when you wake up and I will come get you. Love, Mom."

The phone rang minutes later. "Mom, I want to come home."

I had been to Tammy's house only once. She and her husband owned Castles, the gas station/gathering place for the local farmers. Driving into an unfamiliar driveway in the middle of the night, I felt my fear rise as I opened the car door to the darkness. The faint kitchen light revealed a tired friend with a tearful Mackenzie close behind. I hugged my daughter tightly as she sobbed in my arms.

My sweet girl...no child should have to face this pain alone. How unfair.

Arm in arm, we stumbled to the car, not quite sure which of us was holding up the other. Back at the farm, we climbed the stairs to her room. Not wanting to sleep alone, she curled up in her sleeping bag at the end of my bed. I got myself ready for some much-needed sleep, unpacking just enough to find my toothbrush. As I left the bathroom I heard an unmistakable voice.

"Now the story really begins. Finish the book."

There was no mistaking his voice. I had courageously given my manuscript to Ron earlier that summer. On his last trip to Denver, he had shared his disgruntled feelings about my depiction of our troubles. Through my writing, years of silence had come to an end. Hours of talking and crying over the pain, misunderstandings, and loss offered great resolution to the wall of previously unspoken feelings.

Peace overwhelmed me in that moment. My sealed emotional port, partially opened through my writing and healing, had been blown wide open by his death. I thought of our shared story—our early love that had been strong and heady, productive and ambitious. I acknowledged our divergent paths—his wanting more success, mine wanting more tenderness. Divorce allowed us to see ourselves, our patterns, and discover our truths. Beneath the veneer of protection and hurt, hearts of appreciation and compassion had begun to emerge.

His presence was unmistakable. Free to guide me in a way he could not in life, my transformation was beginning.

Ron Hill, you have just set me free.

Now the real story begins.

Tamlyn Evans Hill's daughter's open-heart surgery and her son's broken neck after a tragic hockey accident led to her path as an intuitive kinesiologist. In their family's time of greatest healing, her ex-husband was killed from a broken neck. Her own heart continued to open and evolve, and in response to these life-changing events, she committed to be an evolutionary heart guide. Through the Soaring Spirit Institute, Tamlyn gently guides others to deeply connect with their hearts in conscious growth and transformation. To learn more about Tamlyn and her services, visit www.soaringspiritinstitute.com. This excerpt—from her upcoming book, The Space Between the Wings*—will be published in late 2012.*

THE HEALING POWER
OF FORGIVENESS

Elizabeth Cuckson

The warmth of the sun shone on my face. I glanced at the clock to see what time it was. I catapulted my body out of bed and ran through the house waking everyone up. I had overslept and would be late for an executive meeting I needed to host, and we had children to get ready. My husband smiled and graciously said he would get the three babies ready so that I could make it to work on time.

My head a clamor of thoughts, I frantically searched the house for my laptop and finally found it next to my daughter Nicola who smiled at me from the comfort of her car seat. She sat quietly, flashing her gummy smile and melting my heart with her twinkling eyes as if to laugh at her silly mommy. I grabbed my bag and yelled to my husband that I was leaving and to have a good day.

I sat impatiently and somewhat restlessly in my car, waiting in the usual heavy traffic. I finally arrived at work, flipped open my laptop, pulled up my email, and read that the meeting had been cancelled. Sighing, I packed up my things and went to my desk. The day continued with requests for presentations and work that was needed yesterday.

At 3:30 p.m., while in a meeting with my manager, out of the corner of my eye billowing black smoke attracted my attention as it ascended up the wall. My manager asked why I seemed startled, and I responded that it was nothing important. Being a Medium, though, I had a feeling that someone close to me had passed. I dismissed the vision and my intuition and figured that my family would call if anything was wrong.

I began packing my things to go home for the day when my husband called to say that something had happened to our nine-month-old daughter, Nicola, and that she'd been rushed to the hospital. He had no other details. Tears welled up in my eyes, my stomach turned in knots, and I began breathing as if it might be my last breath. I intuitively knew that the swirling cloud had been Nicola and that she had passed away 30 minutes earlier. I just knew it was her little spirit.

I rushed to get my things together, throwing papers into my laptop bag, swinging my purse over my shoulder, getting my half-eaten lunch and throwing it away as I grabbed my cell phone to walk out the door. I recall looking at my co-worker and staring blankly at her as I said, "I think Nicola just died."

Shocked, she stopped me. I remember being surrounded by co-workers asking me questions. It seems like yesterday as I recall it so clearly. My heart hit the floor and each breath felt as if it was a struggle to get to the next. I knew that what I'd witnessed and dismissed was my little girl saying, "Goodbye Mommy, I love you."

"Elizabeth, did Lee say she died?" my co-workers asked, jolting me back to the present. I responded that he did not say anything other than she'd been rushed to the hospital. But I just knew. At that moment, my manager walked around the corner to hear what was happening and said, "Don't worry, Elizabeth, Nicola will be okay. Please let me drive you to the hospital."

Being absolutely focused on bringing the breath of life back to my daughter, I jumped in my car and headed for the hospital while my manager followed closely behind in his car. There was a delay with the parking garage when the gate would not open. And then I entered what became one of the longest drives of my life through rush hour traffic.

Looking back, I see that I was in a place of knowing as an intuitive, but being human, I was also having an experience as a mother and wife. My daughter was slowing me down to get me present and focused, but I was not listening. Instead, I picked up my cell phone and called my friend so she could calm me down. I just wanted to see my baby girl and traffic would not move. Then I called my daycare provider to ask what had happened, and with a quiver in her voice, she said the paramedics were taking good care of her. That pronouncement was unsettling for me. I knew what would come next. I was going to hear what no mother wants to hear—that her baby is gone.

I called my husband, still crying and cursing traffic to just get the hell out of my way and move. My husband answered the call but was silent. I asked, "Are you there yet?"

With a pregnant pause, he said, "Elizabeth, she's gone." As my body tensed up and tears poured from my eyes, I was lost in time. My husband said that the detective was standing there and wanted to speak with me. He handed her the phone and she asked, "Are you OK? Where are you?"

"I am five to ten minutes away and will be there as fast as I can."

The detective asked me to drive carefully. She said they would greet me at the entrance to the ER and take me to Nicola when I arrived. Then, the call ended and silence set in. I beat my fists on the steering wheel and experienced the air ripped from my lungs as I gasped and couldn't breathe. I was being smothered by a tsunami wave of grief that shredded my heart and drug me under.

Numb and unfeeling, I sat heavy in the shell we call a body as I continued to drive down the long stretch of highway. My head fell back onto the driver's side headrest as if to support the heavy thoughts racing through my mind. Traffic still creeping along, my eyes were drawn up to the heavens as I peered through my sunroof. Shoulders curled in, my spine no longer wanting to support me, hands clenching the steering wheel, and a baptism of tears pouring out of my eyes, I unleashed a mother's anguish. The mourning from my car sounded like an Indian war cry as I released my pain in prayer.

"Nicola, I want to tell you I am so sorry that I was not with you this morning to give you a kiss and tell you I love you before I walked out that door. I was so preoccupied with my work that I lost focus of my true priorities, my family. I am so sorry that I didn't have time to dress you, that I didn't have time to give you a kiss, and that I didn't say I LOVE YOU. How much time would it have taken from my busy day to say I love you before I walked out the door?"

All I knew is that I wanted to hold my baby girl. To help me be as present and focused as I could be on the road, I called my sister and dear friends of ours to tell them what had happened.

When I arrived at the hospital, my husband, the coroner, and a detective greeted me with long mournful faces. I walked into the room and saw Nicola lying on a sterile metal table. I was back to the cold reality that what was happening was real. She had a shunt in her leg and a tube in her mouth where they had tried to resuscitate her over a long period of time. Strangely, I wanted to pull up the safety rails so she wouldn't roll off the table.

I looked at the coroner and asked for permission to pick her up. I gently picked up my baby in a cherished moment and rocked her to a heavenly peaceful sleep. This would be the last time I would embrace her—my baby—in my arms. As my husband stood next to me, he was shaken and overcome with grief. He had never experienced anyone close to him die. He stared and cried in disbelief. She had been a healthy, vibrant baby only a few hours earlier. How could this be?

I looked down at her angelic face and smiled with the biggest smile on my face. I was so proud of my baby girl. I smiled as memories rushed through my head and the sound of her infectious giggles filled my heart. I was so proud that I had nine wonderful months to celebrate her life, and my heart was wide open and full of bliss.

I cannot adequately describe the feeling, the sensation of that moment, but it was as if her soul went through me and my heart was elated and opened. Yet the physical and emotional part of me as a mother was so torn, broken, and destroyed as I took in the deep knowing that I would not see her grow into the beautiful woman I had dreamed of. It was the beginning of my shock, my disbelief, and my guilt.

My husband went back to the home daycare with my office manager to pick up Nicola's twin brother. He then picked up our two-year-old daughter at preschool. The local Sheriff located my 14-year-old son and brought him to the hospital. As my son walked through the doors of the hospital, the coroner and detective asked me to tell him the truth. It didn't even cross my mind to not tell him the truth. I shared the news, and he fell into my arms and wanted me to take him away.

I looked over at Nicola and told her I loved her and I prayed that she would stay with me. I asked her to help me through my life and be an angel to me and guide me to what I am to do. I promised to open my heart to whatever God's purpose was for me.

My mom, sister, and I went to the mortuary to make the arrangements and then shopped for the most beautiful princess dress we could find. I brought things home and showed them to my husband to get his approval, but he simply wasn't able to sit and look through everything. He just nodded his head and agreed while he stared numbly into an abyss.

My husband and I were wrapped in our devastating loss, deep sorrow, and uncontrollable weeping, but he insisted that we invite the daycare's family to attend the wake and the service. It was only two days after her loss and we had been asked by the detective to remain distant with the daycare provider and the family pending their investigation. As we expressed our heartfelt emotions to our family, a silence filled my head and a flutter filled my heart. I knew I needed to listen within and be absolutely present. It was Nicola. I was still quite connected and open to receive despite the emotional pain I was in. Nicola asked me to wrap my arms around the daycare provider's family and give a mother's love and forgive.

The process of opening my heart, forgiving without knowing why, and trusting was one of the hardest things I have ever done, and I did it because Nicola asked. Miraculously, I experienced immense forgiveness, empathy, and love. I felt that by letting go, I allowed everyone to grieve in their own way. Opening my heart to love and empathy conveyed that whatever they felt in their hearts was forgiven. This was the beginning of my journey to the healing power of forgiveness.

During preparation for the funeral, my husband asked me to help him write a little something. I told him I could not; his daughter wanted him to write it. I knew it was part of his grieving process and that it would allow words of love to enter his heart and pour from his mouth. As a family, we also invited others to add a little "note" for Nicola to take with her, if they felt so inclined.

There are no words to describe the rollercoaster of emotions that my body and soul endured. It was if all of nature's natural disasters were put into one event. A slow, swelling tsunami wave slammed me down, crushed me, threw me up again, and the earth was ready to swallow me whole. The tornadic activity within my head was shredding anything logical and the one thing that saved me was my faith in God. I knew Nicola would not want me to cry for her, but to celebrate her life. I did as I was instructed.

We arrived at the church and added all the notes that people had brought, a few stuffed animals, and a cozy pink ladybug blanket to take with her on her journey. We said our goodbyes to our dear princess. I kissed her on the cheek as tears rolled down my face. It seemed so final, so cold. Our family walked up the aisle of the church and we were taken to the front where my husband would share the most eloquent and heart-touching eulogy I have ever heard. I was so proud of him and so was Nicola.

With numb hearts, we left the church and were greeted by our friends and family at the cemetery. "Canon" by Pachelbel played as it had every night when Nicola went to bed. We could not think of a more appropriate song to lay her to rest. During our celebration of her life, we released three snow-white doves to represent peace. Two of the doves were released when the music began, and we watched them fly away gracefully and fade into the distance. One dove was handed to me and my husband to release towards the end of the song. We released it and the dove gracefully circled above our heads. The sound of the violins ripped through my soul, and I felt as though I was letting go and allowing my baby girl to soar. Tears rolled down my face, and in my head I cheered her on saying, "Go baby, go, you are free! Soar with the angels."

Over the course of the past couple of years, our families have grieved in their own individual ways. I have realized the power of forgiveness and the gift of living in the present moment. In forgiving my daycare provider, I began a journey to forgive myself.

Nicola opened the doorway to letting go and releasing my painful past by breaking my heart wide open. My fragile heart at that time was like a pistachio nut that didn't want to be disturbed. Tightly hidden inside a shell of safety, I was cracked open and exposed. In her passing and as time has allowed my heart began to heal.

And my life continues to unfold. I have been able to see the ways I held on to all the emotional, sexual, and physical abuse that I endured from so many. I realized that forgiving does not mean forgetting. I forgave myself for holding on and wallowing as a victim rather than learning from my experiences and through what I endured, helping others. I have spent the last couple of years giving myself unconditionally to others and assisting them to identify the opportunities and gifts they have. Some may call it paying forward—I call it unconditional love.

Nicola has been an amazing gift to me; her loss opened my heart to love openly, deeply, and unconditionally. Letting go has been the hardest. I smelled the powdery scent of my baby girl's clothes one last time as I packaged them up and donated them to an orphanage. In giving, I gave my spirit the biggest gift. Love. I was finally expressing and allowing myself to be authentic.

Today, I look forward to waking each morning with the sun shining on my face and spending time in prayer and gratitude for all God has given me. I center myself to be a demonstration of peace, love, and joy. And now, in the still of the moment, I continue to soar with my littlest angel by my side.

Elizabeth Cuckson is a talented and trusted Intuitive Solutions Expert for individuals and large organizations, the Executive Producer and Host of "From the Heart" on Transformation Talk Radio, Author, Speaker, and President of ElizabethCuckson, Inc. Elizabeth has been an inspirational role model to many as she shares her touching life story, which includes abuse, divorce, and the sudden death of her infant daughter. In fall 2012, Elizabeth will be featured in the book Awakening the Divine Feminine, The Heart of the Goddess. *She is currently working on her memoir. Get inspired at www.elizabethcuckson.com.*

FOUR DAYS IN OCTOBER

Joanna Hudson

They want his eyes. No, be specific, they want his corneas. Probably the only part of his body that could help anyone now—his eyes. I sign the papers. The doctor with the red nose and whiny voice tells me that I will get a thank you letter from the dead eye society. *They aren't my eyes, why should I get thanked?* I wonder how long they have to harvest his eyes before they get too hard. No one answers me. *Maybe I hadn't said it out loud.* My brain feels as if it is screaming. *Doesn't everyone hear it?*

"Yes, I will see the body now." *It will make the faces in the white coats feel as if they are doing a good job.* The good Catholic sister walks with me through a corridor with polished floors, past the noise of the emergency room, to a crisp beige curtain. The same doctor who gave me the news comes from behind the cloth barrier and leads me gently by the elbow. He is short and haggard looking.

There is someone on a hospital gurney. *Some poor person on a slab like a side of beef. Oh, I remember—it's my husband.* The sheet is pulled down and I touch his arm. He is chilly. *We should put a blanket around him,* I think. *We are both fighting a virus.* The fading tan line stops above his elbow. His white shoulders make him look vulnerable and sad. As usual, he needs me to take care of him. *That's what they said on the phone to get me here—he needs you.* The sister sighs. The doctor coughs. Someone says to stay as long as I need, but I say, "Thank you," and move to return to the room for grieving families. As I do, I look down at my hand because it is still feeling his cool skin. I have never felt him that cool before. Standing upright is suddenly impossible.

The bishop is coming to the rectory to comfort me. *Put on another pot of coffee. What about tea? Cut the lemon poppy-seed cake. Straighten the living room. Clean the bathroom sink. Remember to comb your hair and put on some lipstick. Adjust your best Reverend Mrs. Face. No, adjust your best, recently widowed, Reverend Mrs. Face.*

Open your mouth and say the things that are expected of you.

185

Comfort the bishop. After all, he has just lost a good Christian soldier and they are hard to come by. "You are young enough to have a full life ahead of you," they tell me. Then, they go through a list of things I must listen to so that I can have input into the funeral arrangements.

The bishop has brought his wife and a clerk who will handle the paperwork for me to receive a pension from the church.

"How did you two meet," the wife asks, "at church?"

"No, he was a member of the Board of Education in a small town where I was interviewing for the high school principal's job. After I got the job he dropped by my new office to talk and that was that. Our souls were in love almost a year before our bodies knew it."

"Just sign here," I hear the clerk say. The wife tears up and the clerk clicks his pen over and over.

The bishop is uncomfortable in his black suit and collar. He doesn't know me well and seems at a loss for the perfect combination of words to heal me. "As if they would," I almost say. He blesses me.

More cups, more coffee. *I need to get a quart of Half and Half and more cough syrup for myself. Better make a list and get to the store.* "No, thanks," *Mrs. Bishop,* "a neighbor will do that for us, they have been so supportive today. Thank you so much for driving so far to pray for his soul."

Thank you, sorry, tragic, sudden, shock, disbelief, mistake, too quick, confusion, heart pulled out of my chest and broken like his. These words define me as they whirl in my head. They are the words of the days to come.

A blue plastic bag from the hospital with the clothes he had on this morning sits on the bedroom floor. "His glasses and billfold should be in there, too," I was told by the parishioner who went to get it for me from the hospital. *Later, I will deal with that, later.*

The phone keeps ringing and food keeps coming. Family somehow gets picked up at the airport and delivered to motels. I seem to be automatically organized. My brain noise is still very loud. My doctor, who was his doctor, comes and gives me something to swallow. One pill helps the fever from the virus and one pill is supposed to help me cope. I have lost my voice physically and emotionally.

The deeply saddened child is finally asleep after our trip to her elementary school to pick her up and tell her that her daddy has died, and the bag in the bedroom is still waiting. It is late and the almost winter darkness is upon us. I can just step over it, or move it into the closet, but I fear it will call to me in my sleep. *Please God, after such a day, let me slide into a peaceful sleep with him here and hear his chuckle as he wraps his long arms around me.*

As I unthinkingly get ready for bed, I pick up the bag and when I pull stuff out, I see that everything is neatly arranged in a pile. *Probably the nun—women's work. Shoes—marine polished, black, size 12. Do you bury people in shoes? Socks—worn, gray, mid-calf length. A cleric collar with the hook button missing. He always blames me for losing them—wait until I laugh at him over this one. It is the same one we had to look for this morning. His underwear—briefs, not boxers. His suit pants and belt—he needs a new belt. Didn't we just buy this one in July? His suit coat—wrinkled because he wears it driving in the car.* "Well, a priest doesn't need to be a fashion plate," he would say. His glasses are scratched and dirty from hitting the ground when he stumbled out of the car. His gray cleric shirt and a new white tee shirt both smell faintly of his aftershave. *Why are they cut open? To get to his chest? To his heart that stopped? Why is it wet? Why did I open the bag? Don't cry—people in the house might hear and worry. Let me sleep.* I finally do, with his clothes all around me.

The group with the most names in the guest book at the funeral home must win a prize. Everyone is so intent on signing in. *Oh, they don't feel comfortable looking toward the casket, so they're taking their time. Guest books as part of the ritual of weddings and funerals. This one can go in the box with the one from our wedding only 18 months ago.*

There is a family in a smaller room across the way that lost a great-great grandmother of 89 years, and they seem loud in the celebration of her life. There is even laughter, but it seems like blasphemy to us. *How dare they?*

Lost, loss, lose—I need more words to describe death. I got lost yesterday at the mall when I went to buy my red dress for the funeral. He always said that red was a color of celebration and almost jokingly said to wear it to his funeral. As I walked down the maze of the place, I was suddenly afraid and weak when

I realized that I had lost my bearings. I was angry at myself because he and I had been in the same mall last week at a matinee holding hands and enjoying a couple of hours alone. I pretended to be looking in store windows so the daughter who was with me wouldn't sense my panic. She is very intuitive. We walked for what seemed like hours and people became worried because we were gone so long from the rectory. Now, no one will let me out of their sight. *Did he panic at the pain when he was driving before he went off the road? Alone, he was alone and afraid. At the end did he call the God he loved so well?*

No one is loud in our section of the aging and faded mauve funeral home. The suddenness of his death has caught in their throats like a sob. When the clergy support staff went with me to pick out the casket yesterday, we were asked about how many hours of viewing of the body we wanted. I deferred to the support staff, never having buried a husband before. Because there are so many parishioners and community clergy who want to pay their respects, 12 hours were scheduled for day and evening.

What I didn't know is that the custom at our new church, in a larger city, in a different part of the country, is for the widow to sit with the body during *all* the visitation hours. After the first eight hours, I am convinced that the body with no eyes under the lids is really dead. We do not need to drive a nail through his head or put a bell in the casket to make sure. He is lost to me—but lost is too weak a word.

Family comes, strangers come—people trying to be helpful and those who want me to help them. All hug me hour after hour. I comfort them all with a little voice. I am calm and almost serene. *I am gracious and coping beautifully,* I hear them whisper. Conversation floats in and out. *Thank you for coming and sharing our loss. I know you grieve too. Something good will come out of this I am sure. A door closes and a window opens. He will be sorely missed. Yes, I have a cold, don't worry, I'm on medication, and it sounds worse than it is.* Polite lie after lie just like they want. Our young doctor comes and almost collapses at the casket with guilt and grief. He feels as if he missed the signs of the impending disaster. *Didn't we all?*

My brain noise is medicated down to a dull roar, but people talk to me and I can't understand what they are saying. *Did everyone learn a new language? Is this a foreign film?* I am afraid to open my mouth because a wailing and gnashing of teeth might explode from the back of my throat. I nod and smile and hold hands of the most shaky. People keep handing me things to sign and hot tea and broth to keep the wailing silenced.

I watch myself from afar and think maybe I need a piece of duct tape over my mouth. He and I use the word "duck" as a code when either one of us is on the verge of saying something inappropriate. They do not want the truth of the depth of my pain or our love. I started cleaning out his desk today looking for something of him to hold close to my heart. I found three quotes about dying that he was going to use for a parishioner's funeral that we will use instead for his. He had a small paragraph about sending angels to help those who are left behind. *Could they come and turn back the clock?*

Should I tell them about the dream? He was sitting on a flight of stairs and talking to me, sitting a few steps below. I asked him to wait so everyone could be called and told that there had been a mistake and he wasn't dead. In turning to look for the phone and turning back, he was gone and I was alone on the stairs. Yesterday, after a short rain shower, there was a double rainbow and my youngest son said it was sent from God as a promise. Dreams and rainbows are what are left to me. My love is gone. I am empty.

Two bishops and twenty-three priests and deacons and hundreds of the faithful are gathered to send him on his way after forty-nine years on this earth with his favorite hymns and incense and numerous prayers. There will be bagpipes and the obligatory "Amazing Grace" at the end.

A moderately priced, politically correct, machine gun gray casket—to which we tied two huge, colorful bunches of balloons—contains his earthly remains minus his corneas. He enjoys balloons and they look majestic in the tall, gothic ceiling of the church. My new red dress looks almost festive and a black bra that he loves to unhook is under it. I already miss his hands. A few days ago the deacon at our new church took me aside and told me that he had noticed us during lunch hour walking in the town holding hands and laughing and it made him smile all day.

I hear a noise to my left and see the funeral home workers

bring in the casket and position it next to me in the aisle by the front pew. Then, I hear people sobbing around me and it appears that they are sobbing for me. I feel the thick, woolen texture of the pall on the casket and am stroking it where his arm is under the lid. I can't seem to stop and my fingers are becoming red. I want to hold his hand. I miss his hands. *Can we open the casket again? Who should I ask?*

Our blended family sits close to me and my oldest son takes my hand in his to stop the pain that has been made visible to the faithful by my distress. *Is it embarrassing to the congregation that I am not being the perfectly controlled, recently widowed Reverend Mrs.?* I mentally shake myself and tell myself to get my act together. He deserves my best behavior.

The wind has picked up and is blowing in a late October storm off the lake. The stained glass windows in the historic church rattle a bit over the sound of the grand old organ—getting my attention and helping me focus on the service. We are sending prayers to God for the deceased. The balloons will quickly disappear as the procession leaves the church and we release them. It will seem like a visual metaphor for life and death. He would like that.

At age 44, the sudden death of a man I loved and trusted, especially after only 18 months of marriage, influenced the rest of my life in ways I could have never anticipated. I had intellectually known stress and trauma and in both my private and professional life had faced them many times.

But when this cataclysmic shift became the way I was now identified in the world, I imagined myself cut into small pieces and thrown to the winds of change, with no control over what was happening.

Well, we always have choices, even in the worst of times, and a kind, patient grief counselor reminded me of that. My resilient self, after several difficult starts and stops, picked up her head, squared her shoulders and learned how to create happiness and joy for others, and finally for herself.

Joanna Hudson holds a Master of Arts in Educational Administration and is a lifelong educator. After the death of her second husband, an Episcopal priest, she moved forward to live her best life. For the majority of her life she has lived and worked in Colorado. Her children, grandchildren, extended family and great-grandson are a constant source of awe and delight. Joanna can be reached at jhcreatingsolutions@msn.com.

DIGGING DEEP

Julie Bach

A daddy's girl...

In 1989 my father was diagnosed with cancer. I was 22 years old when he was diagnosed, at the beginning of my career. I was shocked and scared. I cried the entire 18-hour ride home from Michigan to Florida. When I got home, I collapsed from exhaustion.

My dad showed me a thing that looked like an egg near his knee. It was his cancer. He had been to a few doctors. Some wanted to run clinical trials and experiment with him. Others wanted to amputate his leg—making him unable to fly—a hobby he could not let go. This was devastating. My world was changing. Our lives would never be the same.

The next few years were filled with making positive memories as a family. I called my dad every morning and every evening to see how he was doing. Just to hear his voice. To know that things were good, at least appeared to be good. To just hang on, I guess.

A few years later, my father had to retire his pilot's license. It was probably the saddest day for him—far beyond being told he had a rare form of cancer and would die from it. I myself have never flown privately since. It is what my dad and I did together.

A going away party for my dad...

My wedding in 1994 actually became a going away party for my father. He chose everything from the location to the cake. At first, I looked all over town to try and find a "special hotel" for the wedding. After looking at a few places, my dad, who was exhausted by then, said, "Let's have it at the country club." It was where we'd had many family gatherings, including my sweet 16 party. It was where our family played tennis and golf together. And when we grew older, it was where my brother and I met my parents for lunch.

Originally, the date was set for April, but my dad said, "I

will not be here." I asked, "When will you be here?" He replied, "February 19th." So February 19th it was!

Everyone at the wedding knew this was a big going out party for my dad. It was an amazing evening filled with so much love. A horse and carriage picked us up at my parents' house and took us about one mile to the club. The band played. I danced with my father to "Sunrise Sunset" from *Fiddler on the Roof*. My dad twirled me and smiled as his implanted morphine pump dripped on and he felt no pain. I knew he was extremely proud of me and gave his blessing for the next phase of my life. I knew that I was loved.

My saddest 48 hours came a few months later when my father called me on a Thursday afternoon and said he was finished. He'd called to say goodbye. I scanned around the cubicles—I was on the phone at work. I felt nauseous, sat down, and turned white. Kevin—who worked in the cube next to mine and had been through this with his own father—leaned over and said, "You know that you only have 48 hours till he is gone. When they give up, they are ready to go. And it happens quickly."

My dad forbade me to come home and see what he'd become. He was ashamed and just wanted to go. Earlier that day he had taken out his gun but was too fragile to kill himself. He was given a final opiate dosage, and it was over in a matter a minutes. He was out of his misery, and my mother could be out of her pain as well.

My dad passed away knowing his mission was complete. He had left a legacy of his inventions that made the world a better place. The family he left behind all struggled in our own ways after his death. He had been the nucleus, the glue, and he was gone. Even as I write this, an immense sadness comes over me. After 16 years, I still have good and bad days.

My father's death marked the beginning of the end of my relationship with my husband. I took my dad's death very hard—as a result, I put up a wall around me. I would not let anyone in. I thought I was safer that way, but all I did was keep my sadness and anger at bay. And it shut out anyone close to me. I spent the next 16 years trying, without success, to find a replacement for my father and the close and trusting relationship I'd had with him.

A mama's girl...

My mother struggled to live her life without my father as well. She attended clown school and went into schools to make kids laugh. That was my mom—kind and generous, always thinking of others. My mother was also my champion. She sent me cards regularly to convey how proud she was of my accomplishments. She handpicked each card and wrote, "Just another feather in your cap." I loved receiving these words of encouragement.

On her 60th birthday, my mother was diagnosed with advanced stage 3 ovarian cancer. This time, I was not planning a wedding. I was eight weeks away from having my first child. Her diagnosis hit me hard. So hard, that I lost weight during my pregnancy and was put on bed rest. In the end, I was only able to gain 20 pounds with the pregnancy...but I delivered a healthy boy and my mom came to my side within a few days of his birth.

In 2004, my mother came to live with our family in Vail, Colorado, while she underwent treatment. She carried a lot of guilt for outliving my dad. They had been high school sweethearts and best friends. She was not thinking of her legacy, only her loss. She wanted to die.

One specific day will always stand out with my mother—the day she and I talked about her funeral. She told me she'd already made the plans and just wanted to fill me in on the details. I looked at her and said how scared I was of death and asked her if she was too. My mother said she wasn't afraid. I pressed her to reveal her secret.

My mother explained that she'd been there next to my father when he died, and it had been beautifully peaceful in the end. I think that is what she really wanted—peace. Ovarian cancer in Stage 3 is a terrible diagnosis—one where you have to come to terms with your mortality very quickly. That was something my mom accepted without question—her own approaching death. She did the treatments to help others but knew they weren't really doing anything for her.

My mother and I were not very close when I was young, but in the end, she and her death taught me compassion. While my mother was going through cancer, I was not there as much as I could have been. I was busy attending beauty school. I'd also bought a business, lost my consulting job, and had a second baby.

However, even while she was in the cancer center for treatments, she was still my biggest advocate. My mother never made me feel guilty for not giving her more of my time.

I was building a career and birthing children. I was not a very compassionate person. I was very good at compartmentalizing and not feeling emotion and *great* at being numb. I led life through my mind. And yet, my mom saw the promise and potential in me. She knew I could change how I lived. Unfortunately, she had to die for that change to happen.

While she was alive, it was not my care of her that really touched her. It was the treatment she received in my spa. She talked about that treatment over and over, how it was the only thing that made her feel human and allowed her to focus on her life rather than her death.

Another going away party...

There we were, just home from the hospital. My mom sat on the couch, alert and intent on a thought she was formulating. After a few minutes, she seemed to settle that thought. Then, she looked over at me, put her hands up in the air, and said in her Jewish accent, "So, what do we do? Just sit here and wait...?"

Caught off guard, I looked over at the hospice nurse. My face must have said it all. The nurse said, "Your mother knows she is home to die."

I turned and looked at my mom and asked, "You do?"

My mother replied, "Yes, I do."

Earlier that day, in the hospital, my mom's doctor told me that she had no more than 14 days left to live.

"Ok, then," I said, "Let's call everyone so you can say goodbye. And after the last person comes, you decide what you want to do next."

I had my brother call everyone and fill them in while I made arrangements to be there for my mom's last days. Over the next eight days, family flew in and said their goodbyes. In the meantime, I had to make the difficult decision to cut off her food and fluids. The doctor explained that it was keeping the tumor alive, but not nourishing her. I agonized to come to that decision. I remember my mom, being the New Yorker she was, saying, "Julie, do you think I'll ever eat a pizzer again?" I told her I was afraid not.

"As per your living will, I have stopped giving you food and you cannot swallow a pizza." She understood. I felt like crap. One thing I have come to realize is that so much attention is given to the cancer patient, but we forget about the difficult decisions that the caregiver has to make. In my case, I could have lied and said yes, you will have pizza, but I did not want to lie to my mom.

On the eighth night, the last visitor arrived, David. He was my mom's third child—if she could have had a third child. David always looked after my mom just as he did his own mom. I explained that he would be the last visitor. I told her how much I loved her and that she was free to leave when she wanted. (You have to let a person know that it's okay to die. When you ask them not to, it creates a big dilemma for them and they can remain in limbo.)

That night as I slept, I heard the oxygen machine. I listened as her breathing became shallower. I knew this was going to be her last night. I just didn't know when it would happen. I had never been with a dying person, so I didn't know how it would happen either. I just lay in bed and listened for the machine with each delayed breath. Somehow I fell asleep until around 7 AM, when the hospice nurse woke me and said I had just a few minutes. I raced over to my mom. My heart pumped with adrenaline. I searched…scanning the room like I'd done when piloting with my dad. What do I do? No one had prepared me for this. No one!

I noticed Psalm 121, left by the rabbi. Instinctively, I grabbed it in my left hand. I cradled by mom and read it to her. As I read, I became calm and held her until she left—I was very aware of the exact moment she left. I had given her that which she had given my dad in his final moments—permission to leave in peace. And she gave me just what my dad had given her—I no longer fear death. I did not cry in those moments. I think I was completely focused on being a good daughter and staying strong, on telling her that I loved her, and ushering her into whatever lies next.

I wandered for years…

Anyone who knows me knows that I fell into an abyss after that. You had to really know me, though, because on the outside, I was still a strong woman. I took the death of my parents hard.

That, coupled with a divorce, meant that I felt very alone. For the first time in my life I felt isolated and not sure of myself. I had lost my source of unconditional love.

I aimlessly wandered for a few years as a single mother of two small children under the age of five. I lost weight. I wore three shirts at work to appear less frail. I expanded my business and built out a second location. From an income perspective, I was doing just fine. But, then again, I was a business professional and that was easy to do—autopilot. The emotional component of life, however, the battle of the mind and heart…well that I was not prepared for…

And then it happened…

Cancer is a life-changing experience for individuals and their families. It can be a springboard for self-examination, personal discovery, and growth. It can provide the opportunity to live differently, intentionally, and perhaps more richly than before. BUT, someone has to let you know about this secret and help guide you.

For me that person was Felix, a trained monk and Prana healer. I made an appointment. I was in a rage—yelling at my brother that I just wanted to find a place of peace and calm in my life. Dressed in white, Felix led me to a chair and sat in silence for a moment. He then told me he loved me. He repeated it three times. I cried. I balled. I had not heard those words in five years. Before that, I had heard them every day of my life. And every month for my whole life, my mother had sent cards telling me how strong I was and how much she loved me. So, upon hearing Felix's words, I just broke. This was a turning point, the final part of the process that had begun with my father's death. This moment was when I began to learn the power of love and that unconditional love is hard to come by, yet possible to create. Since then, I have learned to live more from my heart and less from my mind.

Felix did not tell me much except that I had closed off my heart chakra and put a wall around me to protect myself. Felix's words changed my life. He said, "Julie, you are an angel. Now go out there and be one."

Digging deep to serve myself and others...

I have learned how to forge forward in a calm, peaceful, and altruistic manner. But this did not come easy. At my Harvard reunion this past spring, my classmate from Africa said to me, "Julie Bach, you look so happy. How is it that you are that way? Please tell me the secret. I want to find it." To which I replied, "Ludvig, you have to go through a lot of crap to get to the other side. You have to face yourself. You have to dig deep."

I am still learning to dig deep. And I embrace each day to learn more about me and the amazing world in which I live. I am doing it. And I have been handed a new life of freedom and higher love to serve others.

I have come to understand that my place in the world is to help people RECONNECT with themselves when they are going through cancer. And although I have never had cancer, I felt the same sort of isolation and need to dig deep to win. That is why I pour my life into Spa4thePink—so that others can be touched while they are finding the courage to fight the demons that come with cancer and to experience the unconditional love and kindness from others, if even for a few brief moments. I may no longer receive a card from my mother each month, but I know she is still my biggest cheerleader. With each person we serve, I pass some of that love and caring back to her and my father too.

Julie Bach is a Social Entrepreneur and founder of Spa4thePink™. From life's experience of losing both parents to cancer, Julie left her corporate career as a management consultant for Fortune 500 companies, turned her business mindset to that of a service-minded entrepreneur, and founded Spa4ThePink. Her MBA from Harvard Business School has been instrumental, as nonprofit and social entrepreneurship are at the forefront of today's evolving business models. As executive director for Spa4thePinkTM, Julie is responsible for merging the "spa and wellness" industry with cancer centers and integrative medicine to support a mind-body-spirit healing approach with cancer patients. Julie has a close working relationship with multiple cancer centers and operates a complimentary spa and meditative center for cancer patients in Vail, Colorado. You can contact Julie at spa4thepink@gmail.com.

HEAVEN HAS TEA PARTIES

Michelle Post, Ph.D.

"Cream and sugar please" is the way I take my tea. I am the daughter of a beautiful woman from Newfoundland. My mom was the ninth child of twelve and grew up on the island speaking with an English accent, having tea instead of coffee, and eating scones and raisin buns. I loved having tea with my mom, just as I loved having coffee with my dad. It was our special time together. We didn't talk about anything of significance; we just enjoyed the comfort of the cup and the conversation.

One of my most favorite memories shared with my mother was having "high tea" at a quaint little restaurant, "The Secret Garden." The Cambridge Dictionary (n.d.) defines a high tea as, "a light meal eaten in the late afternoon or early evening which usually includes cooked food, cakes, and tea to drink." We had to make reservations for a "high tea" and needed to wear our Sunday best. We sat there as the wait staff brought out a carousel of English finger sandwiches and sweets. And the best sweet of all was an English scone with clotted cream, raspberry jam, and lemon curd. My mouth still waters thinking about that experience.

The teas were served in fine china teapots with a cup and saucer that matched. We had our choice of the type of tea we wanted and received our very own teapot. From it, escaped the aroma of comfort. I definitely have my mother's English blood for I love a great cup of Earl Grey—only black tea for me—with cream and sugar. A high tea is heaven on earth. My mom and I would discuss which sandwiches we liked best, and we never shared our scone with one another. They were just too good to part with, even for one bite.

I also found the name of the restaurant, "The Secret Garden," described another of my mom's favorite pastimes. She didn't have just one green thumb; she had two green hands and arms. Every Texas spring, her gardens were beautiful. Her flowerbeds were filled with perennials and annuals of every shape and color.

But it was her rose bushes that were her favorite flower. She could name every species of plant she tended. I remember taking my mom to the garden shop when I lived in Texas. As I pushed the cart behind her, I was continually amazed by her knowledge of the different kinds of plants, whereas I never even knew the difference between a perennial and an annual.

I always had to laugh when she came to my home in Colorado and would ask, "Shelly, what kind of flower is that?" as she pointed to a particular flower in my garden. I would answer that it was a yellow flower, a crimson flower, or whatever color was growing at that time in my garden. I still pick the flowers for my garden by deciding on a color scheme and going with it. Who knew there is a lot more to picking the right species to grow together or the right number of plants? Not me!

I have grown up with many labels in my life: wife, sister, aunt, the baby sibling, teacher, learner, and one of the most interesting, given to me by the government—a DINK (double income no kids). But it is my newest label that I thought I'd never realize in my lifetime, "motherless daughter," which is the most painful of all. I was given this label on Tuesday, August 9, 2011, when my mother died. I don't like this label and still haven't gotten used to it.

As I sat by my mother's bed at the nursing home, the days ran into nights and the nights into days. She struggled for each breath, and though I felt like each would be her last, it was not yet to be—exactly when her last breath would occur we didn't know. While I watched each moment unfold and wondered if this would be the closing act of the scene, I could only feel hurt, loss, and sadness. I watched a once vibrant woman with beautiful brown eyes and a smile that could melt the coldest of hearts, slowly decay in front of me. *This cannot be*, I thought. *This isn't the way her life should end*. I prayed, and prayed, and prayed, but didn't find relief.

Each day brought with it the reality of what was happening—another night of no sleep and another morning of false alarms, for this was not yet to be her final moment. It was as if my family and I were rehearsing the same scene repeatedly, day after day. Our mom would make it through another day, only to begin failing around 5:30 in the morning. "Call your family," the hospice nurse would say. One by one, I would call my siblings and each would arrive shortly after the call. We then rushed to mom's side—crying, whaling, waiting, and waiting, and then she would rally. Five days passed with this same dress rehearsal, but no final performance—at least not yet.

Then we changed the scene, and for the first night since her fall, all her children departed the nursing home, leaving her with two earthly angels, Bill and Troy, her hospice nurses. Our mom completely changed the final scene on the sixth day and decided to go home on her own. We got the call from Troy, "Come quick, she is going." Although we were only 5.8 miles (15 minutes) away, Tuesday morning traffic kept us from her death scene.

As we raced those 5.8 miles, we looked up with tear-soaked eyes and paused in awestruck wonder at the beauty of the morning sunrise. Texas had been experiencing above-normal temperatures all summer and these last six days had been no different, until this one when the morning was cool. Words cannot even begin to describe the sunrise God presented that morning, and we knew before we got the next call, "She is gone," that she had already left for home. We knew this, for morning was my mom's favorite time. She would fix herself a cup of tea or coffee, sit on her back porch, and watch the beautiful sunrises. And this day was to be her greatest sunrise of all.

We arrived a few minutes after the call, running through the nursing home to try to catch her, but it was too late. Her body, still warm, and a final releasing of her spirit was all that remained for a fleeting few seconds. Just as we rehearsed the scene each prior day, one by one her children arrived to say our last goodbyes. Why she couldn't or didn't want to wait for her kids, we will never know for certain.

The subsequent hours were brutal, for the tears would not stop. I had become a motherless daughter and an orphan, all in one day. My siblings and I left the room to make the calls—those dreaded telephone conversations one never wants to face. I had to tell her only living sister that her big sister had just died. And then another call, and another, and another, until all family and friends had been notified.

What I didn't realize until I returned to the room, was that our hospice nurse, Bill, had begun to prepare her body after everyone left. What a shocking site to see my mother so frail and void of life. Then Bill said to me, "In Egypt when they buried the pharaohs, they prepared the body with oils, and that is what I am going to do for your mom too." He gently straightened my mom's broken body, lovingly put cream on her arms and legs, and with extreme tenderness combed her hair back, then crossed her arms, and covered her with one of her favorite quilts. It looked like she was sleeping.

Each of my siblings and I took our private moments with her to say our final goodbyes and held her hand one last time. After we each sat with her alone, we made the call to the funeral home, but we couldn't stay to see her taken away. We gathered ourselves and headed off to make the funeral plans. It was amazing to me how God gave us the strength and courage to handle all of the administrative tasks that were required, especially for a parent — our last parent.

August 9, 2011 ended with us looking through hundreds of pictures and selecting all of our favorites of our mom. What I realized as I looked at her through the '60s to the present was that I had forgotten how beautiful she had been. Oh, my gosh, she was gorgeous! The last few years had taken a toll on her. Her body had become frail and her once beaming brown eyes had taken on a vacant look that left me feeling uneasy, because I knew she was in there but couldn't get out due to the Parkinson's and dementia. The pictures, however, brought back her beauty. The most amazing thing we discovered was that our mom smiled in every photo we had of her. That night I came across my favorite picture of her — she was standing on her back porch with peppered short hair and the most captivating smile. That was and is how I want to remember my mom — not the woman in the bed who had no life left in her eyes.

Wednesday the 10th arrived, with us continuing to make the arrangements. What an amazing blessing we discovered that day! Our mother had planned everything right down to the pillow in the casket. She had given us that gift! We only had to make two decisions; the rest had been done for us. That night, we returned to my brother's home and I tried to sleep, but sleep would not come for me.

I replayed each moment of every hour I had spent by my mom's side and prayed that she knew how much I loved her— how deeply I would miss her. I couldn't close my eyes without seeing my mom lying in that bed with her vacant eyes, gaunt cheeks, and a frail frame. The image was etched in my brain. *Where was the beautiful woman from the pictures?* As I struggled to sleep and fought with this image I could not seem to erase, God began to ease my mind and spoke to me, *"You are seeing your mother through your eyes, but I want you to see her through Mine."*

As God helped me see through His eyes, I began to envision that vibrant woman once again. I saw her in stunning colors with angelic radiance that emitted from her. I watched her walk through the most majestic gardens as she held my Father's hand. He was showing her around, and she was meeting family and friends for a high tea. As she sat there with my dad, they laughed and smiled, drinking their tea and eating scones. When it was time for her to leave, she turned to me, waved, and gave me a big smile. "I will love you forever," she said as she turned to go.

I had watched my mom die through my eyes, not through God's eyes. I couldn't see the beauty of her new life, only the pain of the current situation. I know God provided me this opportunity to see my mom through His eyes so I could find comfort and know that she is in eternal glory, not the fading image of life. I know I will see my mom again, and when I do, we will sit in "The Secret Garden" and share a cup of tea.

But now, for a brief moment, the LORD our God has been gracious in leaving us a remnant and giving us a firm place in his sanctuary, and so our God gives light to our eyes and a little relief in our bondage. Ezra 9:8

Dr. Michelle Post has a broad career that spans more than 30 years in business and technology. She has been teaching in both corporate and now academia on a variety of subjects that include generational studies, social media, leadership, organizational development, human resource development, marketing, team building, and professional development. Dr. Post is also noted for her energetic and demonstrative speaking skills, unorthodox ideas for solutions to problems and possessing a high level of behavioral versatility, providing the flexibility and responsiveness needed to handle a variety of situations or work environments.

Michelle Post, Ph.D. can be reached at mpost.phd@gmail.com or www.ReachYourPotential.info.

HAPPINESS IS
A WAY OF TRAVEL

Cynthia Mabry

It was a beautiful evening on the beach in Destin, Florida. The moon was full, the air warm, and the breeze inviting. I had just celebrated the wedding of our niece with my husband's entire family, siblings, and friends. We had all traveled from Nashville, Tennessee for this special event. A few of us chose to take the week before as vacation and rented a house on the beach, leaving the night of the wedding as our last evening in Destin. Little did I know that returning to the beach house after the ceremony would be the last time I'd see my husband alive.

At the time, he was passed out from doing an unknown amount of "Jaeger Bombs" with the best man of the wedding — chasing shots of Jaegermeister with Red Bull. His sister and I moved him onto the floor of our vacation bedroom and decided to go back out for one last walk on the beach. When we returned, the smell of vomit was so potent it almost knocked us down. My husband and the best man had both thrown up while passed out — there was no telling how much they'd drunk. When I found my husband, he had stopped breathing and his arm was turning blue. We immediately called 911.

I curled into a fetal position under the kitchen table and rocked back and forth while the paramedics tried for what seemed like a lifetime to revive my Rob. When they carried him out on the stretcher, I knew he was no longer with us. I went into complete shock and a state of numbness. I don't remember much about the next eight weeks with the exception of two events. I had to tell Rob's son that his father was dead and I had to arrange the funeral of my husband. Everything else is a blur. I literally shut down.

Have you seen the movie "P.S. I Love You"? This was my life. I was 29 when I suddenly lost my husband — young and at a point in life when one is looking forward to new beginnings rather than endings. Contrary to the heroine's experience in the movie,

207

however, I tried to move forward but got some resistance. Some seemed afraid that I would forget Rob, that I'd move on to a new life and wouldn't be a part of theirs anymore. Although I knew they were grieving, the messages from them that it was too soon to move forward felt like roadblocks I couldn't move beyond. Then, on top of everything else, I lost my job—I believed I'd lost my career—just mere months after I'd lost my husband.

Six months after Rob's death, in November, my family, along with some of his family and my closest friends, threw a surprise 30th birthday party for me. They knew Rob would have done that, and they wanted to make my life feel "normal." I hadn't seen the party coming, and it was a great day in my life—it offered a ray of hope for a brighter future.

With the turn of the New Year 2009, I started getting the itch to move forward. That's when I began the process to reinvent myself.

In the days and weeks following the death of my husband, I was blessed beyond belief to be surrounded by family and friends who took care of me, because I was unable to physically and mentally care for myself. During that time, I received the notification from my husband's employer that his death benefit was worth one times his salary, which covered the cost of the funeral, transportation services, and paid off a credit card we shared. After that, while on leave from work, I lived off two-thirds of my salary, the amount I received from short-term disability.

Following a three-month break from life, I decided to get back in the game. I couldn't be the "spinster"—that wasn't me. Going back to work gave me something to do to keep me occupied instead of being alone with my thoughts. I've always been somewhat of an optimist, and returning to my job was my attempt to get back some of that optimism. However, at that point in my life I wasn't able to create an optimistic mindset after being thrown into the depths of despair. In hindsight, I realize I just didn't have the tools to sharpen such a skillset. That came later, along with the gift of time to grieve and come to terms with my life, which had been forever changed.

I've been in the telecommunications industry for almost 15 years. At the time I lost my husband, I had been with my company for seven. Coming back from my leave of absence, a lot of changes were underway. We had been bought—again. My department was being moved from the Operations side of the house over to IT, and with that move, my department's positions were being absorbed, i.e., eliminated. Less than three weeks after returning to my "career," I was looking at a severance package.

Not only did I just lose my husband, but we'd had no insurance, no will, no contingency fund (most people call this an emergency fund), and now I had no career! I couldn't cry. I couldn't be upset. I literally accepted it for what it was. Actually, I think I just surrendered because it was all too overwhelming. After all, I had no control over the moves and decisions at my place of employment. Once the initial shock wore off, I did realize I had control over how I reacted to this situation.

There was a lot of blood, sweat, and tears that went down the drain with my severance package. I had busted my rump all those years for 12 weeks of "thank you" pay. That was it! And that's when I knew that the past 15 years of modern-day slavery I'd endured were over. Having a job isn't a safety net—it was the largest gamble I had ever taken! I worked day after day after DAY, year after year, putting in countless hours of overtime, but because I was a salaried employee, I got the opportunity to work over 40 hours a *week* all the time and not be compensated for it. I'd done all of that to walk into work one day and be told my department was being transitioned and my department's positions were being absorbed.

Needless to say, quite a few choice words ran through my head initially. It's safe to say that at the time all the words anyone can think of probably went through my mind. And I felt every emotion too. Surprisingly, one of those feelings was relief. After all, the entire time I had been with that company—at my many desks, on just about every floor and in almost every building—I spent most of the day communicating with my Rob via email or chat messaging. The brief time after my return from leave, I remembered things like the time of day when we often checked in with each other, what I would have been chatting with him about, and what I would have made us for dinner the night before that we both would have brought in for lunch the next day. I lived in the world of *what ifs* and *what we'd have done* for all of three weeks, and I was going insane.

So yes, being let go was a blessing.

Losing my job forced me to think about what in the heck I REALLY wanted to do. Did I want to program toll free numbers, run scheduling for call centers, and manage other people the rest of my life? Or did I want to pursue something and be a part of something bigger than little ol' me, something that truly got me out of bed every morning and excited about my day, every day? What a CONCEPT!

The hunt was on.

Rarely, however, does someone pursue their dreams and actually succeed the first go round. Such was my experience. But I possess something significant—the desire to leave a legacy—to create a shift in the way people think about "this happened to me" and instead focus on "how am I going to react to what has happened?" And I have tenacious spirit—to not give up until I do find what it is that will allow me to do just that.

A lot of people know how this higher calling feels, and many have been successful "thought" leaders, shaping the very way we think today. Since I believe completely in not reinventing the wheel, I was on a mission to find them, learn from them, and be a sponge.

In the meantime, I had to support myself!

So what was to be next? I took a break. I started teaching dance again. I created a Facebook account. I took my stepson on a cruise where I met one of my dearest friends. I visited with family. I went to movies and watched pay-per-view movies. I slept. I listened to music. I started playing music again. I did whatever I wanted. And that's when it hit me: I had just tasted FREEDOM for the first time. I had never before known what that meant. I had always had a job from the time I was 15 years old. I moved out on my own at 18, put myself through college, and always worked at a job where other people controlled my minutes, hours, and days. Other people controlled how much I made, when I had to show up for work, and decided IF I could take a day off! And if I went above and beyond my daily duties, trading my time for money, I MIGHT be eligible for a 5% raise...that is, if I *exceeded* expectations.

My phone rang in February of 2009. It was my old company asking me to come back on board. It seemed that their plans to cut resources weren't working out quite as they had hoped. Hello, opportunity knocking! I opened that door and DANCED through it. I didn't accept their offer to be "part of the team" again—not on their terms anyway—but I needed income to live and I was overqualified for the jobs I had been applying for. So I negotiated. I agreed to come back as a private contractor and at a 50% increase in pay. That initial six-month contract has been extended for over three years. Apparently, my services were needed.

Instead of sitting on a log wondering what in the heck I was going to do—or thinking that being a full-time employee was my only option—I chose to look at things differently and took a chance by ASKING if they would be willing to contract. What's the worst they could have said? NO. But if I didn't ask, then the answer would have been NO by default. This one shift in how I thought about my situation and how I was going to react to it has forever changed my life. I've realized the importance of self-worth. I boosted my own self-esteem—corporate certainly has never done that! But most importantly, I've learned to ask.

When I first started my contract with my former company, I was feeling pretty confident. After all, I had just negotiated my first deal on my own and succeeded. Although I was feeling pretty sure of myself, I also felt a little timid, understanding they'd terminated me after giving them years of my life and now I was a temporary contractor. I mentioned earlier that I had been hunting for an open door that would lead me to the freedom I had tasted during my layoff. Well, my phone rang again in April 2009, and it was my former assistant. She wanted me to take a look at something, and I thought, *Why not?*

Being open to that one phone call has, three years later, put me in a position where I now work contracts because I want to, not because I have to. I get to choose how involved I am, to what extent, and even whether or not I go into the office each day. All because I was open.

The industry opportunity was Network Marketing. Never before had I truly understood what this business model was about and how it gives ordinary people a chance to create an extraordinary life. I was looking for a chance to leave a legacy and this was it...this is how I'm able to give back to so many. Before, in a traditional job, I could only work so many hours and then receive the amount of pay for the hours I worked. I could have never worked enough hours to create any kind of freedom, because there was no leverage in linear income — being paid only once for the work I provided. When I dove into the power of leverage and residual income, my world was forever changed. I am dreaming BIG. Because of the power of this industry and my dedication and commitment to excellence, I am able to do many things for many people, including donating a percentage of my income to serving young widows.

It's not about the amount of money I can earn...it's what I'm able to do with it and who I'm able to help. It's what I'm able to spend my days doing instead of looking at a "cubicle farm" nine hours a day! Today I am fortunate to be in the business of serving others, truly helping other people get what it is they desire by Changing Skin, Changing Lives.

In the last three years since coming out of my fog, I have been forever changed. Once being a shy introvert, timid and insecure, I've transformed into a strong and outgoing woman. After all, I now have nothing else to lose. I no longer recognize the person I used to be and for that I am grateful. My life today is much more enriched, full of life, love, and joy. I've let go of the people and things that were a constant killjoy and now focus on simply being happy, regardless.

Unfortunately, most people don't go straight to happy. Most people think of success and happiness as conflicting forces. Why? We've been conditioned to believe that success is a destination...a result. I view success as a journey and challenge myself to enjoy the ride.

People will change their lives because they are either inspired or desperate. It is my heart's desire to educate as many people as I can about the possibilities that are available to them. Things don't have to be the way they've always been...in so many ways. I first changed my life out of desperation — my personal and professional lives were turned upside down within six months of each other. After watching others live their dreams I was inspired to do the same.

It's now my passion to be the point of inspiration so that no one ever has to get to the point of desperation like I did.

What areas of your life can you afford to take risks in? Be bold! Are you in a job where you feel undervalued? Have you been laid off in the last 12 months? Consider that however painful your life's circumstances, they are opportunities to uncover the possibilities available to you. Maybe you'll decide to contract privately as I did. Maybe you'll discover something that's even better for you.

Whatever you do, your actions may very well give you a glimpse into the world of establishing yourself as a business owner and introduce you to the beginning of the greatest incorporation known to man: YOU, INC. As Brendon Burchard says, "There are only two things that will change your life: either something new comes into your life, or something new comes out of YOU."

Cynthia Mabry is radiating with joy—she has truly found her transformation platform in her Rodan + Fields business. Formerly an IT Executive, Cynthia reinvented herself after her personal and professional lives halted in 2008. Today Cynthia is an inspirational speaker, marketing strategist and choice advocate. Cynthia's candor about her life's events coupled with her tenacity and successful reinvention has truly struck a chord and is creating a movement across the country. Cynthia is committed to being the source of inspiration for others to make change and regain control of their lives through time and financial freedom. Cynthia's book Straight to Happy *is scheduled for release winter 2013. To interact with Cynthia, go to https://www.facebook. com/cynthia.mabry, email CynthiaMabry@me.com or call her at 615-202-9765. To learn more about Cynthia's business, visit her online at www.CynthiaMabry.com.*

MY CARVED HEART

~~~~~

Veronika Jacob

It was a couple of days past my thirteenth birthday. I was young, naïve, and excited that I had finally become a teenager. I was not sure what my life would bring when I went to California to experience my first summer camp.

Like any camp, I was in a cabin with other girls my age. I quickly became particularly close with a girl who was a couple of years younger than I. Although Lily was only eleven, we instantly bonded and she became my best friend. I called her my little sister, and I vividly remember sharing my red Crocs with her and teaching her how to put on liquid eyeliner, which I wasn't particularly good at as a thirteen-year-old.

Lily and I continued to bond and learn more about each other's lives over the next couple of days. She had a wonderful family, many of which joined her at summer camp. Her mom Laura, or as I like to call her, Mama Murray, was one of the advisors in our cabin. Mama Murray, just like Lily, quickly became a figure of inspiration. She was beautiful, full of wisdom and love, and always had the perfect words. I loved this family! I knew it from the moment I met those two that they would remain forever in my heart.

Like any normal thirteen-year-old, I devoted more time at camp scoping out all the hot boys than I did diving into camp activities. I spent my free time in the craft room or on the open grass laughing with my friends and flirting with the boys. You could say I was a little boy crazy, but at that age, who wasn't? Lily joined me one afternoon, and as we discussed our "perfect boy," she looked at me and said, "You have got to meet my brother." I was a little flustered and a lot excited! As boy crazy as I was, though, I didn't really know much about boys beyond having a twin brother.

Synchronistically, and just moments later, Sam walked toward us. Sam had shoulder-length, wavy hair, and bright

215

blue eyes accompanied by a silly green fedora. He was tall and skinny with a great smile and a personality just like his mother. Lily introduced us, and I instantly went from outgoing, silly loud Veronika to quiet, shy, bashful Veronika. I didn't know what had come over me, but I knew in that moment that I was feeling something I had never felt before. Sam ran off, and Lily and I both went our separate ways. I found my other group of girlfriends and couldn't help but tell them about this "super hot" boy I had just met.

Dinnertime was quickly approaching, and we all lined up to get food. I spotted Sam standing in the line for salad and quietly pointed him out. The girls I was with snickered and thought I was gross because Sam had hair as long as mine. I brushed off their jokes, and before I knew it one of my friends was dragging me to the salad line. I tried my hardest to squirm my way out of her grip, but the next thing I knew she was asking Sam to be my date to the camp dance the following night. Sam started blushing and replied with a bashful "yes." I stood there laughing nervously. *Lucky me*, I thought. *Now I have a date to some stupid camp dance.* I was excited and terrified at the same time.

I spent all afternoon getting ready. I told Mama Murray and Lily that I had a date to the dance, but I didn't tell them who he was. Sam told me he would come to my cabin to get me and we would walk to the dance together. Everyone around me could feel my excitement. I was under a love spell that seemed to be spiraling out of control. Sam knocked on the door of my cabin, and who better to answer than his mother? She gave Sam a hug and asked what he was doing. Little did she know he was going to the dance with me!

When I came around the corner, Mama Murray had tears in her eyes. Of course, we had to take a picture. It is still one of my favorites. We stood there, two tall, skinny thirteen-year-olds, incredibly awkward, yet young and loving. It was dance time, and instead of actually dancing, Sam and I snuck off and spent the evening talking about life. As thirteen-year-olds, we obviously had a lot to talk about. We laughed as we shared stories about our friends, and we understood each other as we talked about our families and what we wanted to make of our futures, which would of course change drastically over the years. I was thirteen, and I was in love.

The way I see it, love is a strong and passionate word. It's a feeling I believe everyone should be blessed to experience. I always felt silly telling people I fell in love with someone so quickly, but when love strikes you, there is really nothing you can do to stop it. We had such a strong connection right off the bat. We sat under the stars talking for hours; it was an experience I will always cherish.

The next day camp was over. Sam and I spent the whole morning together, and I was miserably sad saying goodbye to him. We exchanged numbers and promised to talk with each other every day. Sam held up his end of the promise—he called every single day. Our relationship continued to grow stronger, developing a deeper connection every time we spoke.

Sam was such a special person to me, and I loved nothing more than to talk with him. We shared everything with each other, and I always knew I could call him to laugh, cry, vent, or simply say, "Hey, how's it going?" He always kept me centered; he had the perfect words when I was upset or when I was flying high on life. Sam was fast becoming my best friend.

I told all my friends about Sam, sharing how amazing he was and telling them how I loved him. My friends were skeptical about how I could have fallen in love already. I simply couldn't explain it to anyone; all I knew was how I felt and that it was incredible. That first year I knew Sam we talked pretty regularly. Because he lived in California and I lived in Colorado, we knew it would be hard to see each other until the next summer camp.

The following summer when camp came around Sam and I both attended, sharing an even stronger bond. We were inseparable. I spent my falls, winters, and springs anticipating summer camp. I couldn't wait to be back in the arms of the one I loved.

As we grew up we kept a very open relationship. My favorite moment with Sam was lying under the stars one night. He reminded me that he loved me and shared with me that no matter what our situation was, I would always have a space in his heart. In that moment, I couldn't have been more in love with Sam Murray.

It got harder as we grew older because we both wanted to

meet other people and enjoy all of life's opportunities. Sam was such a ladies' man; he could charm just about any girl who passed. Needless to say, he had several girlfriends. We still talked, and we always exchanged "I love you's." Lily continued to be one of my very best friends, and for that I am forever grateful. It can be extremely hard when you love your best friend's brother, but she never held that against me.

There were times when Sam and I tried to make our long-distance relationship work. When I was fifteen Sam was my valentine. He made me the sweetest gift I have ever received. Sam loved trees and he was also very creative. He carved S + V into a heart that he had carved out of tree bark and mailed it to me for Valentine's Day. This gift still remains on my nightstand. It's a symbol of our friendship, young love, and his passion and huge heart.

As Sam and I grew older, we started to grow apart. The phone calls went from an everyday occurrence to maybe once or twice a month. Both of us started to get into more serious relationships in our hometowns, and boyfriends of mine didn't really like that I was saying "I love you" to a different guy. Sam and I occasionally Skyped or had really long phone calls. The connection was always there, and I dreamed of making it work later on in life. I was still young, yet still in love with a guy I had fallen for years earlier.

I went to college at Colorado State University while Sam stayed in Southern California to attend community college. We continued talking and always tried to convince each other to come visit our respective hometowns. Timing never really worked, but I never held it against him.

Sam was born on April 1st, which is somewhat ironic. Because of Sam's great sense of humor, he was always playing little tricks on those he loved. April 1, 2011 rolled around yet again. It was Sam's nineteenth birthday and so crazy to me to think about how time flies. We had met at such a young age; it was hard to believe we had known each other for six years. Over the years we had stayed close, and he still remained one of my best friends and of course my first love.

I was running around like a crazy woman that day and texted Sam to wish him a happy birthday. We exchanged a few short texts before I simply said, "I love you." Sam responded with an "I

218

love you too." Things between us were wonderful. I felt blessed and happy with our exchange. His life seemed good. He was happy and I was happy. It was a joyous day. Little did I know, this would be the last day we'd interact, the last time we would say "I love you," and the last time I would feel truly happy for a very long time.

Sam passed away a few days later on April 5, 2011. I had just finished taking a French test when I walked out into the extreme wind and beautiful sunshine of Fort Collins. I looked at my cell phone and saw I had a text from Lily. I glanced down quickly and was so excited that my best friend had texted me. We talk quite often and usually send each other cute texts filled with "I love you's" and silly smiley faces. This text had no smiley faces. I opened the text and my stomach fell into what seemed like a bottomless pit. It read something like: "Vee, Sam made his transition this morning. I am so sorry."

Sam had passed away that morning due to a rampant staph infection. The medical examiner later discovered that the infection took over his body as quickly as it did because he had a rare form of leukemia. My eyes flooded with tears, my body froze, and I became speechless. I reread the message a couple of times before I burst into tears. Frantically, I walked away from my French class friends. The wind was so strong that it blew my hair all around me. I felt lost.

I hate showing emotion, especially in public, and there I was, close to running through my college campus balling. The world as I knew it had abruptly come to an end. I called Lily. I was in shock and could only find the words, "I love you, I love you, I love you." No words were said after that. Just two teenaged girls crying. Lily finally mustered up the words, "I know you loved him, Vee. He loved you too. I am so sorry." In that moment, there were no more words to exchange, no more I love you's to be spoken. We ended our phone call.

This was by far the most painful moment of my life. I had experienced death before, but nothing like this. Sam was after all my first love and one of my best friends. We had grown up together and shared a friendship for which I will be forever grateful. After the shock and through the furious winds of northern Colorado, I finally made it back to my freshman dorm room.

I fell into a deep depression. My room remained dark for weeks. Nothing and no one could find the right words or actions to comfort me. I wanted to be alone, I wanted to reflect on our relationship, and I wanted to hear his voice again. The tears didn't stop for what seemed like an eternity. Losing Sam has been the hardest thing I've had to overcome.

I attended Sam's memorial service in California and spent the weekend with his incredible family. Being with them was beautifully healing. Eventually, I started to talk to people. My mom supported me more than anyone, and my spiritual community held me in a high space while I took time to recover. Many of my close friends had also been close with Sam, and their support and love reminded me that Sam was a blessing in my life. They reminded me that Sam would hate to see me this miserable. I needed to get out of my funk and love my life just like Sam had done.

His death made me closer than I could've imagined to my dearest Lily, who to this day is still my very best friend. As time moves forward, I celebrate Sam's life and constantly give thanks for the impact he left. My mom and brother planted a tree in the backyard of the house where I grew up and named it Sam. Sam loved trees. At his memorial the Murray family encouraged everyone to plant a tree for Sam.

The tree remains as a symbol of our love, growing strong and living on. Over the summer, the Murray clan came to visit the Jacob clan. Mama Murray honored our unique relationship by bringing some of Sam's ashes. Together we sprinkled them around his tree. Now, his tree is even more special! I know that Sam is with me. As my dear friend Jami Lula sings, "He's waving." Whether the wind blows or the sun shines, Sam's waving. Sam is always around me and continues to bless me with his unconditional love and inspiration.

Although times can still be rough and tears still fall, I am finally in a place of peace and love. A year later, I am starting to heal and show strength again. I am grateful that I got to say "I love you" once more before he passed. I am grateful for his love and compassion. Sam will forever remain close to my heart.

Veronika Jacob, is currently a junior at Colorado State University majoring in communication studies with a minor in peace and reconciliation studies. She is a member of Delta Delta Delta at CSU. Veronika has attended Mile Hi Church of Religious Science since she was nine. The summer camps she attended were affiliated with the Centers for Spiritual Living. She has traveled to Uganda, Africa, and Thailand and loves serving others internationally. Feel free to contact her at vljacob@comcast.net.

Defining
Moments

PUT A SMILE
ON MY FACE

Mary Liu

That smell. The clean fresh scent of Dove soap makes my
stomach turn even today. I can still remember the large white tub
when I walked into the room. My mother came inside with me
while the big nurse turned to close the door. I hesitated to remove
my clothes, so the nurse pulled my shirt up over my head and
down my arms, then tugged on my pants until they were around
my ankles. I crouched down, trying to cover my body. The cold
air raised goose bumps on my skin. The nurse lifted me into the
cold, ceramic tub—her fat hand held my arm tightly as she rubbed
my body with the sandpaper-rough white washcloth. My feet slid
along the bottom of the tub as I struggled. She moved the cloth in
tight little circles, over my legs, stomach, arms, and face. The soap
bubbles left a bitter taste on my lips. I didn't dare kick up a fuss,
but I felt my cheeks getting hot. I wasn't used to being bathed by a
stranger. I wanted nothing more than to go home. I was five years
old, entering the hospital for my third surgery.

I and my family immigrated to San Francisco when I was
two-and-a-half years old. My first two surgeries had taken place
in Hong Kong. On the day I was admitted for my third surgery,
we enjoyed a warm San Francisco morning. I remember the sun
on my cheek as my mother and I rode the bus to Saint Francis
Memorial Hospital. When we reached the hospital, my mother
spoke in Chinese to another woman; then that woman repeated
my mother's words in English to the woman in the colorful shirt
behind the desk. When they finished, someone came and took
me for my bath. After the bath, I ran to my mother's side and
reached for her hands. The lady with the dark hair then took my
mother and me to a room with two beds—the one near the door
was mine.

In a nearby room, there were children playing; some blond,
some with black hair like mine. Their mothers played with
them, sitting on the floor with crayons and blocks. My mom took

my hand and led me into the toy room. As I sat down, she said goodbye. I looked up and saw her back as she walked out the door. At the time, I didn't understand her reason for leaving me there—she had four other children at home who needed her attention.

The next morning, a flurry of people came in and out of my room checking the machines and the needle in my arm. One of the nurses pulled a plastic thing out and placed it over my face. It smelled like a mixture of rubber and plastic. It made my mouth and nose dry. Afterwards, the nurses lifted me onto another bed; this one had wheels. I shivered under the thin blanket as the bed rolled down the hallway. The overhead fluorescent lights rushed by like the passing headlights on cars at night. I began to feel sick. As the doors opened, the ding sound sent a shiver up my spine. They rolled the bed into a big metal elevator. The ceiling looked high above me. The cold metal room was like a big hollow tomb. Another ding sound and we were off again into an even colder room where I was lifted onto another table. Then it went black.

After that surgery, I never wanted to see another hospital. The sterile smell made my stomach queasy, the wheelchairs were chariots of pain, and those large elevators led to darkness. As I got older, the memories associated with my surgery faded away, but my fear of hospitals remained. To me, the fears seemed unfounded. I didn't recall the surgeries from my youth until I was twenty—I had apparently blocked those memories from my mind. Once I remembered, I hoped knowing where the fear had come from would enable me to deal with my fear of hospitals better. After all, if I ever wanted to have kids of my own I would have to go to a hospital.

Born in Hong Kong, the sixth child out of eight, I was the only one in my family with a birth defect. Unlike my sisters, I didn't like looking at myself in the mirror. Seeing the scars on my upper lip and my crooked nose reminded me I was broken. When the other kids ran around the school yard playing tag in the warm sun, I sat on the bench, feeling the sun warm the top of my head. When my brothers' friends came to visit the house I stayed in my room, not wanting to be made fun of by them.

My mother always told me to look at people when they addressed me, but I saw how her brown eyes drifted to my defective mouth every time she spoke to me. She couldn't take her eyes away from what I wanted to keep hidden even though she saw it every day. She continually told me how much trouble I was to her. Subconsciously, her words and expressions got buried deep within my soul.

In school, I never raised my hand. I kept my head down, hoping no one would notice me or make fun of how I looked. My heart began to race whenever the teacher called on kids. I didn't want her to call on me because I knew I couldn't speak right. One day, she did call on me. I remember the giggles of the girl in the desk behind me. The answer to her question was six, and the letter "s" made me instantly nauseous. I whispered the word into my hair. "Speak up," the teacher said. I could feel her eyes burning into the top of my head. I tried again, but the "s" wouldn't come out right, and I slid further down in my seat. All the students' heads tilted down; I could hear their giggles despite their best efforts.

Growing up, I didn't know there was a name for my condition. My parents never told me anything. After dinner one night, when I was eleven years old, I sat at the pale brown Formica kitchen table. My mom was at the sink washing the dishes. I listened to the dishes click against each other while I bit at my fingernails. Although I sat quietly, I was trying to gather my courage. For years I had wanted to ask my mom what happened with my nose and lips. *Why was I born different?* As the question rolled around in my head, I blurted out, "Why was I born with a crooked nose and lips?"

A plate slid from her hands and fell back into the water. It seemed like forever before she spoke, but she finally said, "I was cooking dinner one night and the cleaver I was using slipped. It injured my pregnant stomach and that's how your lip and nose got cut." At that age, I didn't want to question her answer, as ridiculous as it sounded to my young mind. In all honestly, I was somewhat terrified of the truth. I felt some relief, however, because I *finally* had an *actual* answer—no matter how silly it was—to the question I'd yearned to understand my entire life. I realize now that my mom didn't know the reason for my condition. The doctors didn't know either.

As I grew up, I stopped focusing on the way people looked

only at my nose and mouth and not at my eyes. I overlooked the way they stared at me no matter how hard I tried to hide. Then, one afternoon when I was twenty-three, while babysitting my seven-year-old nephew, we sat in the living room with the sun coming in through the window, hitting the mirror on the back wall. Suddenly, out of the blue, he looked up at me and asked, "Auntie Mary, how come your nose is crooked?"

It felt like someone had hit me in the stomach with a bat. Tears welled up in my eyes and I turned my back to him. Once again, I wanted to hide. His question cut through all the walls I had built up over the years and brought back a flood of memories from my childhood. I rubbed my finger over the rough fabric of the chair. With my back still turned, I managed to quietly reply, "I was born like that." My simple response satisfied his seven-year-old curiosity, but there was no way for me to avoid the truth any longer. I had been born with a birth defect. I would always be different.

What I didn't realize until that moment was that in burying those memories, I had been holding myself back. Not long after my nephew opened my eyes, I found the courage to correct the asymmetry of my nose. That of course meant entering a hospital. Despite the nagging fears, my desire to have the corrective surgery was stronger. I studied surgeons and finally made a choice.

My heart raced with nervous excitement as I sat in the waiting room to meet him for the first time. When I finally made it back to the patient room, I studied every surface. The walls were pale peach. Glass containers of cotton balls and a bottle of hand sanitizer stood on the counter. A basketful of magazines sat on the floor. The cool air brought goose bumps to my arms. I studied the artwork—a print displaying a field of wildflowers. When the door finally opened, I saw his friendly smile and gentle brown eyes and knew I had made the right choice. It turned out he was the same surgeon who had done my last surgery as a child. What a coincidence!

When the day arrived, I drove myself to the hospital. It was a crisp San Francisco morning, the fog settled over the city like a blanket. Once I parked the car, I took a deep breath and walked quickly through the hospital doors, scanning everything around me. The check-in process was quick and easy. The nice middle-aged woman directed me to a prep room to wait for my surgery. The air was biting cold and I really could have used another blanket. I fidgeted and paced until someone finally entered the room.

My ex-brother-in-law worked as an operating room assistant at the hospital, and he came to take me to the operating room. It calmed me to see a familiar face. As I slid onto the gurney, I felt my heart start to race. We began to move and my breathing became shallow. I sat up. We stopped. After several minutes my breathing calmed and deepened. I knew the only way for me to make it to the operating room on the gurney was if I sat upright so I could see where we were headed. There would be no overhead florescent flashes of light coming at me this time.

We talked about my sister and the latest news in the family. Because I was able to see the elevator as we approached it, I expected the ding sound and wasn't shocked when the large doors opened. The elevator still felt large and hollow, but I didn't feel so small this time. Once in the operating room, the nurse placed the oxygen mask over my face. "Count back from one hundred," she said. I don't think I even made it to ninety-four before everything went black.

The surgery went well. A week later, I returned to the doctor's office for my post-operative checkup. I remember grabbing a mirror immediately after the bandages were removed. *Where was my new nose?* It looked the same. My stomach dropped. *Was it all for nothing?* My surgeon reminded me it could be weeks before my nose took its new shape; I had to be patient.

For the first time in my life I wanted to look in the mirror—I did it every day for almost a month. Then on a Tuesday, as I dried my face, it dawned on me that my nose was semi-symmetrical. It wasn't perfect, but it was good enough! I was happy with the results. In that moment, I knew I'd undergone the last surgery I would ever have on my nose and lips.

Something changed in me the day my nephew made me face my truth. I didn't realize it at the time, but I see it now. And after standing up to my fear of hospitals, I found myself looking at fear in a different way.

In 2009, I attended a workshop. There were over 500 people in the room. As the days passed, people stood up one after another to share their deepest secrets. The more I watched and listened, I felt energy building up inside me. It continued to build and soon I found myself raising my hand to be called upon by the facilitator. To my surprise, he pointed at me and I rose. There were hundreds of faces looking at me, most with sincere eagerness to hear what I had to say.

My heart pounded so hard I thought it might leap out of my chest. The sounds of shuffling and side conversations disappeared. I felt the little girl inside me wanting to duck her head and whisper. Although my speech had improved over the years with the surgeries and speech therapy, there were some words that still sounded...off. But, despite my fear, I heard a voice from deep inside announce to this room full of strangers that I had been born with a cleft palate and a cleft lip, a deformity caused by abnormal facial development during gestation, which leaves a large opening in the roof of my mouth. I let out a gasp. This was the first time I had spoken these words aloud to anyone.

Because of the encouragement I received as I spoke, I further declared out loud that I had been supporting Smile Train for years and would continue to support this organization. It was a way that I could give back and support others born with this condition. Smile Train's mission is to provide a child born with a cleft the same opportunities in life as a child born without; by providing free cleft surgeries to children who can't afford it. As a result of speaking out loud to this large group of people—no longer silent, no longer hiding—I felt better than ever. It was a tremendously empowering moment in my life.

As the workshop ended, people came at me from all directions. Some had lived through the same experience; others mentioned friends or relatives who had been through it. "You are so inspirational," one person after another said to me.

Today, at age 48, I have finally come to accept who I am, including my birth defect. I went from *being* a shy, low-self-esteem, no-confidence girl who didn't want to be seen, to *becoming* a Visibility Business Coach, Speaker, and Trainer who helps aspiring women speakers and entrepreneurs be more visible in their business. With my business, Empowered Women Speakers, I hope to inspire, motivate, and empower other women to speak their own truths by sharing my story of how I overcame my struggles. My goal is to help these women step into their power, embrace themselves as they are, and stand out in the world so they can spread their messages to others. One of the visions I hold for myself is to be Smile Train's spokesperson.

Sometimes what we see as our defects are the things that actually set us apart. After years of inner struggle with myself, I finally have a smile on my face and am ready to Be Seen!

Mary Liu, Founder & CEO of Empowered Women Speakers provides a community for aspiring women speakers and entrepreneurs dedicated to building relationships focused on collaboration, support, and business growth—women from across the world sharing in wisdom circles to empower, educate, and mentor others. Her passions include traveling and spending time with her family. Mary resides in San Francisco, CA. You can reach Mary at Mary@EmpoweredWomenSpeakers.com and learn more about the work she does at www.EmpoweredWomenSpeakers. com. To find out more about Smile Train visit www.SmileTrain.org.

WHAT I KNEW THEN
AND WHAT I KNOW NOW

Andrea Costantine

The A-frame building always felt like a prominent symbol, even as a child. The roof towered high above, coming to a peak just underneath a triumphant oak that was left standing amidst the concrete parking slab in the back of the building.

We pulled up to the back door. My dad had the day off but needed to swing by the restaurant to check on something. He parked the car while my mom, siblings, and I waited for him to return. From out back, we could hear the "ring-ring" of the drive-thru bell as well as the sound of the creaky door when it opened. We waited patiently for my dad to return, which took only a matter of minutes. As he sat down in the driver's seat, he noticed a homeless man rummaging through the trash. He immediately jumped out of the car.

"Hey. Hey! Stop that!" Dad called out.

It was hard to tell whether he was mad or just didn't like watching some man go through the trash. We all looked on with curiosity.

"Stop," he continued, his voice getting louder as he walked back inside the building.

Would he call the police? Was this man doing something wrong? My five-year-old mind began to question both my father's and the man's motives for digging through the garbage.

"What's he doing, Mom?" All three of us inquired.

"He's looking for food," she said matter-of-factly. *Food? Why would someone look for food in the trash?*

Seconds later my father emerged with a box of fresh fried chicken—the box decorated in the traditional yellow and gold logo that's been around since the restaurant started in the '70s.

"Here, take this." He handed it to the man. "Now go on. Get out of here."

We then went on our way, heading off to do what we'd planned for the day.

I knew then that I should always stop and take the time to help someone in need.

"Everybody, let's GO! We are going to be late for church."

My brother, sister, and I did our best to hurry and get ready, but it was Sunday. *What fun was it to rush on a Sunday?* Besides, we'd stayed up late the night before and fallen asleep inches from the television set. We'd slept there until morning, when it was time to wake up and get ready for Sunday school. The hour drive to our church just added to our morning rush.

"Okay guys, come on," my mother encouraged us.

Finally, we were ready to pile into our 1975 Oldsmobile Tornado—a sleek, black, two-door car with a blood-red interior. As we opened the front door to head towards the car, almost out of nowhere a couple appeared. Breathless and visibly anxious, they stood right in front of us.

We lived in a remote part of town. Only 10 or so other houses were scattered along our road, each sprawled out over a few acres. We had horses, many cats, and dogs. This was a quiet town of people who knew each other. Yet, all of a sudden, these people appeared. People we didn't know.

"Help us," they said. "Please help." They turned, looking over their shoulders, scared and frightened. Even then, at five, I could tell what fear looked like.

We children clung to our mother. "Get in the car guys," she said. I could hear the fear in her voice as well. But we didn't move.

"Please." The woman pleaded. "We just need to hide, just for a few minutes. Please."

My father looked to my mother, who looked back with a "Don't you dare think about it!" look.

"Well, I have my kids," he started. "And, we are just going out the door for church. I don't know what I can do." I could see his anguish. Torn between helping and potentially putting us all in danger, he wavered.

"Do you have a place we could hide? We just need to hide. We promise we'll be gone before you even get back. Just let us hide." The man and woman were visibly upset. Sweat was pouring from their skin and their voices shook.

"Well, I guess…well, okay. Come on," my father motioned for

them to follow him into the house. We all followed. The couple. My mom. My sister. My brother. And me. We all walked down the hallway. The first room was my brother's, which contained a crib, a dresser, and toys.

"This will do." The woman said. And the couple crouched together in the corner of the room. They squeezed between the four-drawer dresser and rocking chair, as if that would keep them safe.

"Um, okay." My father's eyes darted around the room, apparently assessing what it was in this room that would protect them, our house, and his family. He eyed the window. The shades were closed. "Well, we'll be going now. Be safe."

And just like that, we walked out of the house and went to church. I can only imagine the prayers that went through my parents' minds as we left and throughout the time we were gone.

Hours later we returned to the house. On the way back, I asked, "Do you think those people will still be there?"

"Let's hope not," my father replied.

I knew then that it was okay to help a stranger and do the right thing, even when it was scary.

My father—Ricky, as his friends and family called him—was sensitive. He would help when he could, but more often than not, bad things seemed to happen to him. Once, his wallet was stolen after he accidentally left it on the counter. He returned only minutes later, but it was already gone. The money in his wallet was the only money we had at the time. Because we lived on less than "from paycheck to paycheck" and barely made our bills even in the best of times, he was more than devastated.

On another day, we came home to find droplets of blood splattered all over our front porch. Our dog, Pepper, was nowhere to be found. My father drove the long dirt road back and forth. He found Pepper dead alongside the road. Pepper had been shot by one of our neighbors. Again, my father was devastated. He was hurt, confused, and unable to understand how people could do the things they did. Each act chiseled away at him, eventually leading to his suicide.

After his death, we were treated as "special" children, so much so that when I enrolled in a new school a year later, I insisted that I was indeed a "gifted" child and should be put in "gifted" classes. I thought being "gifted" was why I had been taken out of my normal class every day the previous year. During the year following my father's death, a woman took me from class and I'd join a different group of students. We were treated like we were special. Or, at least the teacher made us feel that way. As a result, I thought I'd been placed in the "gifted" program.

The woman looked like your typical teacher from the early '80s. She had short brown hair, wore large circular glasses, and pencil skirts. She was "nerdy" by today's standards. But beneath her appearance, she was pure love. I could tell by the way she looked at me that even though she felt sorry for what I'd experienced, she still wanted me to have the best life possible and she believed in me. I even remember one day when my sister and I went to her mobile home and watched movies at her house. It was as if she went out of her way to ensure that we knew we mattered.

I knew then that when, through your actions, you show a person they matter, you make an impact.

By fifth grade, I was well-adjusted, a teacher's pet, and a good student. I was the kid who got picked by the teacher to do just about anything—clean the chalkboard, boot up the MS-DOS computers, and run errands to other classrooms. One day, my teacher approached me to see if I would be interested in doing something else. She wanted to know if I'd volunteer in one of the other classrooms on a weekly basis to work with students who had mental and physical disabilities. I agreed. It was the first time I found myself giving back "officially," and I immediately liked it. Each Wednesday I'd spend my afternoon in the special needs room to interact with kids who were truly different than any from my previous experiences. I took my role seriously. I was curious, but kind—loving, but firm. Together, we'd do puzzles or read or build with blocks and other toys.

There was one boy in particular who I especially connected with. I could tell he was unique. He had a very limited vocabulary, so most of our interactions were through play and work. He was a lot older than I was, even though we were in an elementary school. The elementary school was the only place that had a program for students with disabilities. He towered over me and was strong. When he wanted to, he could get physical. Sometimes, he'd get mad as hell and throw a temper-tantrum. He also had frequent seizures and had to wear a helmet 24-7 because he could fall down and seize at any moment. The first time I witnessed him have a seizure in front of me, I was completely terrified. He was at least 15 inches taller than I, double my weight, and fell to the floor right before my eyes. The teacher reacted immediately. Luckily, she knew what to do.

I knew then that I wouldn't always be able to help everyone, but I could do my best and be there for them when I could.

As a pre-teen I was forced to hang out with my parents on the weekends. One night my mom and step-dad decided to get out of the house and head down to the Daytona Beach Boardwalk. It was filled with carnival-type rides, video games, and all sorts of people.

That night we found a parking space not far from the boardwalk and began to make our way over to the activities. As we approached the boardwalk we noticed a group of people gathered in a dense circle. The closer we got, the more we could tell a scuffle was going on.

Two men were in the center. One man stood over another who was down on the ground. Although the man on the ground looked barely conscious, the upright man continued to pummel him. The victim struggled, yet the man brutally punched him over and over again as the crowd looked on. They hooted, hollered, and seemed to enjoy watching the fight transpire.

In seconds my stepfather responded. He'd had formal training in tae kwon do with a third degree green belt in karate. Almost 20 years in the military, and the youngest of his siblings, he didn't hesitate for a moment to jump right in and stop the fight.

"HEY! HEY!" He yelled and moved between the two men.

"Mike, NO!" My mom called after him, trying to pull him back towards us.

His voice reverberated through the crowd. With sheer force he wrenched the man off the other, pushed him away, and tumbled to the ground himself to get the aggressor to stop. The man then turned on my stepdad. Mike, my stepdad, put his hands up; ready to defend and fight back, when the man ran away.

Mike immediately turned to the crowd and yelled, "You are

all just standing here?! You're disgusting." He turned to the man on the ground and again addressed the crowd, "Someone, call an ambulance!" A few people left to do just that. The man on the ground had been beaten badly and was covered in blood. Who knows what would've happened if my stepdad hadn't jumped in when he did.

My stepdad also had a chance to stick up for me as a teenager. Luckily, he was a tough, street-smart man. When girls from high school planned to jump me by coercing me to go on a walk where we could "talk" about our issues, he saw it coming and wouldn't let me go. Moments later, a car full of girls drove by the house. That day, I would've personally been beaten had he not stuck up for me.

I knew from both experiences that we need to stand up for some people and stand up to others.

Over and over, I look back at my life and see the many pieces of a puzzle that have led me to the place where I am right now. What I witnessed throughout my youth greatly influenced me. From my father's sensitivity and desire for a better world to the experiences I had with my teachers and school—many of which I have not included here—to witnessing my stepfather stick up for the man on the boardwalk and for me later on, I see how the pieces have fit together.

What I know now is that we all have gifts and abilities to give back, to do what's right, and to do our part. While these examples may seem dramatic or even extreme, they are a part of my story—part of what make me who I am. They are why I am committed to seeing the world become a better place. They are why I believe we each must act as if every person matters and that we all belong here. My experiences are the foundation from which I've built my life—to live in a place where people don't commit suicide because of the hurt they feel by other people's malicious acts, to live in a world where we care more about the collective than we do about our own personal agendas—a world where we take the time and make the effort to simply do what's right. That's what I learned then, and it's what I know now.

Andrea Costantine inspires others to make a difference in the world by getting involved and creating community through compassion, contribution and connection. She believes that when we come together, change can be made. With a sense of community, separation dissipates, leading to happier, healthier, more compassionate human beings, who can then contribute back to others. Andrea is a speaker, author and workshop facilitator. Her books include: Speaking Your Truth (V1 & V2), How to Bring Your Book to Life This Year, Soulful Marketing, *and* Connected: 101 Ways to Be of Service and Create Community. *Learn more about Andrea at www.andreacostantine.com.*

YOU'RE THE BEST!

Summer Johnke

Celebration means something different to everyone. To celebrate is to honor in ceremony, to perform a rite, to break from one's routine, to engage in festivities. Along the lines of engaging in festivities, one of the biggest celebrations on earth takes place during Mardi Gras, or fat Tuesday before Lent. Of all the possible places to enjoy Mardi Gras, New Orleans is certainly one of the wildest.

Having moved down south to attend Tulane University in the lovely Big Easy, the anticipation of Mardi Gras began the moment my plane landed. Everyone could hardly wait or stop talking about it. Even the trees swayed to the rhythm of Mardi Gras as the beads tossed into the midst of their branches the previous year jangled in the wind. Everyone joked how life was the training ground for Mardi Gras.

After eighteen years and seven months' worth of training, Mardi Gras finally came. When asked to explain Mardi Gras, I can only shake my head and laugh. What is Mardi Gras? Mardi Gras is six days straight of parades, beads, plastic goods galore, cheap concerts, parties at fraternities, and many other things that one can't seem to remember the morning after. Mardi Gras is people of all ages and demographics coming together and sharing the streets of New Orleans, as even the drunk college kids respectfully hand down their best catches from the floats to the children in the family next to them. Mardi Gras is ton after ton of waste, most of which is picked up by a second procession of prison inmates that come by after the main parade. Mardi Gras is a way for the city of New Orleans to unite and rebuild itself after the devastating effects of Hurricane Katrina. Mardi Gras is whatever you want it to be.

To most students at Tulane University, Mardi Gras means getting up in the morning, drinking, going to a day parade, drinking more, going to a night parade, drinking yet again, going to a party with even more drinking, stumbling back to bed, waking up hung over, and allowing oneself a few hours of recovery time before the drinking recommences. The essential thing is to make sure that you are drunk enough to finally let loose and take the scariest of all risks. Being yourself.

Although I will openly admit to participating in a great deal of this, sometimes the whole process of dumbing myself down and waiting for others to do the same seemed ludicrous. I had to ask myself, why is opening up to the world such a terrifying process for so many teenagers and young adults growing up today?

In trying to answer this question, I found myself studying teenage behavior, attitudes, and definitions as to what it means to be cool. What I realized is that being cool is all about being detached, superior even, to the people and things around you. When placed in uncomfortable situations, many teenagers revert to safe topics such as what movie is coming out, how classes are going, or the crazy party they went to last weekend. One of the most frequently used safe topics involves complaining. "Oh my god, I am so tired. You wouldn't believe how late I was up 'til last night!" Or, "Why can't the weather just make up its mind? Does it want to be sunny or rainy?" Throughout it all, you have to be careful not to say anything original or too self-revealing.

Along these lines, it is cooler to say you don't like something than to admit that you do. The person willing to declare, "I'm a huge fan of [insert band]" is placing themself in far greater peril than the person who claims in a blasé manner, "Oh really? Yeah, I heard of them like two years ago. I used to like them, but, I don't know, they just kinda got old." After all, saying you like something is offering the listener valuable information about yourself that he can then do whatever he wants with. Whatever he wants often involves dismissing what you like as unimportant or outright putting you down in an attempt to make himself feel better about his life. Many people just prefer not to bother sticking their necks out in the first place. Why should they when it's so much safer to retreat into their shell and judge others from afar?

All of this may sound ridiculous. I mean come on; modern-day life in America isn't a jungle where you have to be worried about your safety! Or is it? Could the lions and tigers have been replaced by insecure teenagers trying to work their way up a different food chain, the popularity chain? Given the fact that teenagers are willing to put themselves through the process of throwing up and blacking out over and over again just to be themselves for that short window of time under alcohol's effects, one would certainly think so. Most people will acknowledge that growing up is a roller coaster of ups and downs with many rough, bumpy parts. Sometimes kids can just be plain mean.

This led me to my second question. Why? Why are we so mean to each other, seemingly unnecessarily? I've touched upon this briefly before, but the answer can be spelled out in four words. We are scared shitless. What it all comes down to is a lack of self-confidence. Every human being needs love—lots of love. I like to imagine everyone having their own personal love tank that fuels them and keeps them going throughout the day. Like a car that runs out of gas after a certain number of miles, everyone's tank needs to be filled on a regular basis for them to keep functioning properly. Once your tank is filled, you are then able to go out and start filling up other people's tanks with the love their hearts are crying out for.

Most people think that in order to fill up their tanks they need other people's attention and approval, so they go out and put themselves through the terrifying prospect of rejection just for the chance to finally find someone who cares. They are forgetting two things. The first is that most people's tanks are just as dry as theirs; therefore, they are far more prone to hurt you than love you. When someone gets hurt, this only serves to further drain the meager stores of love that they managed to salvage. However, the second thing that most people forget is that if they look inside themselves at who they truly are, they will find an infinite supply of love at their disposal. In order to feel whole and complete as a person, the only person whose love matters is your own.

Alas, the majority of the Tulane population has yet to remember these two simple facts and moves about in the drained manner of a zombie looking for the next kill. This creates the phenomenon of what I like to call the Tulane bubble. Not only are Tulane's students mostly white and Jewish in a predominately black and Catholic environment, but the bulk of them are too intertwined in their own problems and drama to really appreciate the culture around them. Sometimes all it takes is stepping out of the bubble of campus to feel the rush of energy you would usually associate with a breath of fresh air.

One of my main objectives during Mardi Gras was to branch out and connect with local New Orleanais. My status as a white, blonde girl and reputation as a student at Tulane preceded me, making this a far more difficult feat. Resigned to the fact that I seemed doom to fail, I nonetheless set out for my umpteenth Mardi Gras parade, still determined to make a night out of it and have fun. Yet as I watched the parade go by, I couldn't help but be struck by how tired all the people in the parade seemed. Their cheeks stretched in forced smiles as they rallied on in an effort to provide all of us onlookers with the experience we were looking for. It was a relatively cold night, and many of the girls wore skimpy clothing with nothing to keep them warm. Many of the passing band members had to carry heavy instruments and play for miles and miles without stopping. As far as the float drivers were concerned, nobody really acknowledged their existence. The only thing that seemed to matter to the crowd was beads, beads, and more beads.

Unsure as to what else I could do, I began yelling out nice things like, "Keep it up! You're looking beautiful!" to the bands' cheerleaders in an effort to support them. Acknowledging the band members as well, I personally thanked as many people as I could for making Mardi Gras as fun as it was, shouting "You're the best!" to everyone walking in hearing distance of me. This became my slogan for the night, and I even told it to some people multiple times. This caused a minor dispute between two guys near me as they asked, "Wait, we can't both the best! Which one is it?" I laughed and said, "No, no, no! Don't you see, there isn't just one best! You're both the best!" And I meant it, genuinely meant it. That night, in that moment, it was so blatantly true. We all make the collective whole of life but are so different in our own right that there can be no higher good or bad. We are all the best.

Repeating this same refrain, I personally went up and shook the hand of every float driver as they drove by, assuring them that, "Mardi Gras just couldn't run without them." I even thanked the police officers standing nearby, although they only shook their heads and looked at me suspiciously. Not letting this or anything else stop me, I clapped and smiled for the people passing by on the floats rather than push and shove in the battle for beads. Ironically enough, I ended up getting more beads that night than at any other parade.

Before I knew it, two friends who had come along joined me in encouraging the people in the parade, cheering and calling out words of praise and encouragement. My positivity spread to the people around me in a different sort of bubble than that usually associated with the students at Tulane. We represented a bubble of people who cared. People became more generous in sharing their catches with others, more people laughed, and we cheered louder than anyone else. Several people clapped me on the back and returned my compliment, telling me, "You know what? You're the best!" One guy even came up to me and took me aside to say, "You've been thanking people all night for making Mardi Gras what it is, but I just wanted to thank you. You made my night because you made Mardi Gras more than what it usually is." To this my reply was a huge grin, and the words "Well, thank you. You're the best!"

My purpose with this story isn't to boast or showcase myself as some incredible person. As I said before, I behaved like most other Tulane students throughout the course of Mardi Gras. That night, however, was different—special. It reminded me that no matter what atmosphere I find myself in, celebration and life in general can be whatever I choose it to be. That night I chose to celebrate other people and how worthy of love each of them was.

And that is what I want to share with you, the joy I discovered by giving joy to others. Making the long trek back to campus after an even longer day, I felt more alive and energetic than I had in a long time. What I learned is that by seeking beauty in other people and the world around me, I will always end up coming back to the beauty that already exists within me. In the end, the world is one big mirror, and wherever I look I am astounded by my own beauty.

Summer Johnke is committed to passion, beauty, and connection. When she wrote this story, Summer Johnke was eighteen and a freshman at Tulane University in New Orleans, Louisiana. Before that, she split her time between the cities of Boulder and Englewood where her parents lived while attending Cherry Creek High School. Although Summer is still uncertain as to what she wishes to study, she loves languages and speaks French, Italian, Spanish, and some Arabic. She spent six months in Paris and a year in Sicily, Italy, and has future plans to travel around India and study abroad in Morocco during her college career. After that, she'll be wherever the wind takes her. Or wherever she takes the wind.

ANGEL OR GOOD GUY?

Wendie Batterson

When I think about it, I guess I've always believed in angels—maybe not angels as we typically think of them—with wingspans and white gowns, but angels nonetheless. I have always seen faces and images in cloud formations as they whisk and change across the sky and have wondered who they might be or have been. I have been fascinated by watching those formations change from or into people, animals, or images—they are here and then become something else, changing constantly in form. Dissipating is the correct term, I think. All I know is that I enjoy watching the energy in clouds constantly move and change.

As a child, growing up on a farm in Pennsylvania in the '50s, I spent a lot of time by myself and was fortunate enough to sprawl in the grass at times—in a pasture, the woods, or around our house—and just watch the clouds. I have not had the luxury to do that much since becoming an adult, wife, and mom, but I still look up and wonder whenever I have a fleeting moment. I'm still not sure if those images are of people "past or passed," but it really doesn't matter much. I have always liked to think that some of them may be angels.

Over the last couple of years, I have been on a more dedicated spiritual journey than before—some of that is because of my own emotional recovery process, but mostly I had been feeling like a "lost soul." I wasn't sure what I believed, whether I was a true agnostic or an atheist, or nothing at all, and I felt the need to figure it out.

An idea that intrigues me, and that I've done some studying about, is the presence of angels and guiding spirits around each one of us. And, as always, as I have become more open to this exciting possibility, all kinds of events have surrounded me and come into my awareness and experience. The one that I am about to tell is very special to me and somewhat unexplainable from a rational point of view—as most of them truly are.

During 2011, my husband was deployed as a contractor to Afghanistan. It was quite an adjustment for both of us, on many levels, but one thing for sure is that I have had to learn and do all kinds of vehicle and mechanical things that I had never done before. Not that I ever wanted to learn this stuff, but I really had to bite the bullet and "just do it." My husband also had a lot of time on his hands, since he was basically restricted to a military base, working 12-hour night shifts. As a result, he spent a lot of time checking the Internet for deals on all kinds of stuff, mostly vehicles, which is one of his passions.

He got wind of a three-horse trailer that someone was selling out of northern Arizona and sent me the ad. We'd been thinking about upgrading our two-horse to a three-horse because our "pony family" had grown to three and because, if and when we ever really do retire, we want to do some road trips with the horses and would need the extra space. So, I went ahead and contacted this person and arranged a meeting to inspect the trailer and possibly finalize the deal.

It was winter when all of this took place. If you have ever lived in Colorado, you understand that the weather is incredibly freaky because of the mountains being so close. I live south of Denver, so Albuquerque is about a six-hour drive in good weather. We had arranged that the owner of the horse trailer would come from northern Arizona and meet me in Albuquerque, which was about halfway for both of us.

I made all the arrangements and was on my way when I started to get sick. It was some kind of nasty flu bug and getting sick surprised me because that rarely happens. I was beginning to get totally leveled by whatever it was. And, since I hardly ever get sick, I was completely irritated. I have known for quite some time that I am not a very good sick person, and I also know that when I get really sick, I go down big time and it takes me a very long time to get back to my "normal" level of energy. I knew I was becoming very sick!

I have a very dear friend who lives in southern Colorado, and I had planned to visit her on the way. As I drove to her house, I continued to get weaker and sicker with each passing moment. When I arrived, I basically crawled into her house, tried to keep my distance so I wouldn't infect her, and went to bed. In the meantime, there was a huge winter storm predicted to rumble into the entire Colorado Front Range, with extremely high wind warnings and wildly low temperatures. I had watched the weather report and knew it was coming, but my German stubbornness kicked in, and I figured I could make it to Albuquerque, get the trailer, and get home before the storm really hit. Besides, it was the only window of time that would work for both the person I was meeting and me.

As is common in Colorado, it was a nice and fairly warm, clear winter day when I tried to drag my sick head, body, and butt to the truck to get on my way to Albuquerque. "Yep, I can make it and get home before all hell breaks loose," I told myself and my friend. Besides that, I just wanted to crash in my very own bed to get through this horrible bug. And so, "dumber than dirt," I left my friend's house in the morning, got to Albuquerque, met this guy, inspected and bought the trailer, and was on my way back home.

The new trailer was aluminum and lightweight, especially when it wasn't carrying horses. From Albuquerque, I had to come back over Raton Pass to get into Colorado and then home. It's a fairly rugged pass, but it's also well traveled because it is part of the interstate from New Mexico north through Colorado. Just before I got to Raton Pass, the storm hit about six hours earlier than predicted. Having lived in Colorado for a long time and having driven in mountain blizzards with my two munchkins strapped in car seats in the back and our dogs packed way in the back, I feel that I'm a pretty experienced winter driver. However, I had never driven a monster diesel truck and an empty aluminum trailer before in high winds and an incredibly blizzard-like winter storm. I felt like I was parasailing over the pass, and it scared the crap out of me! On top of that, I was sicker than a dog and could hardly keep my head up to drive. I do remember feeling grateful that the trailer was empty, though, and that my horses were safe at home.

The storm was worse than they had predicted. The temperature was dropping like crazy and the visibility from the blowing snow was about zero. I made it over Raton and talked to my friend Fran via cell phone. She was very concerned, since she had watched the latest weather update, and insisted that I should not continue driving home, which would normally have taken at least another three hours. I was so sick that I took her advice and went to her house for another night. Welcome "Typhoid Mary," once again!

This storm was wicked. With the wind chill factor, the temperatures dropped to between -30 and -50 degrees. I knew enough to understand that I had a diesel truck and I needed to put additive into the fuel tank to keep the gas from "gumming up," as they say. So, I stopped and got some additive and put it in. I was thrilled to park this "monster rig" at Fran's house, get out of the storm, and fall into bed as soon as I could.

I'm an early riser, so I'd planned to leave as soon as it was light and head home the next morning. When I walked outside the following morning, it looked like one of Ansel Adams' pictures— everything was totally frozen and absolutely drop-dead gorgeous. I always feel in awe on mornings like that, when the world is so still and peaceful, with a coat of shimmering ice that makes everything sparkle. It looked like an angel's paradise!

I warmed the truck, or so I thought, and pulled out to drive through the town and get on the interstate. "Here we go," I thought, "at least it's not snowing." However, it was still -50 degrees, with super-high wind and winter storm warnings. The scenery took my breath away, both figuratively and literally.

I pulled on to the interstate, still sicker than a dog and wishing that I could just beam myself home, like in Star Wars, instead of driving for hours. All I could think about was that I just wanted to get home safely and get into my own bed. I was going slowly because of the ice and wind when a signal light "Engine Getting No Power" came on in the truck. Apparently, it had been so cold the night before that the additive to the diesel fuel had not done squat. So, the fuel had gotten all "gunked up," as I had feared, and it was not getting to the engine. I called my mechanic, a longtime friend of our family, and he assured me that it would not hurt the truck to drive it home, but that I should stop at the first place I found to get a specific kind of fuel additive. He also told me to not turn the truck engine off because it would definitely not start again. "Oh great," I thought. "Now, I'm really screwed. I will probably end up in an actual Ansel Adams photo myself, probably as a human sculpture frozen to a freakin' scrub brush!"

I could only go about 25-30 MPH on the interstate, and the

trailer was still flapping in the breeze like a kite behind me. I took deep breaths and tried to stay focused. I stopped at the first auto stop. Of course, being in a rural area, they didn't have what I needed. And so it went—driving between 25-30 MPH on a 75-MPH interstate, sailing in the wind!

Many hours later, I got to Colorado Springs, which typically has a lot of high vehicle and truck traffic circulating around the city. Since the interstate is a major truck route, there are always tons of trucks "hauling butt" around there on their way north to Denver and Wyoming. I had my blinkers on to give warning that I was going extremely slow, but these 18-wheelers consistently came screaming into my side-view mirrors, realizing way too late that I was barely moving, and then careened over into the passing lane to get by me.

The momentum of the heavy trucks, in addition to the already strong wind, made the horse trailer react like a whale flipping back and forth. I watched out of my mirrors and thought, "Oh this is not good." I said out loud, as my angel teachers had told me to do, "Angels, please help me. Come and protect my back. It wouldn't be intentional, but it feels like someone is going to ram me from behind and cause a terrible accident." It was really the first time I had asked angels for help. Well, the first time I'd asked out loud anyway.

The traffic was heavy. When there was a quick break with no one behind me, I looked straight ahead for a short distance. I thought, for just an instant, that there might be a moment of relief from the heavy traffic. When I looked back out of my mirrors, probably no more than a minute later, a little white car had unexpectedly appeared with a small figure at the wheel. All of a sudden and out of nowhere, it was as if this car magically materialized. This little white car had its warning blinkers on and was following me closely. I gaped and then remembered my call for help.

This little car followed me all the way through the "Springs" to the other side, until I was past the really heavy traffic. I needed to stop to get gas and put in more fuel additive, so I pulled off at the next auto stop. I finally caught a glimpse of the "person" driving—this little car zoomed past me with what appeared to be a small man driving. He had on a white jacket and little spectacle-like, dark-rimmed glasses. He did not make any eye contact with me and kept his eyes straight ahead on the road as he turned off his blinkers. I waved to him and thanked him, but he never once looked directly at me.

I stopped and got out of the truck to take a break. I left the truck running, went inside to find the restroom, when it finally dawned on me. I am now totally convinced that this was an angel, my angel who came to help and protect me. Many soothsayers would say, "Yeah right, it was just a good Samaritan." Possibly, yes. And maybe I was too stressed to actually see this little car drive up behind me. I'm sure there are a million rational reasons for what happened to me in those few minutes as I drove around Colorado Springs that day. Those few minutes seemed to stretch like an eternity for me. I can only go with the feeling that I had at the moment I saw that "good guy" or angel behind me—it was a feeling of relief, peace, and comfort that was new for me.

Since that experience, I have done more reading, trying to understand and learn more about angels in our lives. There are many "experts" out there who are willing to educate and guide all of us, if we choose to learn. As always, or so it seems to me, my experiences seem to multiply when I am open to receiving them. I choose to be open. For "feeling" reasons that are spiritual rather than rational, I know that this was an angel who answered my call for help—in a little white car with its blinkers on, going around Colorado Springs that day. And I am incredibly grateful for that one little angel in a little white car who protected and kept me safe in those moments on that special, sparkling Colorado winter day.

Wendie has been a teacher in some way, shape or form most of her life—with experience teaching French and English in the public school system, teaching English to Spanish nationals while living in Madrid, and working in corporate America for years in Training and Organizational Development. She holds a B.A. in French, English and Education, an M.A. in Counseling, and a second M.A., with a double major, in Management and Human Relations. She and her husband "Bat" have been married for almost 40 years and live in Franktown, near Denver. They have a grown daughter and son and daughter-in-law, Shayne, Cayce and Staci, who also live in the Denver Metro area.

They are a family of animal lovers and have had horses, dogs, cats, and critters forever! She volunteers with Horseback Miracles, Inc., a life values equine therapy program for "at risk" adolescent girls from local residential treatment centers, as well as with the Alzheimer's Association "Memories in the Making" art program.

BELONGING

Deanna Stull

My voice cracked as I tried to keep my composure. Thoughts flew through my head. *Just hang up. Say it was a phone issue. Ask, "Are you there? Are you there?" and pretend you can't hear her. Do anything to stop this conversation.* I had my headset on and was fidgeting with my hands—wringing and then wiping them on my pants. They were cold and clammy. *What is happening to me?* I thought to myself just as she asked another question, "How are you feeling right now?"

I didn't want to tell her the truth. I wanted to lie and tell her I felt great, fabulous, totally self-assured, and in control. Instead, I heard myself say, "I feel really uncomfortable."

"Describe it," she responded. Two simple words that changed my life forever. As I started to describe the actual physical sensations, I became nauseous. The feeling was overwhelming and I began to cry. Tears slowly rolled down my face as I told her how I was shivering and my stomach felt queasy and tied in knots. She asked me to be present to the physical sensations. I felt extremely vulnerable. My body was shaking like a leaf. I wanted to slam the phone down, pretend none of this ever happened, and go back to not knowing.

"When did you first feel like this?"

My voice was shaky as I said, "I don't know."

Suddenly, a series of scenes flashed before my eyes. One after another. All with the same pervasive message. All equally powerful.

"You don't belong."

I am in kindergarten, wearing a little dress with red, blue, and yellow daises on it. I am seated at a table with my hand raised. My teacher calls on me, and I excitedly tell her I want to play with the building blocks. I loved them. They were grey and covered with a velvety flannel cloth. I wanted to stack them to make forts and houses. I couldn't wait to play with them. "I want to play

255

with the building blocks!" I say. She laughs, "Deanna, you play with the blocks too much. They're for the boys. Come over to the kitchen and play with the girls."

"You don't belong."

Next, I am in grade school sitting beside Gary, the boy who always got in trouble. We are in the back of the class because our names land at the end of the alphabet. He whispers to me and I whisper back telling him to be quiet, but my whisper is too loud. Mrs. Young yells out my name and tells me I need to go out into the hallway for some quiet time since I can't seem to pay attention like the other kids.

"You don't belong."

It's summer and I am sitting in the kitchen filling out paperwork for college. Supper is on the stove—the sun is streaming through the window. My dad is just in from work, smelling like sawdust and tool grease. He sits down and asks what I am doing, then very casually replies, "Women don't belong in college. You will fail."

"You don't belong."

I am walking through the mall dressed in a Sid and Nancy t-shirt deliberately torn and held together by safety pins, a pink spiked bracelet, and a leather jacket with band names painted all over it. A woman and her children walk towards me. Her son smiles as they approach. The woman pulls her son close and they veer to avoid me. She whispers, "Stay away from people like that."

"You don't belong."

All of these moments played out in my mind like a movie. I felt like I'd just been hit by a truck. I started sobbing and wasn't sure what to do as she told me to just be with the process for a minute. My head was spinning and I thought, *I'm super self-assured. I believe I can do anything. This is crazy. This is just wrong... this is not the truth.*

She asked me to share what was happening and I started to talk. I told her about the flood of memories and their primary message: *"You don't belong."* I can't remember what her response was, but I do remember my reaction—total disbelief. I was stunned, scared, and completely and utterly spent.

There were only a few minutes left for our call. I tried to calm down, yet I was still shaking and crying. I couldn't seem to catch my breath. I tried to let what had happened sink in, and I heard her tell me we were late and we would have to call back in to the main room. I hung up. *I don't have to call back,* I thought as I dialed the number back into class.

I knew Coach Dave was talking, but I heard nothing he was saying until he asked, "Does anyone want to share?" I'm not even sure why I started talking because I felt so vulnerable. To try and keep myself from crying in front of the whole class, I clenched my fists and dug my nails into the palms of my hands as I began to speak. I had to tell them. I needed someone to know what had just happened because as soon as I hung up the phone I would be on my own with all of this, which made me feel really odd and exposed.

I cried as I told them how I had lived with the inner belief "I don't belong" for most of my life. I opened up to everyone, sharing the belief that had both wildly limited me yet also oddly empowered me for most of my life.

I have no memory of the rest of class, just a sense of me being in a place of utter surprise. Class ended and I sat there quietly for a long time. I felt paralyzed. *Could this really be true? My life has always been about individuality, possibility, and strength. Is this really the belief that has been driving me the entire time?*

Over the next few days, things started to make more sense for me. I thought about grade school and how quiet I was—I did everything possible to blend in. I never wanted to bring attention to the fact that I didn't belong, so I quietly hid in the shadows.

In sixth grade, as I sat next to my best friend, our teacher, Mr. Massimini, asked for suggestions for our class project. My inner belief of not belonging ran so deep I couldn't raise my hand. Instead, I whispered my idea to Beth and she raised hers. Mr. Massimini looked me directly in the eye and said, "If you have an idea to share, Deanna, it should come from you." With that statement, he changed everything.

Suddenly, I did have a voice and I wanted to share it with the world. My thoughts and ideas were valuable, and I no longer wanted to be silent. But there it was again—strong and pervasive—I don't belong. It was a part of the very core of who I was. I went from shy wallflower to the exact opposite—outgoing, boisterous, and rebellious. I became a rebel without a cause. I grew up in a rural area with quiet farms and quiet people, and I became the opposite—very loud in both action and appearance.

I dyed my hair magenta, put on a zebra-striped shirt, some combat boots, and a leather jacket. In my town, no one looked like me—I went from being quiet, so as not to attract attention, to proclaiming as loudly as possible to everyone that **I did *not* belong!**

I was in a constant state of flux between proving I didn't belong and wanting to find acceptance, so I found a tribe to fit into—the art and music community. It seemed the perfect place for me, in the company of many others who were also part of the same rebellious movement. Yet even within groups of seemingly like-minded individuals, I still found ways to keep myself separate.

In art school, I refused to choose a major, which was how students normally formed meaningful connection. I wavered back and forth between painting, photography, and design, never quite committing and never quite fitting in, always emphasizing the ways I was different from my peers. Even in the music scene, I had a difficult time being part of the cohesive group and I always gravitated to the outsiders so I could remain separate. If my crowd chose a super grungy rock 'n roll look, I threw on a big floppy hat, baby doll dress, and a peace sign necklace so that I never really belonged.

Each time the message "you don't belong" was communicated, I embraced it even more deeply. Subconsciously, I had stepped into the belief and made it part of who I was and then set about to prove it to people each and every day. I adopted this belief and ran full steam ahead—shouting at the top of my lungs, "I do not belong!" Punk rock Deanna, rock 'n roll Deanna, art school Deanna—all the aspects of me that I thought proclaimed my uniqueness were in actuality declarations of "I don't belong." Awareness came as the result of a phone call, and over the course of the days following that class, the subconscious patterns of my life continued to reveal themselves more fully.

On the phone that night, when I learned that not belonging had been an underlying thread for much of my life, everything changed. It was an instantaneous and sustainable change that continued to unfold over time. As I peeled back the many layers of not belonging, more truths about who I really am became apparent. I was desperate to understand and uncover my "becomings" in a lifetime built on separation. Who had I *become* because of this belief—not in spite of it, but because of it?

I became a strong-minded woman—a woman who believes in all things possible. I am a creative powerhouse who can always think outside the box and a coach who is able to bring about mindset change because I lived outside of convention my whole life. I've learned to pay attention to what no one else notices, and I see possibility where most do not.

Stepping into the beautiful perfection of my not belonging was powerful. My strengths came out of my life experience. Embracing judgment-free awareness allowed me to move from that tearful night of overwhelm to this place where I now feel strong and assertive about who I am. I believe that my "becomings" were an important step in a whole new level of self-awareness.

It's been a few years since that moment, and I've since created a new pattern of my own making, a powerful pattern of I *belong wherever I choose to belong.* As a result, life is different and much more open to possibility. I feel extremely fortunate. So many people never fully embrace all of who they are. Now I see the power behind all my life experience—this is profound and life-changing.

And yet, the message of not belonging is still there, dormant but ready to return at any moment. When the opportunity to become the general manager of CoachVille was offered, I said yes without thinking twice. It was a goal I had set for myself after my very first class, so I was thrilled to be offered the position. As soon as I hung up the phone, BAM! The fear started to creep in. The inner voices started to scream, "YOU DON'T BELONG!!!" I was driving and had to pull off the highway. I put my head down on the steering wheel and sat there. As cars flew by, I thought, *What have I done? I can't do this! I don't belong in a leadership position!* Then the new me, the one who gained so much awareness during that phone call years prior, the one who did belong, spoke louder. *Wait a minute. I do belong and I do want this.* "I am a leader! I do belong!"

That was the first significant moment of change—the "not

belonging" voices spoke but I spoke louder. After that moment, awareness came faster, but the truth is each time I step outside of my comfort zone, it all surfaces again. In response, I acknowledge the old pattern, see possibility, and make the conscious choice to belong. Fortunately as I grow, awareness comes more quickly and I gain more power in my life.

Recently, I was invited to attend a weeklong conference by one of the leaders of an organization that sends students to our school. I was about to meet a large group of students in person for the first time, which brought my older inner belief back with a vengeance. As I pulled up to the conference hotel I thought, *I need to get to that registration desk fast. Run to the elevator quickly, find my room, and shut the door so that I will not see any students.*

My plan was to order room service, watch a movie, and stay safe and quiet in my room until Monday morning when my boss Dave was due to arrive. I turned on the television, and the hotel station announced a pre-registration for the conference that evening. I stood there and stared at the television thinking, *No one told me about the pre-registration. No one knows I know—I don't have to go. I can stay in my room, hide, and no one will know the difference.* Instantly, my hands became cold and clammy. My stomach started to churn and deep inside, "I don't belong" started to gain foothold. I sat down on the bed, laughed, and thought, *Is this really happening again?*

I took a deep breath, opened my door, walked out into the hallway and down to that pre-registration. I introduced myself to many of the students, had wonderful conversations, and really connected with the group. The rest of the week was extraordinary because I felt I belonged—I was part of the team.

Learning about this underlying belief was important, but remaining judgment-free has been even more significant. Instead of looking back and lamenting about the past, it has been extremely powerful to honor who I've become because of the old belief. "You don't belong" served me well, as I am an inspired, unique coach with a creative mindset and an authentic, unique view of the world. My successes have come from my "becomings," who I become because of this belief. Now that I am more aware of my inner voices and patterns, I choose where and how to belong in each situation. I recognize that my vulnerability makes me a better person, and I feel eternally grateful for all that has happened.

I have always been a woman of possibility, but now I understand that looking back in blame or anger limits in ways I never fully embraced before. The experiences, though hard, were truly a wondrous gift. Those remembered moments were painful pieces of my past and have become the defining moments that made me who I am today—an authentic, creative, funky woman with a strong sense of belonging and a mad desire to change the world!

Deanna Stull, PCC is a coach, author, speaker, and the general manager of CoachVille. Educated first in art, then in life, and now in coaching, her years of experience walking the talk and her 20+ years of business development provide an enormous box of tools to draw from. She honestly believes the answer to every "Do you think I can?" question is "YES... if you really want it!" She is eternally grateful to CoachVille and Dave Buck for the class that changed everything—Inner Freedom. She hopes to inspire women to find their inner freedom and authentic voice with her coaching practice. www.LuminousLife.com or Deanna@LuminousLife.com.

THE LAW OF MARVIN

Jennifer Lewis

My cat, Junior, with me almost 18 years, is dying. I'm watching him get weaker each day, his illness taking him farther and farther away from me, his death inevitable despite my best caretaking. My mother had three strokes last year and has struggled since, turning me suddenly into her parent of sorts as she deals with her first major health crisis and several hospitalizations. My older sister, a confidante and touchstone to me for many years, has just been diagnosed with breast cancer and is struggling to survive radiation and chemotherapy.

And worse than any of the rest of it, perhaps worse than anything ever before—Charlie, my lover, soulmate, partner, and best friend of almost ten years, seemed to wake up one day not long ago and simply decide he didn't want to be with me any longer. Before I could understand, much less accept what was happening, he was gone. First emotionally, then physically, gone.

Driving to my apartment one night recently, I fell into mental autopilot and drove to our former address. On the land where our cozy, white, two-story rental once stood there was nothing to see but dark blankness. The house where we made our home and family together for so long had been taken down. The lot looked huge, like the black emptiness left when a tooth falls out.

A friend tells me not to repeat a list of these awful events in my mind. "It will only bring you down," she says, after hearing my litany one afternoon on the phone." *Bring* me down? I almost laugh. I can't imagine I could descend any further. Indeed, I try not to think in these terms, afraid to provoke the universe into another laugh at my expense.

The truth is, I find my list strangely comforting. It helps me to explain, to codify, the emptiness and pain that dominate my heart right now. If I don't remember these events and how they have all happened within a short space of time, I am inclined to think each day that how I feel now is all there is, that this darkness is permanent, and finally, that there really *isn't* much of a reason to stick around on this particular planet.

Which brings me to the story of Marvin...

One sweltering, summer, North Carolina evening, when Charlie and I had first moved in together, I stopped to gas up at a convenience store, on my way to an appointment. When I walked in to pay, I noticed a large gray-and-white tomcat pacing beside the store. The dusty wiregrass-covered area where he'd apparently been living was a minefield of empty milk cartons, cellophane Nab cracker packages, and tinned meat cans. Refuse from meals people had fashioned for him out of convenience store fare—small offerings of compassion and connection, but each one isolated and brief. It looked as if he'd been there for some time.

I asked the cashier if he'd noticed the stray cat outside. "Yep, he showed up awhile back," he said, "seems OK though, people are feeding him."

Stepping back into the heat, I returned to the side of the store. The cat, a large-boned male, was skinny and jittery; his taut face reminded me of the exhausted tension that people living on the street exhibit. But he walked right up to me and meowed, trusting me to scratch and pet him. In fact, he seemed more in need of this affection than of the food I'd bought him. Over and over he returned to me, butting his head against my knee as I squatted beside him.

I began to feel sad about leaving him there. I knew that cats are not as independent and solitary as most people believe and stray cats actually lead a miserable life, scraping by and suffering from loneliness as any other homeless creature does.

I tried to get myself to let it go. As usual, I'd been in a hurry to get somewhere when I'd stopped. Did *I* really have to be the one to take some extra step beyond spending a bit of change to keep him going? Did it have to be me to get involved, to take him somewhere he might stand a chance of being adopted? No, I decided, it didn't *have* to be me—nevertheless, it was *going* to be me.

I called home to Charlie for reinforcements, and a half hour later he arrived with a cat carrier. Since we already had two cats, my plan was to take the stray to the shelter where he'd be safe for a few weeks until I could find a home for him.

Just after dark, we delivered the cat to the night deposit box at the shelter nearest our home. On the way there I named him Marvin, after "Starvin' Marvin," the store where I'd found him. I was already doubtful about whether I'd done the right thing; he'd been none too happy to be contained in the carrier and looked nervous when we left him. I told myself that slowly starving to death on convenience store food had to be a worse fate than a limited time in an animal shelter.

But when we returned to check on Marvin the next morning we heard bad news—the shelter could only keep strays for five days before euthanizing them. Suddenly, I had a short amount of time to find a home for an older, male cat—not an easy task. To make matters worse, a volunteer wondered aloud whether we should have taken Marvin to a facility closer to where I had found him, one where his former owners would be more likely to look. This had not occurred to me in the drama of the night before, and to move him again seemed cruel. We had a moment of hope when the woman at the desk remembered some people who had been in a while back, looking for a grown male tabby like Marvin, but when she pulled the record, it was not a match.

For the next few days, Charlie and I made it a point to visit Marvin every evening. But with each passing day, all three of us felt a little worse. Marvin, it seemed, *had* preferred living alone and hungry outside as opposed to being well-fed, but in a cage surrounded by frightened, lonely animals. Each day he looked worse and worse, and each day he ate less and less, until on the fourth evening he lay in the cage with his back to us when we arrived. He appeared to have no intention of ever getting up again.

The shelter staff wondered if he might be sick. But I feared his spirit had been broken by my misguided attempt to "save" him. Had I actually made his life worse by taking him from the store? I knew we would take him in if we had to, but our own two cats were still adjusting to one another. The last thing we needed was another distressed animal added to the mix.

On the fifth day, we arrived at the shelter to find Marvin's cage empty. My throat tight, I walked up to the desk, terrified he had taken a turn for the worse in the night and died—or worse, that we had somehow gotten the euthanasia date wrong.

The desk attendant looked Marvin up by his assigned number in the files and turned to us matter-of-factly.

"His owners claimed him," she said. "They came in this morning."

Charlie and I looked at each other, astonished. How had this happened? There had been no matches for Marvin. But the night before, a volunteer had ended up with time on his hands. Like us, he had noticed that Marvin was polydactyl, sporting an extra toe on each paw, and he remembered a couple coming in many weeks before, looking for such a cat, lost during a move. By cross-referencing and sorting only the polydactyl records, he had found a matching report. The couple was thrilled when he called; Marvin *was* their cat, lost months ago. They had given him up for gone. Now, he'd made it home to them.

Charlie and I had been around and around in our conversations, rehearsing various possible grim outcomes and discussing strategies to deal with them. But in the end, the least likely, most wonderful, and most unexpected thing had occurred.

All the way home from the shelter that day we talked about how we needed to remember this. Ever after, when things looked bleak and unsolvable, Charlie and I would remind one another, "Don't forget *The Law of Marvin*. Good things can happen unexpectedly too."

Now, years later from the night I first found Marvin, I sit alone on my apartment porch and let these memories drift around me, ghostlike, in the late evening air of a very different summer.

Junior, my beautiful, old, cat friend—and one of the last links to my former life, my home, and little family—sits calmly near me. He appears to be unaware, or at least unconcerned, that he is slowly dying. Because of his sweet, calm, and patient nature, I've always considered him a few lifetimes ahead of me, somehow more evolved. The thought of losing his gentle form and presence in my life fills me with sadness and dread.

Still, he is here now and seems to be enjoying the deepening night. I see his ears revolving to pick up tiny sounds. I know that where I am beginning to see darkness, he can see detail, and I wonder what scents he is taking in on the breeze that barely shifts his whiskers.

Soon, it will be time to coax him to eat some dinner, his appetite ruined from his illness. Lately, I've been feeding him anything he will eat on clean, white china saucers with golden trim, the faded but still colorful flower patterns on them seem appropriate—special dishes for the last weeks of his life.

Looking at Junior in the twilight, I think again of Marvin. Then I remember how I met Charlie, who I shared many shining years with, at a time in my life when I had become convinced that I would always be alone.

I think of my sister telling me how the long, lonely drive to her radiation sessions unexpectedly reunited her with certain music she hadn't listened to in almost thirty years. How these rediscovered songs, so deeply engrained in her from an earlier time, helped sustain her on these frightening commutes.

I see how my mother's recent time in the hospital has allowed me a way to express the love and loyalty I feel for her, despite our many clashes.

None of these thoughts takes all my pain away; it is far deeper than that. And it's not that I imagine that everything has happened "for the best." No, that's not what comes to me in this moment.

It has more to do with poking a hole in the strong, even, cloak of gloom that builds when hard things happen in a seemingly unending series. I realize then that I can no more know what brilliant, light, and lovely things are in store for me than I could have predicted the dire events that have darkened these last two years.

As I stand up to go inside, I see Charlie's face and hear him say, "Sometimes wonderful things happen unexpectedly too."

I am remembering The Law of Marvin.

Postscript from the Present:

I wrote The Law of Marvin over eight years ago now and find myself again in need of remembering its message. While my sister has miraculously survived not one, but *two*, series of treatments for metastatic liver cancer (most certainly an example of *The Law*... at work)—my involvement with my mother's situation had only just begun.

During these more recent years, serving as the primary familial support person for my mother—as she transitioned from independence, through numerous blows to her health and related hospitalizations, to finally having to leave her home of 50 years—has been one of the hardest things I've ever done. In large part, this has been because I have borne witness to how agonizing this decline has been for her. An especially difficult evolution has been my slow and tortuous acceptance that I never have been, or will be, able to heal another, but can bring only small offerings of compassion and connection.

Perhaps, like my mentor who guided me to the opportunity to submit a chapter to this series, the chance for me to contribute has come at the perfect time. Working with the tale of Marvin once again, I have been reminded that I must take what comfort and sustenance I can from remembering that, although the future is unknown—sometimes wonderful things happen unexpectedly too.

Jennifer (Jenny) Lewis lives and writes in the Chapel Hill/Carrboro area of North Carolina. Always attracted to the written word, she insisted on learning to read at three years old and completed a novelette at the age of 12. In recent years, she has primarily written short, nonfiction pieces. Almost never without a cat in her life, Jenny now enjoys the company of her first female feline, Rudy Willow. You can reach Jenny at: jlew11x11@gmail.com.

HIGH AT FIFTY

Liz Hafer

Living life and embracing adventure across the globe would make celebrating the half-century mark an extraordinarily epic event, wouldn't it? After celebrating my 49th birthday, I had a year to consider that question and the possibilities. What type of experience would touch my soul as I pondered the future and relived the memories of the past?

Reflecting on my many remote and exotic travels around the world, the images that kept coming back were the landscapes of the mighty Himalayas. Hiking mile after mile along the rocky terrain, passing through villages perched at 14,000 feet, trudging up the steep 18,000-foot passes, winds blowing the brightly colored prayer flags as each summit was reached. This was a simple existence with nothing to distract me except the question, "Who am I?" Such experiences invite the question.

What if I gathered a group of friends to share a trek in the Himalayas and celebrate my 50th year? It most certainly would be epic! Two-and-a-half weeks of pushing physically and mentally to the edges of self-imposed limits. An opportunity to drill into the deepest core of being and to discover that which is waiting to be unveiled. What could be better than the opportunity to sleep in a small but cozy two-person tent, trek for ten days without running water or a shower, and trudge up four 17,000-foot Himalayan passes?

I longed to share this journey with others—an experience that had touched me deeply each and every time I witnessed the wonder of the Himalayas. But who would be up for such a commitment? This wasn't a cruise ship experience where you pack your bag and prepare yourself for relaxation and island hopping. A trek in the Himalayas would require a minimum of eight months of physical and mental conditioning. And it wouldn't be easy. Workouts and preparation would become an integral part of life as each day would bring us closer to the time of our departure.

I realized that if I was to make it happen, I needed to get a move on it. Summer is the best season to trek in the Ladakh region of the Himalayas, and this was going to be our destination. Just west of Tibet in Northern India lies a high desert plateau of such beauty, it takes my breath away just thinking about it. I first traveled to this spectacular area five years earlier, and it was tugging at my heart to return for another adventure.

I wasn't exactly sure who or how many friends would jump at this opportunity, but I had a colorful combination of friends as possibilities. The group of candidates included those who had trekked with me in the past along with college buddies who I thought were unlikely to commit. I wanted to put the invitation out to them anyway.

In the end, there were nine of us in total—Ramona, my life partner; Cindy and Pan who had trekked with us five years earlier; Lynda, a good friend from our Wisdom Community; and Christine, Molly, Jen, and Maureen from my old college days. I was so grateful and honored by their commitment. It was a blend of spirits coming together—a small group that I hoped would connect deeply during our time together.

December was soon upon us, which meant we had seven months left to prepare. The challenge of physically conditioning for 17,000-foot peaks when living at sea level was a major undertaking. Since all but four of us were at sea level, it was critical to engage in a combination of cardio and endurance training to build up the body. This, of course, was only a guarantee that one might make it through the entire trek. By no means, was it a guarantee that our trek would be a leisurely walk in the park. It is impossible to imagine just exactly what will be required until you actually lace up those hiking boots and begin the steady climb to a distant Himalayan pass. All I could do was support the process by keeping everyone on a regimented fitness plan and help with the gear preparations that would keep us comfortable.

As we approached our departure date in late June, the anticipation was growing exponentially. Regular communications engaged all of us from coast to coast as our group bonded across the country. Conditioning kicked into fifth gear and gathering our gear became a flurry of phone calls as we wondered how we could possibly fit everything into the initially large but "growing smaller by the day" duffle bags. It would all seem so insignificant when we finally rendezvoused in the Delhi airport as we awaited our flight to Leh.

Our gathering point was in Delhi for a short overnight before our early morning flight. As we each arrived, we greeted old friends and began the process of making new ones. Our group had come together with anticipation and excitement that was no less than incredible.

Leaving the air-conditioned airport, we were immediately engulfed by the heat and humidity of Delhi. Crowded streets were filled with honking cars, billowing black clouds of exhaust from Tuk Tuks, along with oxen-drawn wagons and the occasional sacred cow roaming aimlessly in search of non-existent scraps of food.

Those of us who had not yet witnessed Delhi on a past trip were awestruck and wide-eyed. For the rest of us, we felt we'd come home. And being surrounded with this incredible group of women, about to embark on a journey of a lifetime, I had never felt so excited. We were all together as a group for the first time and this dream adventure had become "real."

The next morning we arrived at the domestic airport for our flight to Leh. The high mountain gateway to the Himalayas sits at 11,500 feet. This would be our home for the next three days as we acclimatized before heading out on our trek. Our only real objective during this time was to rest, hydrate, and enjoy the many colorful sites of Leh. This isolated town, virtually cut off from travel during the harsh Himalayan winters, was just beginning to show signs of life as the Ladakhis filled the streets and trekkers arrived from all parts of the world. Storefronts began to reopen and displayed their wares for the short season that would support families through the long winter months.

Each day became a bit easier to breathe the high mountain air. We took in the beautiful green of the early summer countryside along with the majesty of the many ancient monasteries. We spent hours visiting with one another as we began to share our deepest fears about what lie ahead on this journey.

June 30th was Day One, and we headed out to begin our trek. Last-minute preparations had us taking things in and out of our duffels and backpacks as we tried to make those eleventh-hour decisions about what we thought we could live without. Once on the road, we began our journey with a terrifying three-hour drive up into the highest reaches of the northernmost territory of India. Narrow dirt roads were carved into the jagged mountainsides, leaving steep drop-offs into the Indus River valley far below. Our drivers, well-adjusted to this type of terrain, didn't seem to mind at all as the rest of us in our three-car caravan held on, white-knuckling in anticipation of each blind curve. We all wondered if we would actually make it to our starting point in Lamaryu.

After holding on for dear life, we rounded the last rocky curve that brought us our first glimpse of Lamaryu with its renowned ancient monastery perched high on the mountainside. We had arrived safely and were ready to hit the trail. As we unloaded our gear and loaded our packs, we could hardly believe this was it. We were going to take our first steps into the Himalayas. Our first day was just a warm-up for what was ahead—with a small pass of 13,000 feet and approximately four hours of time on the trail. We embraced each other in support of the efforts it had taken every one of us over these past months to reach this point. We were ready. Each of us settled into the steady rhythm of putting one boot in front of the other while we inhaled and exhaled, allowing our lungs to adjust to the lack of air. The day was here that all of us had spent eight months preparing for.

Up and over the mini-pass, we made it into our first camp. We had just experienced a taste of what was to come and the realization that this was going to be a big push. There is no way to prepare for this moment as the imagined becomes the actuality of the experience, in the same way it is often impossible to ready oneself for life's challenges.

I looked around at this amazing circle of women who had agreed to be a part of this feat and milestone in my life. Each woman had significant reasons for being there—each was in the midst of major life transition. Here I sat, about to turn 50 years old, surrounded by friends who were questioning what was to come next—on many levels. Breast cancer treatment, recovery from alcohol, sexual identity, divorce, empty nests, career shifts, physical abilities—each of us had a major challenge to wrestle with and would hopefully find a way to come out on the other side.

Even with our individual thoughts and the life stories we'd brought along, we were all feeling reasonably well, likely more tired from the mental anticipation than the physical demand of the day. All of us, that was, except Jen. Jen continued to experience altitude sickness just as she had since she first arrived in Leh. Severe headaches and nausea continued to beat her body down. This first day's trek had been short and at a relatively low altitude. If she weren't able to build her strength back, it would be impossible for her to continue. How do you tell someone who has prepared for eight months that the best bet would be for her to return to Leh and not continue with the group?

I struggled through the night, contemplating what would be best for Jen and the group. By morning, I knew in my heart that I needed to give Jen an "out" and allow her to decide. We were at the only camp that was accessible by road, and she could be picked up and taken back to Leh to rest. She could rejoin the group on our rest day halfway into the trek where we would be resupplied.

Our tight-knit group was extremely emotional as we said our goodbyes to Jen, knowing that it could happen to any of us at any time. As we headed out to tackle Day Two, all of us felt a tremendous loss in leaving Jen behind. Once we hit the trail, we also knew there would be no turning back. Each of us dug into the depths of our souls, believing that we would make it through the next five days before reaching our rest point where we would reconnect with Jen. Focusing on the trail ahead, we wound our way through the Hinju Valley with five hours of steady trekking before arriving at our camp located at the base of Konze La pass. As we reached our home for the night, our eyes couldn't help but look up towards the high 17,000-foot pass that would test our endurance the next day. But for now, we could rest, relax, and enjoy our time together. Tomorrow would be another day.

As daylight arrived, we ate a hearty hot breakfast of eggs and pancakes before gathering up our things and heading out for our third day of steady climbing to bring us to Konze La pass. I knew this day would test our stamina with an incredibly steep four-hour ascent to the top before descending for another three hours to reach our camp. Those months of walking the treadmill at increasing higher inclines would now pay off.

We naturally split into three groups as each of us moved into a pace that was comfortable. There was a steady, cold wind that pushed us to the top. Heads down, bundled in our warmest gear, we moved forward one slow step at a time, each of us lost in our own thoughts. I wondered how each of my friends was doing. What were those who had never done anything like this thinking? Were they wondering when the fun would begin and why the hell they had put themselves through this? Or were they digging deep and pushing through those internal limits to make it to the top?

I reached the summit with Ramona and Christine as Pan and Cindy, who had been the first to arrive, greeted us with big smiles. Hugs of celebration and high fives of accomplishment were exchanged. We hunkered down against the giant rock cairn as the brightly colored prayer flags fluttered against the fierce winds at the top of the pass. Then the five of us cheered Molly, Maureen, and Lynda through the endless last hundred feet to the summit. They arrived with tears in their eyes, standing in a moment of silence, taking in the valley we had traveled below, and looking beyond to the magnificent range that would frame our descent into camp. Stunned by this unimaginable scene, Molly captured it perfectly by simply saying, "It's all so beautiful."

Our gift to leave at the summit was our own set of brightly colored prayer flags. We signed our names on the flags along with those who silently journeyed with each of us along the way as a testament to our accomplishment. We acknowledged our dear friend Jen back in Leh who was with us in spirit. The prayer flags whipped in the powerful wind, sending our prayers into the mighty Himalayas. Our journey together began eight months earlier, but this was truly my culmination of bliss. We were standing on top of the world. We had done it—together! Looking out across the expanse beyond this first pass to those summits awaiting us, we now sensed we could do anything. With fierce determination and moving forward just one step at a time, life's challenges were just another summit to be conquered.

Liz Hafer is Chief Adventure Officer at Corporate Teams (www. CorporateTeams.com) providing outdoor teambuilding experiences to corporate teams and leaders. In addition, Liz is Chief Adventurer of Soul Adventures (www.SoulAdventures.org) leading travelers on transformational trips to the remote reaches of the globe. Liz's passion is to provide individuals the opportunity to tap into their inner resources and explore the bounds of their physical, mental, emotional, and spiritual being. Whether or not it is with a corporate group or a team of excited travelers, Liz pushes the preconceived limits that each of us hold and helps transition to the next level of awareness.

Relationships

MEMORIES
OF A DISTANT SUMMER

Olivia Pohl

My body was a container. Fireworks of emotion were fighting to burst out, but the lid was sealed shut for my own safety. I wanted to miss him, to let the emotions out, but I had to stay sane. We weren't right together. The dance we used to do side-by-side felt disjunctive and wrong.

The feelings threatening to escape could slowly kill a person if not handled correctly. I was afraid for myself, but also for him. I knew he was feeling the same way, only ten times worse. All I wanted to do was comfort him. I wanted to tell him how special he was every moment of the day and put together the broken pieces of his soul. The only trouble was that I'd been the one to shatter it.

He was my dream guy—perfect smile and beautiful blue eyes. He was tall and athletic; basically, the kind of guy all the girls eyed and never thought they would end up with. I'd never had a boyfriend or even encountered someone of the opposite sex I wanted to talk to as badly as I did him. When I finally did, every word seemed to be weighed down by an elephant of pressure to impress. It was impossible to have a normal conversation without an eruption of nervous, flirty laughter. I never thought someone like him would go for a girl like me. I had watched him from afar for two years, two years of wanting to approach him but holding back. It was not until the summer after high school graduation that I finally opened up, with just three months left before each of us headed off to college.

When I was in middle school I had been the queen of crushes. I "fell" for a guy almost immediately upon seeing him, while he never knew I existed. I let my imagination run wild, buying into the Romeo and Juliet notion of love at first sight. Once in high school, I could at least spot that train coming and stop myself from falling before I started. However, what hadn't changed was my shy, middle-school girl attitude that assumed every male on the planet was a hot jock with a jackass personality. My expectations about him were swayed by these long-held beliefs.

But he turned out to be different. And during those three months, my opinion of him changed exponentially. He was sensitive, he was passionate about everything he did, and he always found ways to be active. It had been years since I'd spent much time outdoors during summers. He saved me from my normal sluggish state where I sat wrapped in the world's modern technology without the mental motivation to go out and see new things.

He loved photography and showed me some of what he enjoyed through his photos. We walked to the wetlands behind his house and took pictures of unappreciated slices of nature. He also loved to learn about other cultures. He used to speak to me in French and would tell me that he wanted to live there some day despite the fact that he had a broken bank account. He was working to build it up.

I am embarrassed to say that at the time working was something foreign to me. I liked to consider my feeble babysitting job...well, a job. But the truth is I had never done anything where I had to show up consistently. I would opt out of babysitting frequently to go on vacation or hang out with friends, yet I called myself dedicated.

He worked for more important reasons—to pay for college and live out his dreams. And he loved his work. He talked about it all the time and made cleaning tables and grilling meat sound exciting. He also made me want to learn about every aspect of his life, such as the fact that he had lived in China when he was younger or that he had two small dogs he loved tremendously.

He thirsted for originality. His biggest fear in life was to be predictable. He was afraid people wouldn't find him unique. He loved it when I said his humor was unparalleled to anything I had ever heard before. For him, it was the highest form of compliment. But above all else, his ability to forgo judgment in almost any situation was something I'd never seen replicated in anyone before I met him. No normal high school student was able to go a day without talking about someone behind their back. However, I barely heard him talk about anyone the entire time we were in high school.

He was the first person who really held me. It is hard to believe, but as a result of being the touchy-feely equivalent to an unfriendly porcupine, I hadn't been held by someone since I was a little girl. Yet, it felt safe in his arms—a haven I longed for whenever I was away. I had never shared that kind of physical relationship with someone before. It is funny looking back through all the great times we shared to realize some of the times I miss most were when we just lay there saying nothing and he held me. The comfort I felt in his arms made it easier for me to say "I love you" to him.

Those three words had almost been taboo in my middle years. I think I recall saying it when I was very young, but my parents said it to me so much over the years that eventually the words "love you" simply became an automatic response to any family member. I never placed the word "I" in front or initiated saying it to anyone because after so many automatic responses it became unnatural.

Loving him made me realize that perhaps before him, I had lost the appreciation I once had for my family. Unconditional love can be wonderful yet dangerous. If you know that someone will love you unconditionally it is possible to stop giving your love. You know that no matter how you treat them they will always love you. Being with him reminded me that love is an act. It is a verb. If someone loves you, you have to love them back. It takes some investment, but in the end it is worth the effort.

I soaked in everything during those three months—the times we spent together, the experiences we shared, and all I learned from him. I spent a lot of time marveling at life. I thought the summer we'd had together would be enough as I prepared to go away to school. Sadly, reality proved different. The last night before I left for college, I cried like I never had before. Having to say goodbye to someone I loved so much without the promise of ever seeing him again was overwhelming.

But now I know. Parting to go to college did not mean our connection had to break. I could continue to see him. We could continue to spend time together. It was not until I broke things off permanently that he was truly gone.

During our first year of college, we talked almost every day.

We saw one another over breaks and briefly went back to that amazing summer before we parted. Early on, I had many sleepless nights and was consumed by the paranoia that he would start dating someone else. I wanted to stop caring so much—to stop the desperate longing for his presence. In my attempt at self-protection, I convinced myself I no longer loved him and didn't have any remaining feelings. Thinking how good independent life would be, I broke it off with him forever.

After the breakup, the truth set in. I actually cared about him more than I'd imagined. I had freed myself from paranoia, worry, loneliness, and fear; however, I realized I'd lost more than I'd gained. I no longer had my best friend.

When my friends get broken up with, they usually come calling on me and ask things like, "Wasn't he such an asshole?" I always agree with them, whether or not their ex did anything wrong. I know they are dying inside and grasping at that idea as a mechanism to rationalize their feelings. I know having everyone else agree that "he was an asshole" will eventually convince them he was.

That is why I found it especially difficult being on the other side, being the one to do the "breaking up." There is no one to support you. You are the bitch. You are the brokenhearted without the benefit of friends by your side who truly understand why you are upset. And…someone you once loved with all your heart can only think of you negatively. It is a lonely and frightening situation to withstand.

I went through stages of great struggle. At first I tried to keep myself busy. The day I broke up with him I found out I'd been wrong. I did have a heart. A heart that controlled my head beyond what society deems acceptable. I became depressed. I used my work and petty errands as weapons to cope. As long as I was doing something I didn't have to feel the pain for a while. Any time I was alone, however, I got distracted. I wanted to concentrate on myself, but my mind would wander to that numb place in my heart and I would become incapacitated by overflowing tears. Sometimes I cried without apparent reason. That is when it started to scare me. I didn't want my emotions to control my life.

I began seeing a therapist who gave me tools to clear my

mind. Not necessarily to make me instantaneously happy, but just to have moments of relief. I talked and cried to her, trying to use up all my tears before I got home. When I did get home and felt tears coming, I went into my room and performed the rituals she had taught me. I tapped on my temple, tapped on my wrist, and recited mantras to make myself feel better. Eventually, the moments of relief grew longer. I was able to go into long, empty periods before I felt the swell of tears again. Then I moved on to my hibernation stage.

Like a bear, I curled up and fell asleep whenever I felt the winter coming on. I didn't allow the desolate feeling to envelop me. It crept up on me less than in the beginning, and I began to know and feel when its presence was seeping in. At first I tried to push it back. The feeling would come, and I would literally use physical strength to retract it. In the hibernation stage, however, I tried to avoid my feelings rather than resist them completely. Whenever I felt the impending infiltration of emotion, I went to sleep. In sleep, I thought nothing could touch me. What sleep did provide was a reprieve, as well as a means of surrendering to that which I couldn't keep away, and a time to rebuild.

Ultimately, the day arrived when I woke up from my hibernation and recognized something was different—something had changed. I sensed a strength within that I did not recognize. I started to listen. I began to truly invest myself in the moment. And I used everything I had learned from him to my advantage.

I established my own gardening company. Through hard work and dedication, I found joy in my own accomplishments— internal joy that sprang up from within me. I purged my life of dramatic people who talked badly behind other people's backs. I started to feel normal again and became an even better version of myself. I still thought about him, but the memories were more fond and easier to talk about. Then came the first day I didn't look at old pictures of us, the first week I went without tears, the first month I went into a cosmetics store and didn't spray his cologne, and the first time I didn't think about him at all.

The fireworks had exploded and they broke me open. They pushed at the walls of my psyche until I reached the brink of collapse. I was exhausted from trying to fight them. Instead of working to create more walls, I allowed my emotions to burst forth.

Memories are powerful. They can cause great pain, but they can also create great strength. I now see the dazzling display of who I am and the brilliant spectacle of who I am becoming. I'm not going to lie, there are times when the sadness comes back, but I now have the tools to transform those feelings and find the good instead. Those feelings that nearly crush you can end up being the best tools you have to thrive in life.

Olivia Pohl grew up in Santa Barbara, California. When she was 14 she moved to Dayton, Ohio, where she attended Miami Valley High School. Throughout her years in school she always enjoyed reading and writing. She has begun writing a few novels of her own in her spare time, and she plans to complete one by the time she graduates from Elon University in North Carolina, where she is now a sophomore.

MS. CHARLOTTE AND HER "WEB"
– A LIVING TRIBUTE

Wendie Batterson

She's "no bigger than a New York minute," as the saying goes. And yes, she was raised in upstate New York, near the small town of Franklin. She turned 90 last September (2011), and she reminds me of the "Energizer Bunny" who just keeps on going and going and going! She is an amazing woman and this is part of her story—a story that I am writing to honor her and thank her for being one of the women who has made such a difference in my life and taught me so many wonderful lessons.

I often refer to her as being my very own guardian angel and have known her now for over 40 years, from the time just before her oldest son and I got married. She remains a constant and incredible teacher and mentor, not only to me, but to so many others who have become part of her "web."

Being the next to youngest of 11 children, she grew up on a farm that her widowed mom maintained by herself, which in part explains her "can do" attitude. Her mom must have been quite a woman raising all of those kids, most of them by herself, while keeping the farm running at the same time! I really don't know much about "Gram," other than she must have been quite a role model of strength, courage, and a will to live and survive— some traits that Ms. Charlotte inherited, absorbed into her belief system, and then demonstrated throughout her life.

After growing up on the farm, Charlotte got married during WWII and then went to nursing school in New York City. She and Bill were high school sweethearts, and he deployed for Germany immediately after they got married—a fairly common occurrence in wartime. Charlotte became a registered nurse and continued that career until she "retired." After Bill returned home from the war, they had three children in rapid succession, with only about five years between the oldest and youngest. She balanced a career and motherhood long before the rest of us even figured out that attempting to do that was, at best, overwhelming!

285

Bill was in the Signals Corps during the war and eventually became an air traffic controller with what is now the FAA. At that time, the early 1950s, it was apparently necessary to move to other locations around the country, either to get promoted or for more responsible jobs, so they moved constantly while their kids were growing up. I've lost count of how many times exactly, since they all have a different version, but the number is somewhere between 18 and 30! And, they went all over the country, from the East to West Coasts and many places in between.

In most cases, these transfers meant that Bill needed to be at his new job immediately, which in turn meant that Charlotte was responsible for "packing up and moving out"—all the belongings, the kids, the dogs, and whatever else needed to be uprooted. And, this happened time after time after time—they all became "los vagabundos." Charlotte, the "working RN mom," changed jobs and hospitals every time they moved, which also meant different places, different houses, different jobs for both of them, and different schools and activities for the kids.

Being flexible and adaptable are just two of Charlotte's greatest traits. It's hard to imagine how difficult it must have been to keep moving constantly, and especially during a time when the majority of American families lived in one place for a lifetime. Yes, she was way ahead of her time in many ways, and that is just another example—the word "trooper" describes her perfectly. She also has always seemed to have that wonderful gift of looking at most situations and finding the positive side of whatever life presents. This is just one important lesson that I have learned from her.

She has been an incredible guiding force for our kids as well—we have a daughter and son, Shayne and Cayce, who are now fully grown. Charlotte and Bill were avid campers when their own kids were growing up, and they owned just about every make and model of camper that ever existed on this planet! Even after they both retired in their 50s, they became wagon masters for RV caravans to Alaska and Mexico and continued to camp, travel, and be "vagabundos"!

When our kids were growing up, we all spent many special times with them—on camping trips, fishing, hiking, and just hanging out in nature together. Bill died from cancer in 1992, and

Charlotte continued to take the kids on camping trips by herself, creating more and more wonderful memories. This has also been another important lesson for me—that time spent together, making memories, is really what counts in life.

Above all, Charlotte has been and is a caregiver. After she "retired," she became a "volunteer with a vengeance" and helped charities and people wherever they lived. She took care of Bill when he was sick with cancer and she then took care of his mom, whose name was Rose. Rose was a pistol—I called her "Rosie," the grandkids called her "Grandma Great."

Both Rosie and Bill were characters, and neither one was exactly what I would call "an easy keeper." It's a family joke that Charlotte probably deserved a Purple Heart just for taking care of those two, but then she's taken care of many others as well. She volunteered and helped so many that she set an all-time record in the last place she lived. The Senior Center gave her an Outstanding Contribution Award for being the "volunteer with the most hours—ever"! Another lesson learned—to be of service to others helps us all learn that to give is to receive.

Things were clicking along pretty well in Charlotte's life until the day of her accident. She lived in a little apartment in the small town close to us, but she was always at our house—gardening, planting flowers, and tending to her little patch of vegetables that she loved to "putter" around in. She came over that day, bringing a flat of flowers to plant, and parked her car in our driveway as always. We aren't exactly sure what happened, but we've pieced the sequence of events together as best we could. I was out of town at the time, and my husband, "Bat," was doing repair work on our deck.

The flat of flowers was in the backseat of her car, and when she got out and into the backseat, the car started to move backwards down the slight curvy incline. What we think happened was that the car wasn't completely in "Park," and she got stuck in the backseat as the car drifted. Then, the car door knocked her down and dragged her as it gained momentum, going backwards across the sloped driveway toward the barn. The thought of her being pulled down and dragged through gravel that far still makes me cringe even today. "Bat" saw the car moving and immediately ran over—he saw her on the ground, thought she'd had a heart attack, and called 911.

Charlotte was in the ICU for more than three months following the accident, and it was a continuous daily "touch and go" situation. She contracted ARDS, a respiratory syndrome that usually causes the other organs in the body to shut down. We, as a family, had several conversations about what to do, and there were times when we were almost at the point of "pulling the plug," or at least we prepared ourselves to do that. We all knew that our Charlotte would not want to live that way, nor be a burden to anyone. But of course, we were talking about Charlotte the Trooper, the Energizer Bunny, the "I Don't Give Up" person, Charlotte the positive energy and spirit.

After a very long three months, she pulled out of the trauma, the induced coma, and ARDS, and then went on to months and months of varying levels of rehabilitation. It was a miracle on many levels—but the real miracle was that she continued to work hard, get stronger, and stay positive. Another important life lesson—it's all about your attitude!

There was only one time when she headed "south" on me— Charlotte and I are very close and we've always talked about anything and everything. One day, she got frustrated with the pain in her hip and pelvis, where the car had rolled over her. She looked at me, a bit teary, and said, "You know, I should've just died." I took one look at her and said, "You know, Toots, you're the spiritual one here, so I guess you aren't quite done yet. You obviously have more work to do, so guess you get to stay here for a while longer. And, oh by the way, you never finished folding the laundry at my house the day of the accident either, so you better cowgirl up!"

We both immediately went into one of those belly laughs that simultaneously takes your breath away and makes you cry— and that was the end of the "road south" for her, at least with me anyway. At the time of the accident, she was 70-something. Perhaps a mutual lesson? I think so—that there is a humorous side to any situation—sometimes you have to look hard, but it's always there.

Fast forward to a couple of years ago. She volunteered at hospice, several programs at the Senior Center, and also with me at one of the care centers, helping with the Alzheimer Association's

"Memories in the Making" art program. This program helps Alzheimer patients "remember" memories through painting with watercolors. Because we worked together on this program, I got to observe and watch her in action. She taught me so much about compassion and about how to take the time to actively listen to each one of these afflicted, special "artists." She was literally "hell on wheels" as she met their needs, held their hands, and attentively listened to whatever "memories" they could begin to share. Her hearing had almost totally diminished to the point of being deaf, but it didn't seem to matter. She was a total inspiration to all of us—she heard with her heart! What an incredible lesson I learned about listening and being present for others!

At 87-ish, she decided to put herself into an Assisted Living facility, to give up driving before she became a threat to anyone else, and to move to Billings where she could afford the facility and be close to her daughter and family. So, once again, she sold and disposed of whatever she had that she couldn't take with her and was "on the road." This was a huge and difficult decision that involved a ton of changes—a new place, new friends, new state, new everything, and no car.

We, meaning my immediate family, were devastated when she left—she had been with us for almost 15 years, and her absence left a huge void. The people and her friends in our community were amazed that she would do this at her age—pulling up roots and moving on once again! She had made a commitment to herself that she would not be a burden to her children and, by God, she made sure that she kept that commitment! Some more lessons— change is inevitable, so embrace it and keep your commitments.

Fast forward to today. She is now 90-something, living happily in her Assisted Living residence and has a wonderful new group of new friends. She has terrible osteoporosis, which gives her a lot of pain as her bones become more and more brittle every day, and her old injuries, hip replacements, and countless broken bones are now arthritic and hurt a lot. Yet, she is now working in the daycare service of her complex—she holds and loves the babies and reads stories to the "munchkins" whenever she can.

She gets on the computer at the complex, sends emails to her friends and gets online to research whatever interests her. She is not only an avid reader but a dedicated student and keeps her mind alive by being so active. She loves to play games and has a couple of favorites—she also learned how to be a "master cheater" from her mentor, "Rosie aka Grandma Great." She is an absolute hoot when she gets caught cheating and will deny it to the bitter end! She "boot scoots" around the halls with her walker, going at least one or two miles each day for exercise, and she goes on almost every outing that is offered. In fact, she was featured in a recent article when she caught the biggest fish at a nearby lake!

Our son, Cayce, got married this past summer in Costa Rica to a wonderful young woman named Staci. Charlotte was a bit hesitant to go this "destination wedding," especially after her last trip there when she fell, broke her hip, and had to have a hip replacement in a Costa Rican hospital. I called her and asked her to wait until we got closer to the actual date to make her decision. Well, she mulled it over and made her decision—there was no way in hell she was going to miss this celebration! She made that very long trip, had a total blast with all her own and "adopted" grandkids, and even boogied with her walker at the reception. She certainly "cut the mustard" that night, becoming the "dance floor darling." Another lesson? Yep! Stay young at heart by "keepin' on," being active, and by being a constant student of life.

So, how should I describe Charlotte? A web of positive energy? A love force? An angel in disguise? I can't decide, but it really doesn't matter. She's made a difference in so many lives, and yet she is incredibly humble and probably clueless about the extent of her "web" of influence over her lifetime. She is a living, breathing example of what love is, what love means, and what love can be. She constantly gives to everyone around her and is a bundle of gratitude and positive attitude to boot! I have learned so much from just being in and around her presence, and I'm sure that I am just one of the many who feel that way.

So, thank you, Ms. Charlotte, for being you and for the legacy that you will leave for all of us who have known you—to be the best each of us can be, to choose to have a positive attitude, to be grateful, and to "keep on keepin' on" when life gets difficult, hard, and even overwhelming.

And, from me to you, my dearest Charlotte, thanks for being my incredibly special teacher and my very own "guardian angel"!

Wendie has been a teacher in some way, shape or form most of her life—with experience teaching French and English in the public school system, teaching English to Spanish nationals while living in Madrid, and working in corporate America for years in Training and Organizational Development. She has had her own consulting business for over 15 years and holds a B.A. in French, English, and Education, an M.A. in Counseling, and a second M.A., with a double major, in Management and Human Relations. She and her husband "Bat" have been married for almost 40 years and live in Franktown, near Denver. They have a grown daughter and son and daughter-in-law, Shayne, Cayce and Staci, who also live in the Denver Metro area. They are a family of animal lovers and have had horses, dogs, cats, and wayward critters forever! She volunteers with Horseback Miracles, Inc., a life values equine therapy program for "at risk" adolescent girls from local residential treatment centers as well as with the Alzheimer's Association "Memories in the Making" art program.

LAURA'S JOURNEY

Barbara Thompson-Glatter

Laura and Lisa, more like sisters then mother and daughter, shared a unique relationship into which I landed professionally. Laura—some twenty years my senior—and her daughter Lisa—nearly that many years my junior—hold a very special place in my heart as a result of what evolved between us.

Lisa called me in a panic. "Mom's kidney is shutting down! The doctor gives her one to seven days. How long does she have, really?"

For years I'd broken a massage therapist's Cardinal Rule. Well actually, the number one rule is: never date your client. I merely made one of them a friend. Laura, my friend and client for more than ten years, had been in, though mostly out of, a cancerous state for the past seven. She would hear none of my professional protests on keeping a discrete distance. Everyone was her friend. Period.

So, when kidney cancer was diagnosed, I continued working with her every week after the operation. And when it returned in her lungs three years later, we worked together through the chemo process and the deplorable state experimental drugs left her body in. We prayed and cried and loved each other while doing what I could to alleviate her pain. And when she finished all those rounds and her body began to heal, we continued working and sharing our lives.

"Oh Lisa!" I shuddered. *Mumble something about traffic,* I thought, though the darkened suburban street was nearly empty at that hour. "Please, give me a moment. I need to pull over," I told her. To myself, I commanded, *"Breathe, Barbara!"* Pulling my car into a deserted Lowes parking lot, I wondered ruefully if they had any tools to fix this. No, I'd need to rely on the skills developed through prayer, meditation, and devoted study of various forms of Energy Medicine. But, could I achieve adequate perspective?

The cancer had returned. This time in her spine and before

Laura could be accepted for a robotic operation, another spot was found in her brain. Seven years she'd faced this possibility and seven years she'd laughed at the doctors' prognosis that she wouldn't last three.

This past year my support had shifted slightly from mother to daughter. I'd added Laura's daughter Lisa to my list of weekly massage clients and of course we were now friends too. In addition, Lisa and I explored subtle realms of healing. We had deep philosophical discussions about energetic imbalances, family histories, and karma. We added various forms of what might be called Energy Medicine to her massage sessions, and I taught her ways to work with Light whenever fear reappeared.

I took another deep breath. Lisa's question filled me with dread. It didn't matter. I'd supposedly prepared for this moment. I felt like a boxer's Everlast bag that's been socked in the stomach with a resounding Whomph! I allowed myself to feel shock, grief, and despair, and then watched as they passed through me. I prepared to do the work I'd trained to do, connecting energetically with people and assisting with their healing agenda. Only Laura wouldn't let me connect. I asked for and received an energetic gift from God. OK, check again. Again, "no" was Laura's response. "OK", I said, trying to avoid feeling as panicky as Laura's daughter sounded, "Let's try this."

I offered Laura an energetic gift, which I sensed she'd accept, and again asked permission to connect. *Halleluiah, she agreed!* With a sigh of relief, I felt myself hurrying before she changed her mind. "OK Lisa, she's ready now." My voice sounded more assured than I felt. "I get yes. She's leaving form soon." I tested, listened, repeated back to Laura what I heard and then conveyed this back to her daughter, "Yes, she is ready to go, but no, she doesn't want to."

"Should I tell my brother? I mean, why upset him if there is nothing he can do?" Lisa asked.

"Yes, call your brother, let him help you."

Lisa was doubtful but then asked, "Does she want me to spend the night?"

"Yes, she wants you to spend the night with her tonight. That feels clear. But she reiterates, call your brother too." And that was all she allowed for one night.

Regretfully, I disconnected from Laura and then hung up with Lisa, promising to be at the hospital the following afternoon. I sobbed all night with the pain of losing my friend and the feeling of powerlessness. *What good is having all these skills to reshape energy patterns if I can't even save my own friend?*

The next day, following directions from the nurse's station, I passed by an elderly woman held limply upright in a wheelchair's safety straps. Desperately, she tried to move forward while completely unaware she was actually pushing herself backward into a wall. I commiserated with her for a moment and watched the nurses slowly shake their heads, indicating not to interfere. I left, but not before wishing her well.

Whispering in the doorway of her mom's hospital room, Lisa and I gazed unbelievingly at Laura's peaches and cream complexion that glowed beneath the baby-blue chenille blanket. Vital signs were good. Heart rate, respiration, blood oxygen levels, all normal. She looked ready to order a four-course meal, but she'd taken no nourishment for three days. How could she be dying? It was hard to fathom she was even sick!

In a soft voice Laura's daughter asked, "Will you check in with her? Is there anything you can do?" *Oh,* I wondered to myself, *is it ethical to do this again without Laura's expressed, verbal permission?* Voicing my concern, Lisa laughed, "When has Mom ever let anyone do anything to her she didn't want?" I smiled. She was right, but I still wondered how objective I could be while loving them both so much.

"How about outside, on that cute little bench under the trees?" I suggested. We both squeezed Laura's hand and Lisa kissed her brow.

Over the years, different trainings have taught me much about the mutable nature of energy. Aromatherapy showed how effective plants' essences are. Feng Shui demonstrated how the arrangement and selection of items have definite effects on many levels of our being. Psych-K™ taught how thoughts impact one's life experience and how easy changing a belief can be. Holistic Kinesiology trained me in how to connect and test (directly or indirectly) any substance, memory, or conceptuality for its strengthening characteristics on the physical level and/or the seven subtle bodies. Flowtrician coached me in how to be a proverbial doorman; connecting Divine Wisdom with another person on a treatment table and then allowing for their process. And still I study and practice with the intention to discern wisdom, gleaning as much as I can, practicing wherever it feels appropriate.

We sat on the creaky, paint-chipped bench, tears continuing to moisten our cheeks, sunshine peeking through the autumn leaves. I began the process of clearing myself and the adjoining field of Awareness. I shook off memories of long evenings together, the cute stuffed animals Laura gave my grandchildren each Christmas. I abandoned agony and side-stepped the growing desire to do something to stop her dying. *Am I able to let her choose? Can I love Laura AND her choices?*

Laura's daughter wanted to know what her mother's concerns were, and it did seem Laura wanted reassurances. We went through them one by one.

No, the estate will not be held up in probate. Yes, Lisa will be fine after Laura leaves. Laura's daughter described her plans to join their church's childcare program on Sunday. I also spent time being a liaison between Laura and her two cats, Sky and Amigo. I connected their fields of energy and saw Laura sitting in her favorite armchair with both cats in her lap but facing away from each other, like a feline Yin/Yang symbol. Sky was petted with Laura's left hand and Amigo was enjoying a tummy rub with her right.

Lisa laughed when I described the scene. "Yes of course," she said. "When they share Mom's lap, they always lay that way. Neither one likes facing the other!" I finished the dialogue, feeling complete for the evening. Lisa went home for some quality sleep. We agreed to call the next day, Saturday.

"Mom came to me in my dream last night. She demanded to know why the lights were off in her house. Barbara, the electricity is on, what does she mean?" Lisa was beside herself trying to understand her mom's message. Lisa took her mother literally, but I understood it from an energetic point of view. Laura's house, i.e., her physical body, had shut down. Laura's spirit didn't know what to do.

Again, I found myself talking with Lisa while driving home and wondered what on earth to say. I listened while she described details of the dream. And then Lisa did something my teacher told me would happen, but I hadn't believed him. *Your client will provide you with the answer they need.*

Lisa said her mother walked down a long dark hallway with lots of doors on either side. This is exactly what I needed! I recounted for her my first experience with my own energetic house and its long dark hallway, about exploring some of those rooms and how after I'd completed some chakra exercises, the next time I went into my house, the hallway was lit up like a sparkler. I went on to describe the spiral staircase at the end of the hallway and about having an angelic encounter at the top of the stairs.

Encouraging Lisa, I suggested, "Your mother seems lost. She needs to go where the Light is. Give yourself a message tonight before you fall asleep. Tell your mom to climb the spiral staircase and look for the Light."

Lisa agreed but then asked some tough questions. *What is it to be alive? What is quality of life? Would her mother want to be alive even if it meant being on dialysis? Are we, the doctors and hospice nurses, keeping her sedated when she is ready to be up and about? Would she want to be alive if it meant being like that frantic woman in the hospital's hallway unaware of her surroundings?*

I feel heartsick. I didn't have any answers. What I did have was love, and I reassured Lisa and her brother to keep asking these questions of each other. "I'm so very proud of you both. To examine life, Laura's life, in this context demonstrates great compassion." We agreed to meet at church the following morning.

Sunday morning, driving back into the city, I found myself going over the past few days. *What had I missed? I didn't hear any more questions from Laura and yet she hadn't made her transition. Did it have something to do with her house being dark? Does she not know the way?*

Returning to the soul level mind-state, I found Laura's house still dark with Laura prattling around inside. I "imaged" for her a heavy-duty, camping-style flashlight with a handle on top. This neon yellow flashlight was also equipped with a small blue LED flashing like a beacon. *There, that ought to do it,* I told myself. Still driving, I suspected it was not a good idea to soul surf while operating a car on the interstate.

Lisa and I met at our usual spot and I sat quietly, struggling over the ethical nature of doing work for someone you love. I prayed for guidance. The choir director began a simple chant. The lyrics appeared on the screen overhead.

Come, Spirit flow through me
As I open up to be
An expression of
Your Eternal Love.

Come, Spirit flow through me
As I open up to be
An expression of
Your Eternal Peace.[1]

We sang it three times through and by the end all resistance to working with Laura had evaporated. I peaked in on her progress during the opening meditation. The flashlight was on but she hadn't found the stairs yet. *What to do?* Spirit somehow knew, and I entered into my Light Body to be a beacon and positioned myself at the top of the spiral staircase in her house.

It's odd to me, this person who frequently questions self-motivation, that while in this energetic state I never question anything nor entertain ethical arguments. I don't even ask if any of this is possible or if it will help. It's just simply: Do This Now.

I came back in awareness in time to sing another song, listening to announcements. The view of the creek outside the nearest window was lovely that morning.

Checking in again, Laura was at the top of the stairs now, but the doors were closed. I telepathically communicated, *"The angels are on the other side of those doors."* And smiling, I went back in awareness to the church, letting Laura decide. I knew she wanted this freedom and I needed to let go of wanting to choose for her.

It was near the end of the sermon when I checked one last time. Laura was not on the landing and the doors were open. *Oh! She's with the angels! Well good, she found them.* And with that, I left that mind-space having no idea what her choice would be, nor

1. Eddie Watkins, Jr., Director of Musical Ministries; The Center for Spiritual Living, *"Spirit Flow,"* Music and Lyrics. Contact information for Mr. Watkins: http://www.eddiewatkinsjr.com/ The Center for Spiritual Living, 5801 Sand Point Way NE, Seattle, WA 98105; 206-527-8801.

did I have a need to know. I'd been through those doors and back again. They go both ways.

After the collection, I headed out for work just before the closing song. The eleven o'clock service had run long and I needed to get going. I felt so grateful for this time and community of loving beings that supported this work. I had a sense of peace.

Work was slow that afternoon, but I managed to keep busy with cleaning projects and long-range plans. At two I checked my phone. Lisa had called at 12:31 and again at 12:38 but left no message either time. Briskly, I walked outside to ring her back. The hospital had called. Laura passed right before I left church.

Sadness welled up. My friend had gone. And as sometimes is the case, responsibility felt overwhelming; mental wonderment and emotional guilt wafted through me. *She stayed with the angels! And I, or some aspect of this self, showed her the way!* It took most of the week to allow the mystical miracle to sink in.

While in my Light Body, I feel completely natural, nothing unusual about it. There's a quality of familiarity, too, like I come from there. Agenda-less, no desire to "get things right." No need to know what's next. Being-ness is not only enough, it's Enchanting! These kinds of experiences have become a part of this lifetime.

I stayed awake long into the night writing and wondering, *How can this be?* And then, its corollary, *Of course! How could I have missed it before?*

Laura's children are both doing very well. We check in frequently and I work with Lisa whenever I'm back in town.

What an amazing journey! Laura's persistent optimism carried me through many disquieting moments. I learned how to love her in many capacities; as a therapist yes, but also as her daughter and as her mother too. I watched my own she-bear reactions well up with each new doctor's suggested round treatment. I also learned Laura's style of quiet grace as she first struggled then accepted difficult news and how she always celebrated each effort no matter how minuscule. But the greatest gift I learned was how to employ Love's highest form: allowing. I learned how to allow Laura to choose. Thank you, Laura, for being my best friend and one of my best teachers.

Barbara Thompson-Glatter resides in Colorado and is sifting through the jovial sea of possibility. She has written extensively on the topic of personal and soul development and is exploring publishing venues. She has an article for Bridges Magazine published by ISSSEEM summer 2009. More of her work is coming to Kindle, so keep checking back. Barbara enjoys folk dancing, photography, gardening, Nature hikes, international music and her beautiful grandchildren. She extends a heartfelt thank you to all the teachers and guides who have generously shared their amazing gifts. For more information about Barbara, please visit: www.dancingchi.com; http://dancingch@blogspot.com/; BarbaraT@dancinghchi.com; 720-839-9473.

SECRET TRUTHS
TO MANIFEST TRUE LOVE

Lorii Abela

Nothing comes about by chance. Everything happens for a reason. Somehow, consciously or unconsciously, I have asked; the answer comes eventually, whether I like it or not. These are some of the truths I have learned through the course of my life thus far. Searching for my soulmate has taught me these truths and many more.

In my 40's I sought and wondered where my soulmate could be. I had ventured everywhere looking for him; love seemed aloof. And because I had this quest lingering in my mind, the Universe secretly continued to weave the path which would ultimately unite us. As the Universe has its own timeframe, however, patience was necessary. The Universe works in its own mysterious ways, and I had no say—it was frustrating at times to not be able to make things happen.

When I first landed in the Financial Capital of the World—New York—in 1998, I came looking for a greener pasture. It was a whole new arena to explore—the people, food, culture, lifestyle, and not to mention the dating world. Coming from an Asian country, the Western approach to dating was a real culture shock for me.

In the Philippines, people generally meet through family, friends, work, school, church, or other organizations. Men usually woo women, and it takes some time before a woman agrees to have a relationship. For some, the parents' agreement is also necessary. Therefore, the man not only has to please the woman but her family as well. In the Philippines, the process of finding one's "life partner" has a prescribed methodology, and Filipinos all know how it works.

Almost everything was new to me in New York. It was quite overwhelming to learn the dating practices and protocols in this land of opportunity. I had to discover things such as speed dating, writing and answering personals in different media (newspapers, magazines, and telepersonals), along with navigating online dating sites. I also had to learn how to relate to straightforward Americans and figure out how things were done in my newly-embraced home. Above all else, I had to learn to *do as the Americans do.*

Among my five girlfriends, who were all new to the U.S., I wondered how on earth they each *quickly* got "happily married." Two of my friends were hiking buddies and another had been a contemporary in a leadership training organization back in the Philippines. I'd met the other two in New York. I had recruited all of these women to work for the same telecommunications company where I worked.

With the exception of one, each met her husband through me. The exception was the last to get married. She met her husband online about six years after she came to the United States—she was also the one who moved quickest from dating to marrying. One of my friends met her husband-to-be almost a week after I recruited her and she'd moved to New York. I literally introduced another to her future husband, thinking they would be a good match. Still another met her husband-to-be when I told her to come to a weekend trade exhibit we were holding. The last met hers during a white river rafting trip I invited her to join me on.

I wondered how they were all married and I *still* was not. After all, I was the most adventurous among my friends and the one willing to try almost anything. And I'd had even more dates than any of them! It started to sink in that even though I had met a number of men *it was obviously not a numbers game.*

In 2006, with nothing much to lose, I packed my stuff, said goodbye to my girlfriends, and drove from the east coast to the Midwest—specifically Chicago—Illinois, for a life change. I'd had enough of a fast-paced environment and I did not want to grow old quickly in the rat race of New York. Chicago appeared as a mini-Manhattan—all the happenings were there, but on a smaller scale. There was also an Old World charm, like the canals of Europe.

When I'd previously visited Chicago with a group of New Yorkers, I noticed a difference in the way people behaved too. For instance, when one of my New Yorker pals screamed at the top of her lungs as she inched her way to be in the next batch that entered the King Tut exhibit in Chicago, the woman at the counter spoke to her in a very calm manner. It surprised all of us. It was very alien to not hear a thunder of rebuttal at my friend's behavior. Not only were people friendlier in Chicago, they were also more family oriented. I thought to myself that maybe I would get lucky in this amazing city and find my soulmate.

Little did I know that after moving to a different city, I would soon discover new truths to help me manifest my true love. Spirituality opened its door for me when I became a keen believer in the Law of Attraction. Like many others, I first learned about the Law of Attraction when Oprah interviewed James Arthur Ray on national television. I'd known about it before because of a seminar I attended eight years earlier, prior to coming to the U.S.; however, it was not called the Law of Attraction in that course. It had been referred to as "science of the mind," "synchronicity," and "positive thinking." As a result of that seminar, I manifested coming to the U.S. six months after I took the course. To test what I'd previously learned, I made up my mind to apply the Law of Attraction to the manifestation of my soulmate.

By nature, I like to spend time evaluating my life. I realized that if I wanted to manifest my soulmate, I couldn't forever think there was something strange about me. I can't pinpoint exactly what my old story was, but somehow I knew I enjoyed my adventures in meeting new men and getting their attention; however, that seemed to be keeping me stuck in "dating mode." I began to understand that if my friends could find their soulmates, it could happen to me, too. The world has an abundance of men who are capable of loving me and vice versa. The belief that all the good men were taken was not true—I had to change that story as well.

In any given moment, the inescapable fact is that whatever is happening is the consequence of my thoughts. Fortunately or unfortunately, it also applied to the story of my romantic relationships. As a result of these realizations, I knew I needed to change my thoughts and my story. I understood that positive thoughts would create a positive result.

I began to apply certain principles, thoughts, and beliefs to my life, which included the following:

What I resist persists. I discovered that pushing generated more resistance. I stopped resisting the question, "Why am I still single?" I quit focusing on the lack of someone special in my life.

I deserve happiness. Like everyone on this planet, I breathe the same air and have the same vision for this journey—to be happy. If I am happy, everyone around me will sense it. I therefore started to practice smiling meditations and became attractive by default. It was surprising to see who smiled back and what impact I was able to make on others.

My past is a part of history. Whatever I've experienced in the past makes no difference in the present moment. What makes a difference is the value I place on it. Instead of dwelling in my mind, I tried to live in my heart. I de-cluttered my apartment of everything that would not serve my future. I let go of possessions that were associated with pain, unworthiness, and other negative vibes.

Close first to open a new relationship. Closing my previous relationships was nerve-wracking; I had never before "done a closure." It is not a common practice in the Philippines. Usually people part ways with angst and nothing more. Being vulnerable to close relationships was uncomfortable, but it gave me freedom from past pain.

Most of my past relationships were from my native land. While attending a course on how to manifest a soulmate, I was assigned homework related to closure. Surprisingly, my phone rang and it was my ex-boyfriend from the Philippines whom I hadn't seen for almost eight years. He called to meet up with me while he was visiting a friend in Chicago. Although I never expected the Law of Attraction to be that powerful, I thought, *How cool is this? Homework completed!*

I followed a specific pattern when I talked to him. I thanked him for the time we'd had together. I apologized for whatever pain I'd caused him. I expressed how bad I felt for things he'd done when we were together and forgave him for the heartache he'd caused. Lastly, I wished him well—it was humbling and liberating all at the same time.

Live as if my mate is present now. I've heard a million times that practice makes perfect. I started conversing with "him" in my head as if he were already there. He became a part of my daily life. I wrote personal notes to him. I thought about the affectionate name I would call him and what he would call me. I was preparing for his coming. I saved a space for him in my bed even before we met and reserved a towel and toothbrush for him too.

Define myself and learn to love me. Who shall I be when I meet my true love? I had to cleanse my energy and get ready for the transformation. I prepared myself for my soulmate by doing inner healing. I did this by changing my thoughts, believing in and loving myself, and making sure that closures had been completed. I cleared all my junk and baggage inside and out. I accounted for all aspects of my being, including the physical, mental, emotional, and spiritual.

I asked myself whether I was the person my true love would want. Was I happy with the person I was? I took care of myself and recognized that when I was happy with myself, only then would I attract my true love. I would not appear to be in a state of desperation and neediness—it was time to step out of victimhood.

I knew I would catch the attention of a person who mirrored me. So, I worked on transforming myself in the ways I wanted to be mirrored. I developed myself to be the kind of person that I wanted to attract. I took pleasure in reading, taking myself to multi-cultural events, and traveling. I noticed that my vibration always came into play. If I felt low, I had to elevate myself from negative to positive feelings. I needed to take action only when I felt great, which usually brought about good results.

I learned that even when I stayed close to home, the Universe provided for me according to what I was looking for. It's how the Law of Attraction works. My soulmate could be anyone—my neighbor, co-worker, a friend of my best friend, or a client whose attention I caught by chance. I wouldn't know if someone was the right person for me unless I opened up to the opportunity.

Wait and expect without being obsessed. While I got on with day-to-day activities, attended social get-togethers, and even networking, I kept in mind that being there did not mean I was seriously looking for my soulmate. As a matter of fact, I tried not to give it any thought whatsoever. My intent was to simply have fun at these events. I surrendered my quest.

Take inspired action. When I least expected it, my soulmate came into my life. I took inspired action by meeting Jerome, a male friend, for some drinks with a group of his friends. I had another event that I'd been invited to. However, I was more inclined to meet Jerome. Somehow, the Universe was directing me towards that encounter.

Though I do not drink alcohol, I decided to go. There were two men and two women in the party along with my friend. The women left early, and I had the chance for more conversation with the men. That night, I met Jerome's friend, Domingo. He pretty much fit what was on my wish list except he wore a beard (I've never been attracted to men with facial hair). After that night we hung out together as friends on weekends. Eventually, I noticed that he was becoming romantic. I asked him what he wanted and he said he was interested in a relationship. Had I not gone to meet Jerome, we might never have met.

What I have asked for will come. It's similar to placing an order in a restaurant—I don't have to keep annoying the waiter to serve my order. I know without any doubt that the Universe will pave the way for my order to be served according to my wishes.

I'd made a list of what I wanted in a relationship and what I expected from a soulmate. I used a vision board to help me manifest my soulmate more easily. While I worked with my vision board, I also worked on my mind and emotions, preparing myself to manifest true love.

I can still remember what my vision board looked like. I had cut out an image of a couple kissing in the rain. Then, I added the crucial essentials to my relationship, including Honesty, Trust, Commitment, and Happiness. Being a travel enthusiast, I also included these phrases: "Going global. Two tickets…one trip."

My vision board was strategically placed in my closet. I could see it every day as I dressed. I gave myself up to the concept that eventually he'd appear. It was a leap of faith, but since I was able to manifest things like parking spaces in the city, why couldn't I manifest a soulmate?

Soon enough, thanks to that evening with Jerome, Domingo showed up. And…surprise, surprise! I pretty much got what I asked for and then some! Having someone who liked to travel was very important to me since I travel frequently. I truly wanted my soulmate to love traveling as much as I do. This was a huge bonus for me. During our first year as a couple, we traveled together to 10 different places. We both enjoyed the trips, including the planning and preparations. My vision board had portrayed that cherry-on-top life, and my life became exactly what I had envisioned it to be.

Domingo and I have common core values such as family, travel, curiosity about many things, diversity, friendship, and love of life. His mother came from Puerto Rico shortly after we were officially together to visit him and meet me. He got to meet a relative of mine for the first time when we visited a cousin in Florida. We went to Puerto Rico for Christmas. Close to our first year anniversary, we traveled to the Philippines for a visit so my family could meet him. We became inseparable.

As the Law of Attraction proves time and again, my true love came when I least expected it—at an unsuspecting time, occasion, and place. The when, where, and how were never my business. There was no need to rush or push. The Universe provides in due time. My main responsibility, like everyone else's, was simply to be happy at all times and align my vibrations to Source. I loosened up and allowed the Universe to work its magic for me. Once I let go of trying to make things happen, they did.

Although I met my soulmate in my 40's, much later than I originally desired for myself, I can say it was worth the wait. Trusting that my soulmate was also waiting and searching for me took a leap of faith. It is said that what you think and believe becomes your reality. I left behind any doubt in the guidance of the Universe; my faith in it became stronger. When I was ready and in alignment with what I desired, Domingo and I crossed paths. The Universe conspired. It was our new beginning.

Lorii Abela is a multi-awarded international leader, coach, speaker, author, and manifesting expert on the Law of Attraction for Love. She found her soulmate using the methods and principles she describes in her book Top Secrets to Manifest True Love. *She has also authored,* Take the Guesswork Out of Finding a Boyfriend, Do You Make These Common Mistakes?, Top Secrets to Manifest True Love, *and numerous articles on love and cross-cultural dating. If you like her story or for more help finding your soulmate and manifesting your own destiny, please visit www.manifestingmydestiny.com.*

INSPIRED TO INSPIRE

Sara Hopley Boatz

Have you ever met someone who you thought really needed your help, only to discover you received much more than you gave? That happened to me recently, and it has changed my life. It all began the day I turned 49 years old—one year away from the big 5-0.

Reaching this age made me take a long hard look at myself, and I had to admit, I felt good about everything I had accomplished so far. Then, in the same breath, I found myself asking, "So, now what?" I had met or was close to meeting all the goals I had set for myself. *What else was left? Was this as good as it gets?* I think I began to experience a mid-life crisis. I said to myself, "Who am I now and what do I want? There has to be more."

It was time for a reinvention. I had spent my career helping companies, leaders, and teams create strategic plans to take them to the next level. So I asked, "Why can't I do that for me?" I took myself through the planning process that so many of my clients have had success with. I was able to articulate some personal dreams and create a plan with a new set of goals to take me to that next level. The hard part was keeping myself motivated to follow through.

I decided that I needed to start with something physical, so I signed up to work with a personal fitness trainer. I wanted someone who would keep me motivated and help me move toward some of these new goals. I started just one month into this "50 is coming" thing and was assigned to work with Eddie as my trainer.

Eddie was unexpected. What I saw was not what I got. And, what I ended up getting out of it was much more than I'd anticipated. Dark eyes, a heavy brow, and built like a brick shithouse, the first day I met him he kind of scared me. This guy was, upon first impression, a good-looking, young beef-cake, body-builder type. He was the ultimate athlete that was going to HATE training someone who was far from that description. It looked like he was perfect and had everything together. So, I braced myself for a quiet, intimidating first session. And, while it did start off pretty quiet, it turned out that he was anything BUT intimidating.

Eddie watched intently and listened as he put me through some torturous exercises. Then, he spoke. In just one-half of a training session, he figured out my physical strengths and weaknesses as well as the problems I would have to overcome to meet the physical goals I'd laid out for myself. He had my attention.

It turned out to be an amazing ride because I received MUCH more than the physical training he promised. Eddie not only helped me become more physically fit, he inspired me to meet a life-changing goal—to one day write a book that would inspire others. My work with Eddie was just what I needed to make that dream a reality.

Eddie was extremely quiet and seemed pretty serious. He was very professional, wickedly smart, and exceptionally good at his craft. He fixed physical pains that had plagued me for years, enabling me to get stronger, more flexible, physically aligned, and on my way to meeting fitness goals I thought could never happen at this stage in my life.

But enough about me... Oh wait—one more thing about me. I LOVE a challenge, and through our time together, I found out Eddie was the poster boy for a challenge. His problem—low self-confidence—and that bugged me because I didn't know why. As much as he helped me physically, I felt compelled to see what I could do to pay him back by helping him. And, how convenient, because then I could focus on helping him instead of me turning 50.

Eddie was introverted and guarded. Professional to a fault, he didn't seem to be the type to let people in. To me, he seemed unhappy, moving through life on a slow-paced treadmill with little purpose. It seemed as though, among other things, he'd lost his joy for life. His lack of self-confidence didn't go with his well-sculpted physical appearance. Well, I decided I'd have none of that. I was going to bring him out of his shell and use my skills and abilities to get inside his world and make him comfortable, and hopefully, somehow more self-confident and much happier.

Eddie became my new project. (I'm sure he'd be mad at me if he knew that's how I classified him at that point.) Someone I could positively impact. But in the end, I got more out of it than he did.

He wasn't at all the hard, dark, tough guy that his exterior exuded. I did get one thing right—he was unhappy and lacked purpose and self-confidence. In my opinion, he was existing—and I had to see if there was anything I could do to change that. Over time, I gained his trust and he started confiding in me. His story was quite amazing. I won't tell it in detail because I know he didn't tell me so I could publish it for all to see, but the main points are these: He had a very hard and lonely childhood. I would characterize his early life as one filled with plenty of neglect and abuse. He didn't have parents who inspired or led him. Instead, they did things that for most would break their spirit and put them on a path resulting in another bad statistic. That's the most amazing part of his story—they couldn't break him. He was—and remains— too strong.

On his own with no parental guidance—other than an example of what NOT to be—Eddie bootstrapped his way through life and drove forward against all odds. He graduated from high school and enlisted in the military. He served in the U.S. Army as an airborne ranger for eight years, some of them on the front lines during wartime. Lord knows what he experienced there. And it gets worse. While deployed in the war, his young wife cheated on him and left, taking his only daughter, who now lives more than 1,000 miles away. He diligently pays his child support but longs to be with her to influence her and give her the love and support he never received.

To make money, Eddie got certified as a professional trainer from the National Academy of Sports Medicine in California. This certification not only taught him his career craft, it also gave him the ability to reinvent himself physically, transforming his own body from overweight and average to lean, sculpted, high-performing, and strong.

But for Eddie, that wasn't enough. Haunted by his upbringing, he was determined to get the right training to help kids not have to endure what he did and have a better life. So, he went to college and graduated with a four-year degree in psychology. He ran out of time and money to obtain the advanced degrees needed to fulfill his dream as a child psychologist (for now) and jumped on the treadmill called life that gets him from paycheck to paycheck and gives him the ability to support and stay in touch with his daughter—but that's all, at least for now.

Enter Sara Boatz.

Once I got to know Eddie, he proved to not only be a great teacher, but also quite a special guy. He taught me so much about the details of my physical abilities and inabilities. I couldn't believe it. He made me understand how things work together, why I had pain, and how to alleviate it so my body can perform the way I want it to and stay healthy. He inspired me to get on a weight loss program (down 25 pounds to date) and helped me get ready for a 10K run and then a sprint triathlon. (I used to run triathlons in my late 20's and set a goal to run one more before I left my 40's. I was about to turn 50 in just a few months. Tick tock.) His training style and technique became metaphors for many aspects of my life.

All the while Eddie was training me, I pushed him to think differently and believe in himself. As he trained me to be ready for my upcoming triathlon, I worked to build his confidence enough to take advantage of all the good that was already in him. I told him he needed to start with one single achievement. Then, one day, he surprised me.

Eddie went with me and my family to ski at Vail. Sitting at the top of Vail Mountain, he said he had made a decision to work hard to be sure people's lives were better because he was in them. He wanted to make a positive impact in people's lives and was determined to find a way to do that.

Today, he is thinking about joining the mentorship program with Big Brothers and Big Sisters of the Pikes Peak Region. He says he wants to impact a boy experiencing a similar situation as he went through, so that boy won't have to endure the same challenges. AWESOME! Who better to fill that void than someone who has been in it himself and emerged successful?

Eddie's epiphany inspired me. As I looked back over those eight months of training with him, I realized he helped me get through a very big change in my life—the "what's next" thing that many people go through at my age. When I thought I had it bad, his story reminded me that I must depend on myself and soldier through to get what I want. As he trained me, his attention to detail and demand for perfection in every exercise reminded me that staying the course, being patient, and working consistently WILL make a difference.

In my new life venture to reinvent myself, his work pushed me to strengthen and consistently lean on my core. A strong core—really knowing the details of who I am and what I am made of—gives me the foundation I need to achieve. Eddie has inspired me to keep up with the basics. Build core strength. Practice consistently. Don't cut corners. Get results.

That's all I needed to move to my next level. As I saw how I was able to encourage and help him, too, I thought I might be able to do this for other people—for a broader audience. Today I am almost finished with the book I dreamed of writing. It is called *What If? What Else? What Now? An Interactive Guide to Reinvention and Living Forward.* It is a workbook designed to walk with the reader side-by-side through exercises that inspire them to set and attain goals. The book will help the reader develop a plan and take action, enabling them to engage in life mentally, physically, and socially—to really *LIVE* life on one's own terms, the way one wants, in a manner that makes one happy and engaged in the right situations, with the right people and in the right places. To live to realize one's dreams. To live forward.

Writing this book has been a huge personal undertaking, and it has given me the confidence I needed to embark on a new career to become a professional speaker. I couldn't have figured out how to get started without the life lessons I learned from Eddie. Because of him, I truly have been inspired to inspire others.

Since this was written: As a quick update, writing and submitting this story a little over three months ago even further inspired me. Just putting this on paper got me excited about really turning on the afterburners to get my book done. And I did it! My book is now published and available for sale online. I also started marketing my book by sending out over 600 email solicitations to speak to area groups and associations and booked 5 speaking engagements in the first week! Looks like my own reinvention is working!

Sara Boatz sees things others don't or can't see. Her talent is looking at relevant information and developing solutions to issues that get her clients off the dime and moving forward in a purposeful manner. Sara turns everything on its side, looks at issues from every angle and approaches client information with a fresh perspective. She has been practicing her craft for nearly 30 years. The secret—it's all inside the client. She perfected the process for getting it articulated and analyzed, then creates the focus necessary to take action and achieve. Owner/operator of S.A.R.A.strategies, Inc., Sara enjoys an active, outdoor lifestyle with her husband and two daughters in Colorado Springs, CO.

HEART TO HEART

Carol Papini

I grew up as a Catholic, all-American Air Force brat with three brothers and parents who truly wished they had been the Kennedys, so much so that they named us after many of them. My oldest brother was named Robert F., next in line was David John; I was named Caroline Deborah, and lastly, came Michael James.

As the only girl, my three brothers thought pushing me around and playing jokes on me was the best way to pass their time. On top of that, my dad constantly yelled and my mom took the brunt of it. I grew up thinking that yelling and beating on girls was normal. This was only the beginning.

My dad told me that as his only daughter, "I will NEVER, not ever, let you marry a Native American!" He actually said an "f----- *Indian*." By the time I was 15 years old, I had met him. Yup, the boy who would later become my first husband, and yes, he was a full-blooded Native American Indian. He was also a terrifically drug-addicted and alcoholic boy who had bad habits that included beating me to a bloody pulp. My first marriage was the source of many crises including the six-month miscarriage of twin boys due to his attacks.

On our first anniversary, my husband's family and a friend came to celebrate. They chose to drink all night and wanted me to join in—I refused. I went to work early the next morning and was so upset that I wished him dead. He died that very day. There were seven people, including my husband, who died in a head-on collision. As a result, I swore I would be careful about what I said or wished for in the future. I also vowed to never remarry or ever let anyone abuse me again.

The first day I arrived in Denver I met him—a handsome, young Spanish-American man built like a rock at 6'4", 225 pounds, with me at only 5'2", 105 pounds. We were a match made

315

in heaven. John and I ended up together and had a child, but I refused to marry him.

Two years later we got the news John had "cancer" in his throat. At only 30 years old, with a family, he thought it wasn't fair and questioned why. I did everything I could to help him through his trying time but he shut me out. John proceeded to turn to alcohol for solace, drinking himself into a stupor with regularity and consistency, and started up his old habit of heavy drugs and hiding them from me.

In this altered state, he began to abuse me, something I'd sworn I would never allow to happen again. I was in disbelief that someone could abuse me yet again. All I could think was: *But now there is a child involved and the guy is sick with "cancer." Am I over-reacting? It's not that bad, is it?* My mind tried to trick me into accepting the abuse.

I had been working at a bank for a couple of years when the day came that would shift my life forever. I was asked to help out a customer with his account. The man was so thankful for my assistance that he said he owed me lunch.

I responded, "Okay, how about tomorrow?"

He replied, "Yes, I just happen to be open tomorrow. I'll pick you up."

He drove up in his 1973 Corvette. This was a car I had only dreamed about before then. He and I went to lunch that day, and what happened next was not something either of us could have ever imagined. My necklace got caught in my hair and I didn't know what to do. I struggled, trying to keep my dilemma hidden, when he asked, "Can I help you with that?" I said he could. As soon as he touched my neck, I thought I would go crazy from a feeling that was completely unfamiliar to me. All I could think was, *I'm in a relationship and happy we have a child together.* He felt it too and started babbling about how happy he was in his 16-year relationship with his best friend.

I left it at that. "It was nice to meet with you, Bill. Thanks for lunch."

"Yes, we should do it again," he responded.

"Sure," I offered, "how about next week?"

That was the start of a great friendship that would turn into much more. From the moment we met, I felt it, he felt it, and we both said to the other, "Whatever you do, don't fall in love with me. It will make things much too complicated."

Of course, that was easier said than done. We met one night for drinks and had a heart-to-heart talk. He dropped me off and said, "OK, I'm sorry, but I love you anyway." *Holy crap!* I thought. *What am I going to do now?* Of course I was fighting my own feelings too. After all, we couldn't do this because I had a family and had to keep things together, despite the abuse.

For months I fought it and pushed the feelings away, but it turned out we simply weren't able to stay away from each other. I knew I had to make some drastic changes or this would not end well. The situation presented itself one night when John was really wasted. Sensing that something was going on, he pulled out a gun and held it to my head. He was ready to kill me, our son, and himself. I pleaded for all of our lives.

I was able to reason with him and get him to give me the gun. To save us all, I suggested that we move far away to where my parents were—in Montana about 1000 miles away. Since they'd been struggling with their health, I knew they would love it if we came to help. I also believed that if I could get out of town, the feelings for Bill would go away. I just needed some time and space. I told myself it would be a good thing for the three of us to get away from all the craziness and have a fresh start and a chance to be a normal American family.

The downside was that Bill and I were heartbroken. I told myself things like, *"No, you can't do this. It isn't right. What are you thinking? You're getting in deeper and deeper. You don't deserve any better than what you have now."* I'd then get a call from Bill and we'd talk. We'd end up scheduling meetings in different places. Sometimes I would show up and sometimes not. Occasionally, I left Bill high and dry.

I remember one time when we planned to meet in Seattle and I didn't show. I was supposed to pick him up at the airport. Bill didn't know what to do. He had no one to call and wondered if something had happened to me. He was extremely distraught and decided he needed to find me. He knew I was with my family but didn't know names, numbers, or addresses. Bill, the engineer, began the daunting task of creating a plan of action. He pulled out the phone book and proceeded down the list of all ten pages of like names and contacted each person one at a time. He called for hours until he found me. I couldn't believe it! *What now and how would I explain this one?*

I thought that if we met, it would be easy. I would just let him know we could not do this anymore—we'd say our goodbyes and be done. Of course, that is not what happened. When our hearts met, we couldn't *NOT* be together! Hours later we came up for air and both realized there had to be a connection to another life that created this strong energy pull.

For the first few years I second-guessed the depth and truth of our relationship, which was interesting since he was the only one who'd never hurt me. Given my past relationships, I questioned whether this was love or addiction. I found myself asking, "Is this love or just another bad decision?" It was very confusing and hard to understand. I proceeded to push that feeling and the questions away for many years—eight long years to be exact.

Yes, Bill and I finally ended up together. It took a long time, but I know now that he is my soulmate. We met 25 years ago and have been married for 14. Over the years, Bill was a successful entrepreneur. From the time he was in his teens, he started and stopped many businesses—a restaurant and bar, gas stations, and construction of all kinds, including the tile and brickwork that were in his blood—this was what his Italian family had done for generations in Italy, New York, and Colorado.

I was pretty successful in the corporate world until I got laid off in 2005. Torn between going to work for another company and starting all over again at over 40—which made me feel sick—I decided to become a sole entrepreneur. My first businesses didn't work, and I was confused, again thinking, *What is wrong with me?* I asked for guidance from GOD after an evening of thinking it might be easier if I changed a few things in my life.

The next day a close friend called and asked me to attend a networking event at a church. I went and knew I'd come home. I sensed that the search for what I was to do in this life on earth was there. In the spiritual journey that started then—five years ago— Bill and I both went through a few years of personal development and learned more about ourselves. We even dreamed about creating a business together, a Spiritual Healing Retreat center.

318

While in meditation, we envisioned creating two centers—one in the Colorado Mountains and one at the beach in Maui (two places dear to our hearts). We weren't sure how this would or could happen, as neither of us were healers or very spiritual, but we knew that "God" had it all planned out and this must be the path. Then, the unthinkable happened.

On February 18, 2011, Bill had a massive stroke, leaving him disabled and unable to communicate. It has been hard to watch this brilliant, amazing man struggle with words he could easily use as a child. I am now Bill's only caregiver, not something either of us thought would or could happen in our amazing life together.

As I've reflected back, however, I am able to see everything God has placed so strategically in our life together, knowing that along this journey we would eventually figure it out, follow our hearts, and learn to stop trying to control our lives. Before the stroke, I'd watched Bill slowly begin to ignore and then eventually completely deny his heart. He became disconnected from himself—from his spirituality, from his heartfelt thinking. He'd taken control of his life and convinced himself that he could force things to happen. I continually asked him to pay attention to what was happening to him and his business. I repeatedly asked him whether *this* or *that* was really what he felt he should do. He was hyper-stressed, over-done, and cooking himself up with worry, fear, and plans to save *it all*!

I know his heart wasn't in what he was doing. It was just his head and ego looking for that almighty dollar. I was extremely nervous because he'd already had a heart attack in 2003 and I could see the stress building. He wasn't acting like the man I had lived with and loved for so long. He kept saying, "Just wait... things will get better! They always have and they will again!" And then Bill had his stroke.

This time, God was in control—not my strong, courageous, and noble husband. Bill and God had to come to terms with who was in charge. Bill needed to make the biggest decision of his life and the only place to make it was from his heart. Ultimately, Bill had to decide whether he was going to stick around and finish what he came here to do.

I inherently knew this...and I knew that as hard as it would be, I had to let go of him. The doctors told me he would essentially "never be the same man." During the first 96 hours, the diagnosis revolved around him surviving. After that, they began to tell me that it could take Bill as long as two years to walk with a cane. I stayed as positive as I could to keep him from falling backwards, although in the back of my mind I was thinking, *There goes our dream of having those retreat centers.*

In the first few hours after his stroke, I remember asking him, "Are you sticking around for me?" I knew I had to accept whatever was going to happen and didn't want to be a factor in Bill's choice—not that choice anyway. "Please don't," I begged him. "If you're thinking about sticking around, do it for you. I LOVE YOU!" I did love him, I do love him, and there isn't a moment in any day that I am not grateful he decided to stick around and finish his life, his purpose.

I was thinking one day about how Bill used to buy flowers and cards for me and leave them around our house. This was one of his favorite things to do. He did it *just because,* just because he wanted to show his love. Now, he sends me energetic love, and I believe that as a direct result of our deep-felt love and his inability to fully express himself, hearts are appearing everywhere. I continually ask him, "Did you do this?" and "Are you sending these hearts?" and he smiles.

There are a multitude of examples of hearts popping up; most interestingly of all are the ones on our ficus tree that a dear friend recently gave us. This tree is growing heart-shaped leaves—not just one, but many! I have researched it, and ficus trees don't normally grow leaves like that. I put pictures of these miraculous leaves on my Facebook page and on my phone's screen saver. I have also found heart shapes—without seeking them—in chips, water, clouds, duck formations, rock formations, and many other places. It's amazing and makes me ask God now, *"What else is possible?"*

I was not conscious of the fact that I'd been so divinely guided throughout my life. I used to believe that my decision-making and personal actions made me the creator of my life and that I could do it alone. That was the way I wanted it in the beginning as well as the end. I had control, or so I believed.

Sometimes I can't believe it took me so long to wake up and

really listen, to allow and know that God is with me and always has been. I now truly *listen* and *hear* what to do. I am guided, and it all starts and stops with the quality of my questions. "How does it get better than this?" and "What else is possible?" are two of my most favorite.

What a journey this has been over the last few years. I am so grateful for all the miracles I've experienced. One huge miracle is that I am still alive! My husband is still alive too and already walking with a cane, learning to talk, and doing much better than expected. We have lost many of our prize possessions, but we are surviving and thriving in ways we never did before.

Our story is a story of love and of the miracles and possibilities that become potentialities by simply coming from the heart. I'm not alone and neither is Bill. We are truly being guided. So are you. Many of us face hardships, but when we surrender to them and find the love within them, we come into the power that can redirect and transform our lives. Simply by living heart to heart…

Many know Carol Santos-Papini, as "Carol the Connector." She is a Wellness Coach and Energy Healer using Reiki and Access Consciousness tools. Carol is a certified Access Consciousness Bars Practitioner and Facilitator, working from home in Westminster, CO, which enables her to take care of her husband Bill. With Balance and Inspiration, Carol is connecting others to transform their dreams into realities. She is also writing the book many have encouraged her to do for years. The ultimate goal is to get back to the ocean to enjoy sailing and scuba diving. A dream Carol and Bill share is to open two spiritual healing retreat centers at the beach and in the Colorado Mountains. You can connect with Carol by emailing her at bcconnectedwithbalance@ gmail.com or check out her website at www.connectedwithbalance.com

PATHWAY TO COURAGE

Wanda McCormick

Imagine driving up a long, narrow hill and your stomach flips a somersault in anticipation of discovering what is on the other side. I knew life could be that kind of drive for me, but I didn't know how to get behind the wheel and take control.

"There are plenty of signposts along our path directing us to work hard, look good, make money, get married, and on and on, but there are no signs reminding us to stay connected to the essence of who we are." Agapi Stassinopoulos

I didn't have the obvious signs or someone guiding me through life and poking me on the shoulder to let me know when I'd taken a wrong turn. Sexual abuse as well as alcoholism, emotional neglect, and the feelings of abandonment were all a part of my dysfunctional world and reminiscent of memories and experiences that replayed through the years as I grew into a young adult.

Growing up, I wanted love, nurturing, and guidance but it wasn't provided by my parents. My father was an alcoholic, and he always seemed disconnected and emotionally hollow, while my mother appeared disinterested in me. My relationship with my mother died a rather slow death. I was appalled by her lack of guidance and love. I couldn't talk about how damaged I was. Frankly, most of the time, I really didn't even know how to feel. I survived on autopilot.

I saw very little intimacy between my parents. I realize how my lack of intimacy stifled and stunted my growth into a well-adjusted young woman. It took me years to work through my experiences and learn how to trust myself and my feelings. Although I realized how overwhelming my life had been, I refused to be a victim of my past. In the process, I discovered that I had extraordinary courage and strength.

Talking wasn't something we did as a family. We ignored

things. It taught me that it was okay to keep my feelings in and not talk about issues. I felt I didn't learn the appropriate should and should not's of life, because we just didn't talk about them.

Another thing we didn't talk about was my brother. In my mother's emotional absence, I spent the better part of my childhood acting like a mother to my brother. I didn't know anyone else who had a brother like mine. He was a year older than I was, but he wasn't like other big brothers. The neighborhood kids called him names and said he was "retarded." I didn't know what that meant, but I knew it was something my family didn't talk about. When I asked why he was so different, my mother would say, "We don't know," and then change the subject. Maybe this is what caused my father to detach from the family, but he wouldn't talk about it either.

I didn't have friends because other children were afraid of my brother. I was about seven years old, and my life consisted of caring for my three siblings. Since I grew up without friends, I "played" with my parents. Every weekend, my uncles came over to play cards and drink. Even as a little girl, I was allowed to stay up while they drank, smoked, and cussed until dawn. I didn't have a bedtime or rules to follow; after all, I was a "little adult." This was the life I came to know as a young child. I enjoyed staying up as late as the adults. I was given permission to feel like an adult and I did.

At other times, however, it wasn't so nice, especially when my uncles got drunk. I remember a few times during the wee hours of the morning, after most everyone left or went to bed; one of my uncles would come into my room. I could smell him before he even hit the door. He reeked of beer and cigarettes. To this day, I still can't stand that smell.

My uncle had come into my room on other nights and touched me with his big, rough hands. He did things that didn't feel right. On one occasion, however, what happened was worse. He whispered in my ear that it was going to be okay. But it wasn't. He hurt me as I lay there, crying and confused. I knew this shouldn't be happening. Was this part of being an adult? I didn't want to be an adult anymore. I wished I could have been that little girl fast asleep in her bed, but the sad part was that I didn't ever recall feeling like a little girl. I was horrified and scared. Was

I supposed to like it? I sensed it was wrong, but this was someone I had trusted and loved.

I told my mother the next morning, and she responded, "Well, it was probably because of the alcohol. He was drunk." No nurturing, holding me close, soothing my wounds, or telling me that I was going to be okay. NOTHING! She didn't say, "Honey, I'm sorry this happened to you," or "I love you and will protect you." I was too young to know that this was a prime example of a dysfunctional family.

I didn't feel my mother's love from that moment on, and I started to withdraw from her. As a child of NOT OKAY feelings, I had reached out to her for realistic reassurances and protection. My mother's response floored me, filling me with fear, anger, frustration, and bewilderment, most of which I didn't come to realize until the next time I reached out to her for help.

Fast forward to age 16 and years of playing the "little adult," with no friends, bored with school, and a guy who was 21 years old and liked me. As a child who grew up with no guidance or rules, I ended up pregnant, and that fueled my desire to change the way I would raise my children. I would be different. After all, I'd been a "little adult" for years.

I tried to tell my mother and again she provided no support and said, "Go tell your father." His response was, "You got yourself into this mess, so now you can marry him." I needed direction and found myself lost in trying to figure out my own journey through life.

I was flying by the seat of my pants, and sometimes I crashed into some pretty deep holes. I was in a relationship that was demeaning and degrading. My husband beat me and threw me down the stairs when I was pregnant and only 17 years old. I have no idea how often he cheated on me. He even tried to make me have sex with his friends. He taunted me and knew just how far he could go to stay out of jail. I tried leaving him many times, but throughout the short six years I had four daughters with him. Just like the saying, "It's cheaper to keep her," he actually caused less trouble when he was around, or so I thought.

I had to start asking myself what was enough. What was it going to take for me to stop the cycle? How much more would I put myself through before I said, "I quit"? Why didn't I love myself enough to leave? Why didn't I love my children enough? Nothing had prepared me for these life situations. I felt driven to behave in ways inconsistent with my gut instinct. I knew it felt wrong, and I wanted to act differently, but I didn't know how to take control without putting myself and the girls in danger. With each situation and each wrong choice I vowed to myself that I was changing—and I was, but just not fast enough. I knew I had to be careful or he might do something else, possibly much worse, which he finally did.

During our last separation, he had agreed to pick up the two younger girls and drop them off at daycare. He had been adhering to his agreement. This particular morning, however, was different. He left with the girls as he always did, put them into the car, but then came back upstairs. I thought he had forgotten their diaper bag or something, and I let him back in. He had other plans. He blocked me from escaping and hit me so hard I was thrown through the bedroom door. Before I realized what was about to happen and could scream, he knocked me to the bed, grabbed a pillow, and put it over my face. He raped me, and I honestly thought I was going to die that day. When he was finished with me, he left, like nothing had happened.

I called the police and reported him. He was arrested and eventually let go. Even an order of protection didn't stop him from continuing to harass me. He was one of those guys that could beat the system and get away with it. I didn't help matters by letting him back into my life, but then again, I understood and resigned myself to the fact that he was always going to be around because he was the children's father. I was humiliated and disgusted; not only by what my parents didn't teach me, but because of what I was passing on to my own children. I realized the pattern of "no protection" was repeating itself, and I could see myself following in the footsteps of my mother. I felt paralyzed by the choices I had made in my life, and I knew I had to do it differently for myself and my girls.

Fast forward about six more months. I started to take control and petitioned for a divorce. He approved the divorce, but only under the condition that I wouldn't claim any wrongdoing on his part. The divorce was granted and the official reason was irreconcilable differences. I also enrolled in college, and he agreed to watch the girls for me at night. I thought everything was finally working out okay. After all, we weren't together any longer.

Then, the most unforgivable act happened. History repeated itself again. I was distraught and devastated because of what he did to one of his own. I hurt more for her than I had for myself, when that same unforgivable act was committed on me at her age, because she was my daughter. I cried so hard my stomach felt like the life was being wrung out of me.

From that point on, our lives were turned upside down. What had I taught my children? I had failed and didn't protect them just like my mother hadn't protected me. This was a turning point in my life. So many things began to happen. That was the last time I communicated with him. His parental rights were eventually taken away and things got very complicated, but once again, he got away with it. No jail time, no conviction of a crime, and no label as a sexual offender.

During the court process and visitations, I found out that my mother was communicating with him. She had done it again too. Once more, she wasn't there for me. Not only was she unavailable to me emotionally, she even crossed the parental boundary by having contact with him. I couldn't understand why she would do that. I was ashamed by her actions and found it hard to look her in the eyes. As much as I felt more deeply wounded by her behavior, we never talked about it. I couldn't believe that while my heart felt like it was being ripped out of my chest, I had absolutely no one to turn to and no one to confide in. I felt helpless and alone.

I asked myself what had been enough. Over the years, I'd made painful choices and compromises, sometimes naïve to the consequences. Enough was a place that I finally arrived at, albeit not quick enough to stop the repeating patterns. History does have a way of replicating itself, but my pivotal turning point was that I would not have the same reaction as my mother. Loneliness, isolation, and hardening of the heart are all parts of me that I hope I've left behind, along with denial and misplaced loyalties. It was no longer about self-destruction and loss of control; it was about creating and passing on loving memories to my children and being there to support them.

Deepening my relationship with me and following a path

that now resonates with my sense of purpose and self-worth has taken a lot of soul searching and is still a very intimate, vulnerable experience for me. I have also made some very good choices in my life. I went to night school and got both my GED and a degree in criminal justice. I also worked for several police departments during my career as both a corrections officer and a 911 dispatcher.

I became a domestic violence and rape advocate to guide and encourage other women that it's possible to choose a different path even though horrible things happen. I now dedicate my life to working with women by empowering them to discover their power within. If we can find the strength and courage to stand up and face what may be happening in our lives, we can make changes that might even break generational patterns. I hope that by sharing my story, it may help others find the courage to create their own positive journey. I smile as I ascend that hill in anticipation of what life has to offer, knowing I am in control of my choices.

Wanda McCormick, Owner of Power by Choice LLC, Certified Personal Trainer, Women's Fitness expert, published author, and presenter, is passionate about helping women discover and transform their body, mind, and spirit into being their most infinite powerful self through lifestyle changes, healthier eating, stress relief, exercise, and self-love. She specializes in women's health and with 30 years of experience she has learned that everyone is unique and has their own story. Wanda's newest program, Roadmap to Change, is designed to create different outcomes by taking action, changing habits, and eliminating the self-defeating thoughts. Life is about choices. How do you choose to live yours? Get fit, stay healthy, and enjoy life. She lives in Colorado Springs, CO. Visit www.powerbychoicellc.com.

LIFE AS IT SHOULD BE

Maria Russo

My parents were on their honeymoon the first time my dad was hospitalized. The doctors called it a psychotic break, likely caused by a combination of the stress of getting married and the fact that the day before their wedding, Germany had invaded Poland. Two days later, Great Britain declared war on Germany. These events awakened the pathology in my father's mind. It was the first sign of his belief that he had an influence on decisions made by governments around the world.

They were in their early twenties when they met. When my dad's family learned of their plans to marry, they pleaded with my mother to reconsider. She refused to listen even when my grandmother told her that my dad had been diagnosed with paranoid schizophrenia. Though medications quieted his self-deceptions, my grandmother knew the progression of this disease could tear a life apart. My dad was also epileptic, but my mother didn't care. The thought of giving up her one true love just because of illness was unthinkable. She believed he had been selected especially for her by God and nothing would change her mind.

The year I turned five, my father had to be hospitalized again. This time his delusions had been triggered by a single event halfway around the world. It was 1948 and Gandhi had been assassinated. My dad was sure his thoughts were responsible for the acts played out by others. It was unbearable for him to imagine that he caused harm to anyone. This break proved to be deeper and stronger.

My mother was devastated when the doctors informed her that they'd made arrangements to send him to the state mental institution. This was virtually a life sentence—once a person was believed to be insane, the prevailing belief of the day was that there was no cure and they should be removed from society.

However, this did not squelch my mother's devotion to my father. She made him the centerpiece of her life, never missing the twice-a-week visitation days. She told me she was sorry that I didn't have a father anymore.

I was seven by the time my dad's condition improved. The shock treatments had stopped and his thoughts were more balanced and realistic. One beautiful, sunny day I was allowed to go to the hospital with my mom to spend a Sunday afternoon with her and my dad.

The hospital grounds were meticulously landscaped with manicured lawns and well-kept flower beds. My dad brought us around the back to the old farm buildings on the property to show us the workshops where he spent most of his time. He was a skilled craftsman. He built tables, bookcases, and wooden lamp bases. He made unique jewelry and inlaid trays and carved wooden candy dishes and figurines. One year, he made a miniature replica of a stage coach. His work was detailed and intricate. When people talked of my dad, they always mentioned the fine line between genius and insanity.

I remember holding my dad's hand tight that day as we walked past the ominous hospital with the caged balconies where patients confined to their rooms stood shouting things I couldn't understand. I felt safe with him by my side, confused about my gentle, soft-spoken father living in the same place as people who seemed wild and out of control.

Later, my parents sat on a bench under a large oak tree while I played in the grass several feet away. I heard my father tell my mom that she should file for divorce. "This is no life for you," he told her. The conversation was short. My mother reminded him of their wedding vows "for better or for worse," and the subject was closed.

By the time I was eight my dad started to come home on weekends and every Wednesday night for dinner. Life was finally returning to some kind of normalcy. He was always attentive, wanting to know what I thought and which "Bobbsey Twins" book I was reading that week. First thing on Saturday mornings, he greeted me with a little game we liked to play. I would make a steady sound come out of my mouth and he would pat my back to make a totally new sound, sending us into fits of laughter.

One Saturday morning, he came home with his arm in a sling, and I burst into tears at the sight. Having no real conception of his illness, the thought of him having sprained or broken his arm was upsetting. To me, my dad was just as normal as anybody else's dad, except for his mysterious seizures.

Besides woodworking, my father could draw beautifully and paint. He played the piano and the trumpet, though he'd never had a music lesson. He often wrote his own music. It took me years to realize what a happy and peaceful man he had been. He lived in the moment and knew life was worth living to the fullest extent.

The summer I turned ten, my mother moved to a rural town 30 miles away. It was too far for my dad to come home regularly, so she took a Greyhound bus every Sunday and visited him in the hospital instead. I only got to see him on holidays when someone made the drive to pick him up.

I was 15 the year he came home for the first time in several months to celebrate Thanksgiving all together. I greeted him with mixed emotions. Although I always felt my dad's caring and love, I also felt self-conscious around him, especially since I'd not seen him in quite a while. I was apprehensive yet excited that we would have this time together. After our initial greetings, he sat down beside me on the couch. "Mom told me you are in a new school this year," he said. My responses to him were short and didn't reveal the truth about my feelings for him. He tried to engage me in conversation, and I resisted letting him get close, even though I loved being in his presence.

That Friday night I found myself alone with my dad in the living room. He sat on the piano bench, patting a spot beside him. "Come sit with me, Maria," he said. "What do you think of this?" he asked as he started to play something from the music book he had scribed earlier. Not waiting for an answer, he began to sing the lyrics he'd written, "Carry me back to Sorrento," and invited me to sing along with him. I felt too shy to sing, content to just be there by his side.

"I bet you never heard this one," he said, leaning into me with a twinkle in his eye as he turned the page to a new song. It was another of his originals. He called this one "The Isle of Capri," and sang in Italian. I might not have understood the words, but there was no mistaking his love.

Then he stopped singing, his fingers frozen on the keys. I looked up to see what was wrong. He was staring off to the left and his body began to stiffen. I screamed for my mom and as she came running I escaped to the far corner of the room, paralyzed and crying. Cowering in the corner, I felt like a scared animal, as if I needed to protect myself. I was terrified, feeling helpless, since I'd never been taught what to do in response to his episodes.

My mother always knew exactly how to care for my dad. Soon he was calmed and resting. Still standing in the corner, my mother walked over to me. "Don't you ever do that again!" she yelled. "You should know better than to get so hysterical. It upsets your father." Her harshness shouldn't have come as a surprise to me. I was used to not being nurtured or comforted by my mother. She had a way of making me feel I had done something bad when I didn't do what she expected.

About a year later, we were all together again at a relative's home for Easter. Earlier that morning, I had heard on the radio that a girl in my typing class had been killed in a car accident. My dad was sitting next to me on the couch that afternoon, waiting to be called to dinner, when he made a simple statement. "You're sad because your friend died." I had become unaccustomed to his attention and could not fathom responding to him or letting him console me, so I walked away.

Three years later, in 1964, the state reevaluated the way they treated people with a mental disorder. A social worker came to see my mom and told her that the laws were changing. Soon my dad would be one of the first to be released from the hospital.

I had been living with my mother since high school graduation. My dad moved in with us the following June. I loved being around him more often, but I still kept my distance, making sure we were never alone in the house together. I'd never become comfortable with his seizures nor my ability to support him if and when they occurred.

When I got married the following May, I moved out of state with my husband and only saw my dad a couple times a year over the next five or six years. Then, just before my 29th birthday, my aunt called to tell me that my dad had suffered a stroke. She asked how soon I could get there.

The thought of going to my father on his deathbed terrified me. What would I say to him? How would I relate to him? *Is it time to take down the walls and be real?* I asked myself. I prayed he would get better and I would not have to face it.

My mother called the next day and begged me to come. When she realized that was not my plan, she handed the phone to one of my uncles, convinced he could talk sense into me. But instead, he told me my dad was doing better. "In fact, he was sitting up eating chocolate pudding tonight," he said. "Why not wait to see how he is doing tomorrow?"

My dad died that night. When my aunt called to tell me, she commented on my lack of emotion. I don't remember much about my father's funeral. I'd convinced myself it was a relief for him to be free of a terrible life.

It was four years after my father's death, when my husband came home with theatre tickets to see *The Man of La Mancha*. While getting dressed that evening, I remembered a conversation my dad tried to have with me about this play when I was still in high school. He had seen it with a group from the hospital and wanted to tell me about Don Quixote, a man who was considered "crazy." That made me especially uncomfortable, so I found an excuse to leave the room.

Sitting in the theatre that night, I was stunned by the messages. I couldn't hold back the tears, listening as if my father were speaking directly to me through the characters. I began to understand what he once wanted to say to me.

Quixote was a man who questioned life and the meaning of what was considered crazy. He wondered if it was not crazy to lock up people who thought differently or who pursued dreams that seemed impossible to others. He wondered if it was not madness itself to take life at face value rather than look at everything from a deeper level. Quixote believed we all had a destiny and aside from winning or losing, following that destiny was all that mattered.

That is how my father lived his life. I started to understand that he probably had the deepest and clearest understanding of life of anyone I had ever met. He never bucked the system. He accepted his destiny, even the judgments. He accepted his diagnosis and never let it interfere with living. He was mindful.

He loved life and lived it to its fullest, never playing the role of "mental patient." When his delusions took over, he received the help to get past them and moved on.

It was hard for me to bear what I had missed with my dad. Despite the way I treated him, he was extremely patient with me. He never pushed me or got mad. He always took whatever I gave him, even if it was the cold shoulder. Over time, I learned to heal many of my father-daughter wounds through a therapeutic journal process, often on weekends in retreat centers. In 2004, I signed up for a five-day retreat at a center in Kentucky I'd been to many times before.

On Saturday morning, a random remark was made referring to *The Man of La Mancha*. Immediately I felt the presence of my father. Throughout the day, my meditations and journaling were centered on memories of my dad. My favorite was how he taught me to roller-skate when I was only four. He literally tied a pillow to my behind, "so when you fall, it won't hurt," he said.

As I got into bed that night, I prayed, "Dad, if there is something you want me to know, send me a clear message. I don't know what to do with all this awareness."

Entering the Zendo on Sunday morning, the wrought-iron dancing figures that had been placed in the room made me smile. The dancers reminded me of a dream I'd had several years before of dancing with my dad. I don't ever remember dancing with him when he was living, not even at my wedding, but this dream was so vivid it was like a memory. I could feel my dad's arm around me and hear the faint sound of the waltz playing. I recalled the vibrant color of his blue serge suit. It wasn't a dream where I could see myself dancing with someone, but a dream where I only saw what I would have been able to see if it were real. It was a close-up vision of my dad's shoulder, and I could almost feel the warmth of his cheek against mine.

Satisfied with the message that my father wanted to dance with me, I waited for the music to usher us into the morning meditation. Expecting soft flutes, tears welled as I heard my father speak to me again through the voice of Lee Ann Womack. The lyrics to "I Hope You Dance" echoed the messages my dad sent to me throughout my life by the way he lived his. He modeled facing each day with an element of surprise and enchantment. I imagined him speaking directly to me that morning, telling me to appreciate it all.

He reminded me that when Life said "No," it would always be followed with a "Yes," bringing something new and unexpected just waiting to be discovered. He told me to trust life to give me just what I needed and to "long for my dreams, knowing nothing is impossible." He knew better than anyone that winning wasn't the point— Living was. He wanted me to understand that it would not always be easy but it would always be *worth it*. He told me, "Don't always believe what you see but come to know life as it *should be*, with all its many treasures."

I had loved this song since my daughter gave me the book with the words and a CD a few years earlier along with a sweet written message in the inside cover that read in part, "...I hope this inspires you to live your best life always!" The following year she chose the song as her father-daughter dance at her wedding reception.

I said a prayer of thanks to my dad. No matter how much I'd shied away from him when he was alive, he never abandoned me. Because of his gentle spirit—his beautiful soul—he never forced himself upon me when he was alive. Rather, he gently reminded me in a myriad of ways that I and those who follow me will *always* have his love and support. My dad continues to be my greatest teacher.

Maria is a psychotherapist with a private practice in Denver, Colorado. She believes the essence of the human spirit is divine energy and that there is nothing but pure goodness and beauty within us all. Her passion is to inspire others to awaken to their possibilities for personal growth and deep spirituality. Maria is one of eleven contributing authors to the International book "Extraordinary You – The Art of Living a Lusciously Spirited, Vibrant Life" and author of her soon to be published memoir, "The Growing Soul". Learn more about Maria at www.MariaRussoLcsw.com

KAMBER, OUR
INCREDIBLE JOURNEY

Gail Hamilton

Have you ever loved someone or something so much you'd do anything for them? My life as a woman who is blind has been hard—surviving premature birth; sexual, physical, and emotional abuse; societal and professional discriminations; loss of romantic relationships and suicidal ideation; deaths of my mother and grandmother; and having both my eyes removed. Yet, through all my challenges I knew I'd make it. I knew someday I'd find my voice, sing my song, and "live my dreams and fly on my wings." Kamber, the dog who opened my heart, is one of the "people" in my life who has given me my wings to fly. This story is dedicated to him with all my love and gratitude.

I met Kamber in January, 1998, at The Seeing Eye school in Morristown, New Jersey. With leash in hand, my trainer explained, "Kamber is a 29-month-old, 52-pound Golden Retriever. His birthday is August 23, 1995. He has a small scar on his head from running into a tree while chasing a tennis ball. Gail, when you're ready, call your dog, Kamber."

Firmly, I commanded, "Kamber, come." In one pounce Kamber flew forward, jumped onto the chair, placed both his front paws on the back, rested both of his back feet on the arms, and stood with his tummy over my head wagging his tail. Laughing, I wondered how to get this huge dog off me.

"Gail, call your dog down."

Oh yeah..."Kamber, down!" Three times I commanded. Finally on the fourth, he at last got the message and jumped onto the carpeted floor.

Later my trainer told me, "Kamber is a follower, not a leader. Every morning, Kamber waited in his kennel for his buddy Boo to come out from his kennel next door and pass him before he ventured out himself. I moved Boo's cage to the other side of the room trying to force Kamber to be independent; however, every morning Kamber sat and waited for Boo. Giving up, I moved Boo's cage back beside Kamber, and the two remained inseparable."

One afternoon while playing in our room, Kamber stood on his head, stuck his butt in the air, wiggled it, and grunted. Not knowing what to do, I reached down and scratched him. As I laughed, he grunted and groaned louder and wiggled himself all over. Later I asked my trainer, "Have you ever seen Kamber stand on his head?"

"Yes, once I was teaching him how to get off escalators and when we got to the top I reached down and gave Kamber a hearty pat saying, 'Good boy, good boy!' He got so excited, he stood on his head right there in the middle of the escalator in harness!!"

Once back at home, my working relationship with Kamber was rocky. I don't know if it was because I made him stop at every driveway and when he didn't I corrected him, because he was my first Golden Retriever, or because he was a male. At any rate, he walked a hesitant step forward and tucked his tail between his legs. Sometimes he angled when we crossed streets and led me into traffic. I rewarded him with treats when he crossed well and gave him a two-handed overhead correction when he misbehaved. Every day I attempted to work Kamber up to my previous guide dog's guiding level and every day Kamber rebelled.

Finally, in the late summer, Seeing Eye sent a representative to work with us. The trainer gave me some suggestions; however, once he left we were back to square one. Twenty-one months after receiving Kamber, upon my request, the same trainer returned for more evaluations. After we struggled down the block he announced, "Here, Gail, come on, take my arm." Realizing this was unusual, I let him guide me across the street for coffee. "You know, Gail, Kamber isn't any better than a year ago when I came to see you. I think you ought to retire him." One side of me knew he was right and the other didn't want to face the facts. After much processing, I officially retired Kamber on November 1, 1999.

Giving up the harness and allowing Kamber to be a regular dog encouraged my heart to love Kamber for who he was, not for what he did for me out of obligation. I chose to have Kamber in my life and to take care of him for better or for worse. Consciously, and perhaps spiritually, I committed my heart to loving Kamber forever. This meant I wouldn't entertain the idea of getting a fourth Seeing Eye dog until he transitioned.

Before Kamber, depression reigned and suicidal thoughts consumed my heart. I did *not* love my Self nor was I capable of fully loving anyone else. Though there were other dogs and people before him, I wasn't present with them and I certainly didn't know how to embrace their hearts and kindnesses fully. From Kamber I learned to love my Self, to laugh and play, to embrace my child within, to be present, and to feel. Kamber's actions modeled pure love and joy, and from him I learned how to live in my heart and soul and to *BE* in the world. His unconditional love, Being, and spirit opened my heart, and to Kamber I'm eternally grateful.

As the days, months and years passed, I loved being with Kamber. I embraced the moments when he curled up in bed beside me at night, lunged for popcorn while I watched football games, chased after tennis balls, scampered after Kongs, and strolled in the park. His loyalty and happy personality never ceased. Though I faced many personal challenges (Mom dying, having both my eyes removed, and having to sell my house due to financial hardships), Kamber was always there, sitting with his back to me wanting his ears rubbed, lying on the floor wanting his tummy scratched, or standing on his head egging me to massage his hips. Our physical, psychological, and spiritual connection was deep. We never left one another except when he had to sleep over at his grandparents' home while I built a Habitat for Humanity house for us. Other than those times, we were inseparable.

One sunny, crisp afternoon ten years later, Kamber slipped out of his front gate and ran three blocks north amidst cars to chase after a cute dog. He couldn't resist! Even as friends and neighbors yelled, he kept running, weaving in and out of traffic, and falling on his wobbly 14-year-old legs. At last, he was captured and brought home. "You naughty boy, you could have been killed," I sobbed into his fur.

Two months later, I had a temporary ramp built over my back steps and bought a portable ramp just in case he'd need it. Kamber's legs were starting to slip while getting into cars, and I had to put my hand under his butt to assist him. My heart ached, watching his body let go. Every once in a while he couldn't control himself and left presents in the house. I never scolded him-I knew he couldn't help it. He took "drugs" for his legs and loved it when I bounced the pills on the carpet for him to catch.

By the next year, Kamber wore "big-boy pants," which helped with the presents. Using both the back-door ramp and the portable ramp was no longer a luxury; rather, it became a necessity. He was on heavier drugs for his wobbly legs and prescription dog food. I allowed Kamber to take charge of when and how much he wanted to eat and sometimes I heard him get up at midnight and have a little snack. He still played ball; however, he'd often lie on his side and watch it roll by. The couch was getting harder to climb onto and many times I found him lying in the sun on the kitchen floor.

By January, 2011, Kamber's little legs became weaker. Though we still walked in the park every day, one snowy afternoon he fell twice and thereafter I cut his walks in half. He loved his porch, and on days when the temperature was above 40 degrees, he lay in the sun and watched the world go by. Most of the time he went in and out my front door and drove me crazy; however, in hindsight, I'd do it all again if I could bring him back.

Finally, on Thursday, February 24, one day following his 15 ½ year birthday, Kamber got up and fell down. After doing this several times, he ended up at the back door with his little nose lying in the crack between the frame and the screen. Even with his blue canvas harness with pull-up straps, I couldn't lift him. "It's okay, Kamber. You can lie there. I'll come back and check on you, okay?" I gave him a pat and with tears left him. Three hours later, after I had made the fatal appointment for him at the vet's office, Kamber got up and walked around like nothing was wrong. He started going in and out again, and with gratitude I canceled the appointment.

Saturday morning arrived and Kamber struggled. He got up and fell down three times. I pushed back tears as I watched him wince in pain when he curled up his legs. I tried to crawl over to comfort him and he moved away.

"It's okay, I won't hurt you baby!"

I called my friend, "What shall we do? I don't want to give him to God and I can't let him be in pain either!"

"I'm sorry to say I think it's time! How about you call the vet and see if they have time today?"

I called and thankfully their next window of opportunity was Monday, February 28th at 7:00 a.m. With heavy heart I made the appointment.

The afternoon went smoothly as Kamber went in and out the front door and lay in his beloved sun on the front porch.

The following day was a good day. Kamber got up as usual with no assistance from me. I gave him breakfast and afterwards brushed him. "This is not for you, it's for me!" I told him. With all four brushes I brushed his ears, withers, back, sides, legs, and tail. Every once in a while I leaned down and hugged him, sobbing into his fur. He would breathe in and give me a contented long sigh.

That evening, I sat on the floor and told Kamber my appreciations, regrets, and hopes. "I appreciate everything about you. Your happy personality, your soft ears, your long silky hair, your love of treats and crackers, your playful spirit, tearing up my pant legs and wrapping paper when you were a puppy, everything. There are so many things I appreciate that it's hard to think of them all. All the companionship you gave me going everywhere with me: grocery stores, shopping, restaurants, concerts, plays, people's homes. You were the best retired Seeing Eye dog on the planet. I regret teaching you to stop for every driveway when you were a Seeing Eye dog. I regret what I have to do tomorrow. I hope you go to God in peace and that you play with all the other dog angels. I hope you are without pain. I hope there is a Heaven! I hope you are happy and love again. I hope you miss me as much as I'll miss you. I hope we see each other again."

The next morning a friend of mine came at 5:45 and read a poem to Kamber and me entitled: "Dog Heaven" by Cynthia Rylant. As she read, I sat beside Kamber and stroked his soft ears. I remembered two days before, another friend told me a story of a woman who had a near-death experience and saw her dog. Suddenly the dog said, "I love you and want to stay with you, but I've got to dig," and with that, he was off and she came back into her body. Soon after, she learned there had been an earthquake and knew her dog was being asked to help save the lives of people or dogs on earth.

Alas, it was time for us to go. Kamber walked with ease down the back ramp and up his portable ramp into the van. At the vet's office the staff was wonderful, touching my arm, speaking words of comfort and apology. We walked into our familiar examination room where a blanket was waiting on the floor. The vet came in and described the procedure in a compassionate yet professional demeanor. He gave Kamber a sedative and left us alone.

Every few minutes he'd come back, "Is he getting sleepy? No? I'll be back." Later, "Is he getting sleepy? No? I'll be back." And still later, "Is he getting sleepy? No? I'll be back." Meanwhile, my friends offered poems, songs of love, touches, prayers, and loving acts of kindnesses.

Kamber took ten to fifteen minutes to react to the sedative. "Atta boy, Kamber, stay awake. Do whatever you want." All the while he went to everyone in our group nestling them and getting treats. He'd go over and drink water out of a bowl, "Atta boy, Kamber, you eat and drink as much as you want." He only came to me at the end when he couldn't stay awake any longer. Sitting with his back to me, I reached out and felt his soft silky ears. "It's okay, Kamber, I love you." He finally lowered to the floor and rested with his head up. "It's okay, Kamber. You're okay." Stroking his ears, I sobbed.

Suddenly the doctor sat in front of me. "I'll soon give the drugs. He's getting sleepy. His eyes are closing."

I felt his head. It was down. His soft ears were lying on his paws. I stroked him. "I love you, Kamber, go to God."

"Are you ready?" I wasn't, and yet I knew I had to let him go. "He has the furriest paws I've ever seen. He's a beautiful animal."

I stroked those ears and sobbed. "He's gone?" I felt his ribs.

"Yes," and with that my favorite vet leaned over and gave me a hug.

Two days later I dreamed Kamber was in my house running everywhere. "What do you have in your mouth?" I felt his muzzle and there was a baby bottle. "You are such a tease! You always like to tease me!" I woke up laughing. Maybe there is a dog Heaven, and just maybe Kamber was up there running and teasing, waiting for me.

Two weeks later I dreamed again. Kamber was in harness. We were walking fast. He was perfect, working like a champion. We were walking and then running, until suddenly, my hands were holding onto his collar and we were flying. Free and happy we soared. With traffic buzzing above our heads, we flew at lightning speed towards the end of a long tunnel. With paws stretched out in front of him, my fingers holding tight to his collar and my feet stretched behind me, we whisked fast towards the light. Just as we got to the end of the tunnel, I woke up. My heart burst with joy. Without a doubt I knew Kamber and I would meet again.

Kamber was a kind-hearted, gentle-loving boy. And a tease! He loved his popcorn while watching football, playing ball at various homes and offices, attending music performances, searching out crumbs under the reception table afterwards, scrounging for scraps, lying on the porch basking in the sun, digging in the snow, standing on his head and wiggling his butt in the air, rubbing his face on the carpet after a treat or while waiting to go to the park, wrapping himself around trees on his 25-foot flex-a-lead, and going swimming. So many memories! My heart and house have been empty, and I feel devastated without my baby boy.

It's now fifteen months later and time has helped heal my broken heart. Though I still long for Kamber, I've started personal training to strengthen my left arm and have begun walking two miles a day in order to go back to The Seeing Eye to train for dog number four. My heart knows there will never be another dog like Kamber; however, I'm at last ready to embrace the love of another. Words can never express how Kamber's unconditional Love, Light, Spirit, and Being opened my wounded heart and taught me how to live on wings of love.

I am grateful beyond measure for your love, Kamber, and can't wait for our spirits to join and for us to fly together one day!!!!

For more than thirty years, Gail Hamilton has been assisting others in overcoming their obstacles, challenges, and daily struggles empowering them towards options, creativity, and spontaneity. Gail is a powerful motivational speaker, facilitator, life coach, author, teacher, singer, and piano and autoharp performer. Holding a BA, MM, and MA degrees, Gail has spoken and performed to audiences on a local and national level. Gail is in the process of publishing her life story in an inspirational nonfiction novel of courage and perseverance, Soaring on

Wings of Greatness, a Blind Woman's Powerful Journey, Vision, and Transformation. *She also has a CD entitled: "Singing on Wings of Love." You may contact her at: gail@spreadyourwingstofly.com or call (303) 922-9269.*

AFTERWORD

It has been a pleasure to bring forth three volumes of *Speaking Your Truth* with over 40 contributors in each one. When I first had a vision for the project in 2009, I had no idea I would have the opportunity to meet such amazing women and assist them in sharing their stories with the world. Many of these brave women had never spoken their stories publicly, and the process of writing was a healing one. Doors opened and hearts were touched as Volumes I and II became available.

In Volume III, we noticed new themes emerge—that of defining moments and relationships. These are stories we can all relate to. All the stories have touched us—quite a few have affected us deeply. Both Andrea and I cried through many of the readings, moved by the narratives and messages that flittered across our screens.

With each volume, we have been surprised by the pure level of vulnerability and authenticity the women contributors have expressed. We've seen so much love and spirit from both the readers and the writers of these stories. It has definitely proven that whenever we allow our hearts to open, the support system builds around us. We just need to trust, share, and be willing to receive.

The original inspiration for the project came after my divorce, when I felt empowered every time I heard a similar story to my own. It was a mirror and a reminder that I was not alone on this journey, no matter how dark my days were, and even though at times I felt my situation was "unique." The more I heard from other women who had also experienced pain and loss, the more I knew that I too would be okay.

Stories are truly a gift. Even the ones we resist most have much to teach us. And our stories and their lessons will live on long after we do. It becomes our right and responsibility to share our stories and let them teach our lessons—even after we are gone. - L.S.

Through the last few years, the journey of *Speaking Your Truth* has inspired my life's work and direction. Bringing women together to share these stories and seeing the connection and community that has been built around the series has been remarkable to watch. It's been an honor to be a part of it. Through it all, I've learned to trust more, open more, dare more, and ultimately, be more.

I am forever grateful that Lisa asked me to be a part of this project in early 2010. It is one of the best decisions I have ever made. - A.C.

*"People are hungry for stories. It's part of our very being.
Storytelling is a form of history, of immortality too.
It goes from one generation to another."*
- Studs Terkel

We wish for you to take these stories and their teachings and receive them with an open heart. Find the story or stories that speak to you, share their message, and share yours as well. In this way, we keep our circle ever-expanding.

Our third volume of *Speaking Your Truth* concludes this series. The community it has created and the inspiration it has shared has been a joy to be a part of. We are forever changed.

A special thank you is due to each of the women in this book and the entire series. You have each contributed to *Speaking Your Truth* in your own special way, and we value every one of you. Thank you for inspiring us and other readers, and may the experience continue to fuel empowerment and the magic of sharing and telling stories.

In gratitude,
Lisa Shultz and Andrea Costantine

ABOUT US

Lisa Shultz conceived the idea behind *Speaking Your Truth* in 2009 ten years after an event that transformed her life, which she wrote about in Volume I. She hoped that by sharing her story, others might gain hope and inspiration in their lives if they found themselves in a similar circumstance.

She invited Andrea Costantine to become her business partner to bring Volume I to completion in 2010. Since that first publication, she has also coupled with Andrea to help writers self-publish their books with Self-Publishing Experts, LLC., their joint venture, www.SelfPublishingExperts.com.

Lisa is passionate about connecting and empowering women and finds the *Speaking Your Truth* and Self-Publishing platforms offer the perfect outlet for her mission. She also enjoys speaking, consulting, and loves to hold workshops for aspiring writers.

She resides in Breckenridge, Colorado and you can find out more about her at www.LisaJShultz.com.

Andrea Costantine inspires others to make a difference in the world by getting involved and creating community through compassion, contribution and connection. Andrea is a motivational speaker and author.

In collaboration with Lisa Shultz, Andrea has also co-written and self-published *How to Bring Your Book to Life This Year: An Exploratory Guidebook on Writing and Self-Publishing*, and solely created *Connected: 101 Ways to Be of Service and Create Community* and *Soulful Marketing: Heart Centered Marketing for Conscious Entrepreneurs*. Andrea resides in Denver, Colorado. Discover more at www.andreacostantine.com.

ABOUT THE ARTIST

Janice Earhart, the illustrator for the book, is delighted to be a part of this wonderful collaboration of women telling their courageous stories.

iZoar is her primary art business and the Village of iZoar is where her whimsical and inspiring characters live. As an artist, writer and the creator of iZoar you will find her witty, profound, funny, insightful and her characters speak volumes. With a succinct writing style she is able to capture big emotions in a simple sentence. This signature style of whimsical characters and simple clear messages makes her work appeal to women in all walks of life. Her prints, cards and gifts are sold all over the world in boutiques, galleries and gift stores.

Her life is her story. iZoar teaches what she has learned. They deliver the messages she uses to make her life remarkable. Her wish is that you receive inspiration from them and her prayer is that you become all that you can be.

When she is not in the world of iZoar, Janice enjoys hiking the mountains of Colorado with her husband and their Golden Retriever. Chronically curious, she finds the world incredibly interesting. Thus, she keeps her life as fascinating as her characters.

Visit her online at www.iZoar.com.

CONNECT WITH THE
SPEAKING YOUR TRUTH
COMMUNITY

If sharing our stories has inspired, moved, or empowered you, we would love to hear from you. Please join us online to connect with other contributors, share your stories, and receive inspiration.

For information about speaking engagements, other books, workshops, and training programs, please contact us directly.

If you are writing your own book and are considering self-publishing, please visit www.SelfPublishingExperts.com for more information and book support.

Visit our blog and share your experiences with our growing Speaking Your Truth community.

Contact us directly:
Lisa Email: info@lisashultz.com
Andrea Email: info@andreacostantine.com
Website/Blog: www.speakingyourtruthbook.com
Facebook: www.facebook.com/speakingyourtruth

We look forward to hearing from you.
Sincerely,
Lisa Shultz & Andrea Costantine

Are you interested in buying multiple copies
of *Speaking Your Truth* for your business,
network, community, or clients?
You can receive special discounted pricing,
great service, direct shipping, and more.
Inquire with us today.

Lisa Email: info@lisashultz.com
Andrea Email: info@andreacostantine.com

Made in the USA
Columbia, SC
10 May 2018